ROUTLEDGE LIBRARY EDITIONS:
THE ADOLESCENT

Volume 4

ADOLESCENT LIFE AND ETHOS

ADOLESCENT LIFE AND ETHOS

An Ethnography of a US High School

HEEWON CHANG

Routledge
Taylor & Francis Group

LONDON AND NEW YORK

First published in 1992 by The Falmer Press

This edition first published in 2023
by Routledge
4 Park Square, Milton Park, Abingdon, Oxon OX14 4RN

and by Routledge
605 Third Avenue, New York, NY 10158

Routledge is an imprint of the Taylor & Francis Group, an informa business

© 1992 H. Chang

ISBN: 978-1-032-37655-4 (Set)
ISBN: 978-1-032-39067-3 (Volume 4) (hbk)
ISBN: 978-1-032-39075-8 (Volume 4) (pbk)
ISBN: 978-1-003-34829-0 (Volume 4) (ebk)

DOI: 10.4324/9781003348290

Publisher's Note
The publisher has gone to great lengths to ensure the quality of this reprint but points out that some imperfections in the original copies may be apparent.

Disclaimer
The publisher has made every effort to trace copyright holders and would welcome correspondence from those they have been unable to trace.

Adolescent Life and Ethos:
An Ethnography of a US High School

To my parents, Chin-Ho Chang and Eui-Sook Cho

Adolescent Life and Ethos:
An Ethnography of a US High School

Heewon Chang

The Falmer Press

(A member of the Taylor & Francis Group)
London • Washington, D.C.

UK   The Falmer Press, 4 John St, London WC1N 2ET
USA   The Falmer Press, Taylor & Francis Inc., 1990 Frost Road, Suite
        101, Bristol, PA 19007

© H. Chang 1992

First published in 1992

**A catalogue record for this book is available from the British
Library**

Library of Congress Cataloging-in-Publication Data

Chang, Heewon, 1959–
      Adolescent life and ethos: an ethnography/by Heewon Chang.
      p.   cm. — (Explorations in ethnography series)
      Includes bibliographical references (p.   ) and index.
      ISBN 1–85000–865–5: – ISBN 1–85000–866–3 (pbk.):
      1. Adolescence — United States — Case studies.   2. High
school students — United States — Case studies.   3. Ethnology
— United States.
      I. Title.   II. Series.
      LB1135.C43   1992
      305.23′5′0973—dc20   91–35956
                                                      CIP

Jacket design by Caroline Archer

Typeset in 11/13 pt Bembo
by Graphicraft Typesetters Ltd., Hong Kong
Printed and bound in Great Britain by
Burgess Science Press
Basingstoke

Contents

List of Tables

List of Figures

Introduction

Negative images of contemporary US adolescents abound. Widely read tomes, such as the sensational *A Nation at Risk* (the National Commission on Excellence in Education, 1983) present high-school aged adolescents as a manifestation of national at-risk phenomena. Among thirteen 'indicators of the risk', four directly concerned this age group:

1 About 13 per cent of all 17-year-olds in the United States can be considered functionally illiterate. Functional illiteracy among minority youth may run as high as 40 per cent;
2 Average achievement of high school students on most standardized tests is now lower than 26 years ago when Sputnik was launched;
3 Many 17-year-olds do not possess the 'higher order' intellectual skills we should expect of them. Nearly 40 per cent cannot draw inferences from written material; only one-fifth can write a persuasive essay; and only one-third can solve a mathematics problem requiring several steps;
4 There was a steady decline in science achievement scores of US 17-year-olds as measured by national assessments of science in 1969, 1973, and 1977 (1983:8–9).

In addition to 'an alarming drop in standardized test scores' and the suffering of American students in 'virtually all international comparison', William Bennett, US Secretary of Education in 1985–89, argued that 'pathologies' have increased among US young people (1988:10). Whatever he meant by pathologies, two of his official speeches addressed drug use and sexuality among adolescents. These teenage problems were presented as quite serious, as is indicated by his statistics: 'Sixty-one per cent of all high school seniors — roughly two million young men and women — had tried illicit drugs' (p. 86); 'More than one million teenage girls become pregnant each year'; and 'Births among unwed teenage girls rose 200 per cent between 1960 and 1980' (p. 93).

More statistical data of high school dropouts, youth crime, and suicide rates worsen the image of the youth of the US. According to the statistics from 1970 through 1986, high school dropouts constituted over 10 per cent of the total population of 14- to 24-year-olds (US Bureau of the Census, 1989:145), averaging over four-and-one-half million. In 1987, almost half of the persons arrested were under 24 years of age; over one-third of them were under 18 years old (1989:173). Although youth crime rate declined slightly between 1975 and 1987, 'a modest reduction during the early 1980s' was viewed as a result of 'the declining numbers of "high-risk" inner-city male youths' (Sullivan, 1989:1). A leading cause of teenage death was suicide. 'Among people aged fifteen to twenty-four, estimates of suicide attempts range from 50,000 to 500,000 per year.... [The] rate of success at suicide attempts is about 5,000 a year' (Allen, 1987:271). Between 1970 and 1986, the suicide rate had increased by 250 per cent for 10- to 14-year-olds and 172 per cent for 15- and 19-year-olds (US Bureau of the Census, 1989:84). Another leading cause of teenage death was traffic accidents involving intoxicated drivers.

No matter how statistical data is interpreted, the numerical presentation of problems seemed to be powerful enough to paint a gloomy picture of US adolescents. Are average US teenagers likely to be academically underachieving, drug-abusing, sexually active, carelessly pregnant, violent, recklessly drunk-driving, and readily attempting suicide? No. Unfortunately, the statistical data of these aspects have been overly exposed, and skewed attention to adolescent at-risk behaviors has produced a misunderstanding of American youth. Two problems occur with the misrepresentation of this kind of statistical data: 1) those who slipped through the statistical grid were often ignored in analysis, and 2) individuals who exhibited at-risk behaviors were quickly labeled as delinquent juveniles.

Who are the adolescents who slipped through this kind of statistical grid? They are so-called 'normal' ones who either fell in the group of a statistically insignificant minority or whose lives were too average to be sensational. This group of young people has often not received enough of the spotlight in educational research. Furthermore, 'the relatively untroubled adolescent is regarded as an anomaly, an unexpected pleasure...[and] has remained an enigma for most adults' (Offer, Ostrov, and Howard, 1981). Fortunately, however, some ethnographies and qualitative studies, unlike statistical studies that single out at-risk youth, have dealt with more inclusive circles of adolescents. Some of them include *The Adolescent Society* (Coleman, 1961), *Inside High School* (Cusick, 1973), *Jocks and Burnouts* (Eckert, 1988), *Elmtown's Youth* and *Elmtown Revisited* (Hollingshead, 1975), *Growing Up American* (Peshkin, 1978), *God's Choice* (Peshkin, 1988), and *American School Language* (Varenne, 1983).

Another aspect of the over-exposure of the adolescent problems is that those who were counted for the at-risk category lost identities other than as social delinquents. Do they not have other characteristics beneath the label, which they would share with 'average' adolescents? Even for those who have experienced one or more of the 'pathologies', are these superficial symptoms all there is to know about them? The overemphasis of their problematic dimensions of life tends to destroy their image as human beings. Some ethnographers who have paid attention to adolescent at-risk behavior have identified discrepancies between statistical reality and ethnographic reality. While statistics focus on an overall picture, ethnography concentrates on everyday reality often hidden under the surface. In other words, instead of dwelling on the superficial phenomena, ethnographers try to understand the inner structure of problems and cultural values of individuals' behaviors. In ethnographic studies, at-risk adolescents transcend their anonymity as statistical objects, coming alive as real human beings. Edgerton, in the Foreword of Vigil's book, assessed the author's ethnographic intent of understanding Mexican youth gangs as follows: 'He is as horrified by gang killings as anyone else, but his purpose is to understand gangs and the young people who belong to them' (Vigil, 1988:x). *Getting Paid* (Sullivan, 1989), and *Barrio Gangs* (Vigil, 1988) are two among many ethnographies and qualitative studies of adolescent delinquent behaviors.

The ethnographic study to be described in the following pages focuses not on the at-risk dimension, but on the overall culture and ethos of US adolescent life. An ethnography is both a process and a product. As a process, researchers utilize ethnographic methods — participant observation and ethnographic interviews — to collect cultural data and to analyze and interpret it in a holistic context. As a product, ethnography presents a cultural description and interpretation. Thus, this ethnography does not evaluate US high school education. It does not diagnose teenage problems, nor does it discuss pathologies among youth. Rather, it describes everyday life of high school students in one United States community and analyzes the cultural values and ideals that guide their day-to-day behaviors.

This study is of adolescents in the United States. It covers a wide range of individuals from 'jocks' to 'burnouts', from 'socialites' to 'nerds', from 'populars' to 'unpopulars', and from the 'successful' to the 'at-risk'. This work is grounded on a premise that adolescents are able to talk about their own culture; the reality they present in their own voices is more valuable than the reality constructed solely by researchers. In this study, adolescents were treated neither as topics for academic discussions nor as objects of scholarly counting. Rather, they were regarded as real human beings able to speak for themselves. Therefore, I tried to include their own accounts of daily lives as much as possible.

This study was done in a semi-rural ethnically mainstreamed high school, here called Greenfield High School, and its surrounding community, conterminous with the Green Lake School District. Some may argue that teenagers from a rural, ethnically homogeneous community do not represent US adolescents.[1] Then a question arises: Are the urban youth typical adolescents of the United States?[2] Academicians and other adults seem to be quite concerned about identifying typical US adolescents. No matter how the outsiders would label Greenfielders, teenagers in this community considered themselves just as normal and average as others in the nation, because their reality is right there with them. The high school principal's claim also gives us insight into a native's view of the community's typicality:

> You found the right community for your study because it's a melting pot of kids from professional families...hippies... lumber mill workers...farmers.... It's like a big family. But there's such a diversity.... This community is a microcosm of American culture.

This study was completed by an Asian ethnographer, a South Korean. Since the report, *A Nation At Risk*, included South Korea as a potential competitor, I feel urged to clarify the educational situations for Asian adolescents and to counteract the negative image given to US youth. Overcriticism of US education and youth and unreasonable admiration for other nations' education, particularly that of Asian countries, presumably derived from blind comparisons between different educational systems. The blind comparison is faulty for two reasons: it does not consider the cultural background of each system, and it often relies on standardized knowledge-based measurements for comparison. It may be true that students of some Asian school systems performed well in some tests because they spent considerably more hours learning basic subjects. They also valued schooling as a means of social upward mobility more than their cohorts from many other countries. My understanding of Japanese education and more recent fieldwork in Korea (Chang, 1989), however, have revealed that Asian adolescents suffered their share of 'pathologies' in these educational systems which overemphasize learning basic knowledge. As a non-native to the American system with appreciation in context of Asian education, I was able to discern positive aspects of adolescent life in the US. I do not intend to compare them, but my understanding of these two systems allowed me to look at these distinct populations on their merits.

This book, an evolution from my dissertation of the same name, consists of four main parts: 'Doing Ethnographic Fieldwork', 'Adolescent Life', 'Adolescent Ethos', and 'Reflections on the Ethnographic Experience'. Part 1 introduces the ethnographic research by describing each step of the research procedure, setting the background and interpreting cultural data. Encompassing five chapters, Part 2 provides detailed descriptions of adolescent life at home, in school, and in the community. In Chapter 2, a brief version of the life history of a female key informant is narrated through the ethnographer's voice. Chapter 3 portrays the surrounding community as a context of the youth culture. Its physical environment, population makeup, economy, and its relation to the high school and students are discussed. Chapter 4 deals with three aspects of the school -- ecological environment, students, and functions. Five roles of the school are discussed — school as a place for theoretical and practical learning, for discipline, for extracurricular activities, for citizenship training, and for friendship and courtship. Chapter 5 illustrates a typical school day from awakening in the morning to bed time, as if the author has physically followed a composite student created from field data. Chapter 6 presents a collage of excerpts from students' journals and essays pertaining to their activities and feelings on weekends, holidays, vacations, and special occasions.

Part 3, 'Adolescent Ethos', includes four analytic chapters which identify three aspects of adolescent ethos and characterize them in relation to social ideals. Chapter 7 discusses 'getting along with everyone' as one aspect of the ethos that the young people valued and tried to live in peer interactions. In Chapter 8, adolescent perception of 'being independent' is examined and five symbolic markers of independence are explained. Chapter 9 discusses the students' zeal for 'getting involved' in activities, social meanings of activeness in the youth culture, and adolescent ways of managing stress caused by multiple commitments. In Chapter 10, an interpretive chapter, the three aspects of adolescent ethos are linked with three sets of ideals such as egalitarianism/elitism, inner-directedness/other-directedness, and competition/cooperation. This chapter offers explanations as to how and why these contradictory ideals guided adolescent behaviors and how the young people tried to resolve the conceptual paradox of the ideals in their daily operation.

Part 4, 'Reflections on Ethnographic Experiences', focuses on methodological and personal concerns with doing ethnography. Chapter 11, written in a 'confessional' style (see Van Maanen, 1988:73–100), is devoted to personal reflections — as a female adult, Korean born, non-native speaker of English — on fieldwork experiences among US teenage informants. It addresses issues such as examination of self, dynamics between self and others, the inequality of languages, and continued friendships with informants after the completion of the fieldwork.

I would like to conclude this Introduction with acknowledgments of those who have directly or indirectly assisted me in completing this work. Special thanks are due to the Greenfield High School students, staff, and community members who gave me tremendous assistance and showed immeasurable patience with this naive student of their culture. Without them, particularly my teenage friends, this study would not have existed. I am also greatly indebted to Professor Harry Wolcott who academically nourished me during my graduate studies in the field of anthropology and education, served as mentor during the whole process of this ethnographic endeavor, and carefully edited the manuscript for this book. His generous time and invaluable comments cannot be overstated. I extend acknowledgments to my doctoral committee members — Professors Philip Young, Ray Hull, and David Flinders, and Mr. Otho (Bid) Sanders — for their continuous interest in the study and valuable input to the original manuscript.

The following individuals deserve my hearty thanks: Dr. Jean Campbell, the late Dr. Grace Graham, Ms. Lynn Search and Mrs. Ruth Ebert, all of whom spent many unselfish hours proofreading my drafts; Mr. Ken Harris, who produced the maps for the dissertation on the computer; my colleagues from Oregon, Dr. Geoffrey Mills, Dr. Letty Lincoln, and Dr. Thomas Schram, who shared their joy and concerns of doing ethnography and provided me with intellectual stimulation and moral support; and Dr. Margaret LeCompte who gave me insightful suggestions for the further improvement of the study. My deep appreciation extends also to Professor Ivor Goodson, editor of The Exploration of Ethnography Series, Malcolm Clarkson, Managing Director and Carol Saumarez, editor of Falmer Press, as well as the anonymous reviewer who gave invaluable suggestions in the course of transforming the dissertation into a book.

My special gratitude is to my parents, Chin-Ho Chang and Eui-Sook Cho, and to my sister, Hee-Young Chang, for their spiritual encouragement, intellectual stimulation, and emotional and financial support throughout my growing up in Korea and graduate studies in the United States. I would also like to express my sincere appreciation to my husband, Klaus Volpert, who has continuously encouraged me as an intellectual partner and showed enormous patience throughout the whole period of the ethnographic research and preparation for this book. The last individual who deserves an acknowledgment is my daughter, Hannah Volpert, who has competed for her mother's time and attention since her birth while the dissertation has evolved into a book.

Although this book was born with all the assistance and suggestions from those mentioned above, I take sole responsibility for the content and the interpretation of data.

Notes

1   After reviewing this work for The Distinguished Dissertation Award, sponsored by a joint committee in the American Educational Research Association, Margaret LeCompte commented that Greenfielders are not 'average' adolescents because 'the rural communities of America are suffering rapid decline and urbanization'.

2   I recall a personal conversation with George Spindler during the 1989 American Anthropological Association Annual Meeting. He claimed that if there is any 'typical American culture', it lies in between the two coasts and thus in non-urban communities.

Part 1

Doing Ethnographic Fieldwork

Chapter 1

Doing Ethnographic Fieldwork

This ethnography is based on a year of fieldwork conducted in Greenfield High School and the Green Lake community in Oregon.[1] In this chapter, I describe five procedural steps taken during the ethnographic study: selecting a site, gaining entrée among adolescents and maintaining rapport, collecting and recording cultural materials, analyzing data and interpreting cultural meanings, and writing up an ethnography.

Selecting a School and its Community

In order to pursue my interest in American adolescents through research, I looked for a small senior high school and its community in Oregon that were willing to tolerate the relatively long-term presence of a quiet 'intruder' — an ethnographer. Two criteria were considered in this searching process: a manageable-sized school of less than 500 students, and location in a small rural to semi-rural community. My preference for a small school was based on the idea that I might be able to make close contact with a majority of students. I also preferred a rural location, because I wanted to experience a 'traditional' way of doing fieldwork. Traditionally, anthropological fieldwork has been conducted in societies where natives live in cohesive communities and share a culture. I viewed high school students as natives of a culture that was formed within social boundaries of a school and, in turn, was embedded in a local community.

A few school districts with those characteristics were contacted but my efforts to gain entrée ended in vain. The emergence of Greenfield High School, a desirable alternative, finally turned my frustration into euphoria. The high school was a variant from the original criteria, in that its enrollment slightly exceeded 500 students and its surrounding community encompassed more than one rural town. The greater community, conterminous with the Green Lake School District, included a small city and three rural to semi-rural towns (see Chapter 3). In spite of the size, the community was often united by its high school activities. Therefore, I settled with this community and Greenfield High School.

In mid-December of 1986, I visited Mr. Smith, then principal of Greenfield High School, for an initial contact. My description of the study as an ethnographic endeavor of a foreigner to learn about the youth culture of the United States was well understood and accepted at this level of the administrative 'gatekeeper'. I proposed to observe and participate in normal student life from January to December 1987. After listening to my brief account of research methods and timeline, the principal told me that he could imagine my presence at the school in the role of a foreign exchange student. Both of us agreed that my appearance (Asian features and young-looking for my age) was credible for a foreign high school exchange student and the role would help me gain access to teenagers and maintain rapport with them.

My ethical preference, however, was to introduce myself as a researcher rather than a foreign exchange student. I was glad that I revealed my true identity as an ethnographer from the beginning. If I had taken the seemingly 'easier' way, I would have not only adopted a stance I find unethical, but also encountered technical difficulties, such as making up a trail of lies and confining myself to school activities all the time like other students. A subsequent Chang study (1989) among Korean adolescents[2] demonstrated to me that this honest approach had more advantages than disadvantages.

Without further probing, the principal approved my long-term presence as an ethnographer in his school. The next step was to seek permission from the superintendent, the next level of gatekeeper in the school hierarchy. My proposed role as a student-like adult puzzled him, because it did not fit the typical structure of an educational institution. In his legalistic frame of reference, a school environment consisted of two constituents: staff (liable adults) and students (legal minors). The superintendent was concerned about my undefined and rather unfamiliar status between the two groups of constituents. I assured him that the in-between status would allow me to gain entrée among adolescents and maintain objectivity by 'detaching' myself from the young people to a certain degree. I was finally granted entry to Greenfield High School after one more discussion with him.

Gaining Entrée among Adolescents and Maintaining Rapport

The morning after receiving final approval from the superintendent I stood in front of a mirror contemplating what to wear to school. I was supposed to be introduced in a faculty meeting that morning and then be left on my own in the midst of students. My field journal entry that day described my ambivalence in choosing my primary identification in the school:

> I spent more than fifteen minutes in the morning [which is long for me], deciding what to wear. I didn't want to over-dress for students [because I wanted to look like them] nor underdress for faculty [because I wanted to be treated profes-sionally]. I first chose a pair of dressy pants and a V-necked sweater with a matching blouse. I thought wearing pants wouldn't make me look too formal to students, but the design of the trousers might be formal enough for teachers. But at the last minute, I decided to choose more of a teenage-like attire. I changed the dressy pants to jeans and pumps to sport shoes. Now, I looked like a high school kid. Especially in a ski jacket!

Who could have guessed that this incident was the first indicator of internal battles that I was to go through thereafter in choosing be-tween adults and adolescents as my associates? The first battle ended in favor of youngsters. I often found myself making similar decisions throughout my fieldwork.

After the initial meeting with school administrators, I began to 'hang out' among adolescents in and out of school. I frequented places where students were supposed to be: classrooms, student lunchroom, student restrooms, student parking lot, halls, school dances, sports events, fast-food stores, a shopping mall, local churches, and other teen activities in the community. As an Asian-looking newcomer, I was readily recognizable in the predominantly white student popula-tion and among students who had known each other well. During the first few months of my fieldwork, several students asked me if I were a new student, a senior, or a foreign exchange student.

In a health class, Tom, a sophomore sitting two rows in front of me, sent me a written note reading, 'What school year are you in?' I returned the note with my answer: 'I'm going to the University of Oregon as a graduate student. Here in Greenfield High School, I attend all levels of classes — one for freshmen, one for sophomores, and one for juniors and seniors.' He sent the note back with another question, 'How old are you?...' Surprised at my answer, he responded, 'You look about fifteen or sixteen years old.' This note exchange continued two more rounds until the class ended. I was concerned about the teacher's possible annoyance if he noticed this minor 'disruption', but I found myself enjoying a feeling of acceptance and the thrill of participating in the teenage note-passing conspiracy.

I took this initial expression of curiosity as a sign of acceptance, but I was soon disappointed at the quickly dissipating interest in me among students. My disappointment was intense because my professional ego had been boosted by several scholars and other adults who implied that teenagers would be delighted to become a part of the research. I noticed that teenagers who approached me at the beginning were mostly newcomers and female students. Agar (1980) coined the term, 'professional stranger-handlers', to refer to the people who first approach strangers and scrutinize their identities. In my case, one of the first approaches was made by Holly, a junior, who had transferred to the school four months before my study began. She was a year older than most of her classmates, because she had been out of school two times (see p. 165). A sophomore who had transferred from a local Christian school also approached me at an early stage of the study.

Unlike Agar's claim that the professional stranger-handlers were likely deviants on the margin of society, my initial contacts were not limited to less integrated students. Actually, some of so-called 'popular' students, such as basketball players and cheerleaders, also approached me at the beginning of the study. Tom, who sent me notes in class, was a member of the rally squad and played football while keeping his grades above a 'B' average. Interestingly, I came in contact with smokers — emic (from insider's view, Kessing, 1976:173) deviants — only later in my study.

Staff cooperation smoothed my role transition into that of a student. I was allowed to purchase school lunches with student tickets. I also was assigned a hall locker and a gym locker. An English teacher included me in class activities with other students. I was given a biology test to take when I happened to observe the class on an exam day. On a day when electricity went out in school and students congregated in the hall, the teachers who supervised the dark hall treated me like a student, not allowing me to leave the area.

The young people observed me participating 'on their side' in activities. From time to time, they rewarded my 'stepping-down' approach with personal invitations: some invited me to sit next to them in classes or school events, which often led me to a 'gold mine' of information, or they included me in family or social activities. Tanya, a sophomore, invited me to her home for several weekends to teach me how to sew. Sewing was her hobby and, at the same time, an economical way of being well-dressed. Charlie, a junior, invited me to observe a 'skateboard session' (see p. 152). Numerous home visits were made by adolescent invitation. Sometimes I was introduced to parents or guardians and became involved in conversation with adults, but at other times, students kept me to themselves. As time went by, I offered rides to some students; others felt comfortable asking me for rides home or to go shopping. The car itself created a private space where I could talk with them.[3] As my novelty among insiders waned, my feeling of familiarity waxed with the teenagers, the school, and the community. By the end of the fieldwork, I was able to recognize most of the seniors and the majority of the student body by both face and name. Unfortunately, I was not able to talk to everyone at least once, as I first expected. Five hundred students proved too many for an intimate ethnography.

Collecting and Recording Data

Participant Observation and Ethnographic Interviews

I collected most cultural data through two main techniques: participant observation and ethnographic interviews. I observed the adolescents' lives in classrooms, on the school grounds, at home, and in the community, focusing on the non-instructional social aspects of their activities. I did not confine my study to the school boundaries, but I spent the majority of my time interacting in school-related activities. During the observations, I employed different levels of participation ranging from 'passive' to 'moderate' to 'active' (Spradley 1980:59–61). At athletic games, for instance, I observed but rarely participated. In classrooms, I observed the students, sometimes participating in class activities. In adolescent social functions, where I was less afraid of interrupting their normal lives, I actively joined their activities. For instance, I participated in school dances accompanied by teenage female friends.

For the first few weeks, I regularly attended four to seven classes a day. Returning to the same classes helped me develop friendships with some of the students. Later in my fieldwork, I made an effort to sit in on different classes, at least once, in order to observe as many as possible. In most classes, I was moderately involved: I listened to lectures, took some notes, and participated in some class activities; I neither engaged in class discussions nor did homework.

During lunch time, I usually bought a school lunch at the student cafeteria, sometimes ate my brown-bag lunch with students in the hall, went out to a fast-food store, participated in intramural sports, joined a student Bible study, or just strolled around the campus accompanied by some students. I often participated in students' social activities actively during lunch, because this time represented the most relaxing and least restricted hour for most students. Some formal interviews were conducted during lunch time.

After school or on weekends, I observed and participated in students' lives outside of school. I visited their homes, watched athletic games, worshipped at local churches, and joined in off-campus school functions, such as dances, rally and music competitions and field trips. I also attended meetings or events in the community, and I interviewed local citizens when I was not engaged in adolescent activities. I was a privileged observer and, at the same time, a passive participant at formal meetings. On most informal occasions I felt comfortable playing the role of a moderate or active participant.

Participant observation was often accompanied by informal and formal ethnographic interviews. 'Informal interviews' refers to casual conversations with adults as well as adolescents. Whenever I had opportunities to meet teenagers, I asked many questions to learn details about their lives in and outside school. Formal interviews were held when the time and place of the interviews were prearranged. Sometimes informants were informed of interview topics, but I did not prepare rigidly structured interview schedules. Interviewing allowed me to explore given topics in informants' terms. Both formal and informal interviews began with an open-ended, descriptive question: 'Could you describe your day?' 'What did you do this last weekend?' or 'How do you spend time after school?' Spradley termed this type of questions as 'grand tour questions' (1979:86–88). New questions evolved from informants' answers during interviews.

During the summer, I conducted extensive formal interviews with Marylinn about her life history, friends, school and home life, and job. The interviews took place either at her home or at mine. Her mother participated in some of the interview sessions, and both took such an interest in the study that they accepted my invitation to attend the oral defense of my dissertation.

Data Recording and Word Processing

All data from participant observation and informal interviews were hand-written in shorthand in the field and transcribed daily on a personal computer with a word processing program. Some formal interviews were dictated at the scene and later word processed using the computer; others were recorded on audio tapes on site and later transcribed into the computer. As many fieldworkers have discovered, the transcribing process seemed endless and tedious; the transcription of a ninety-minute tape took from thirteen to fifteen hours. All the fieldnotes and interviews were stored on disks, identified by the research technique used, date, and page number.

I discovered four advantages to word processing my fieldnotes and interview transcripts. First, I did not have to worry about producing clean fieldnotes on site, which freed me to better concentrate on participant observation and interviews. Second, the illegibility of shorthand fieldnotes protected the information from being inadvertently read by others in the field. Third, processing the information twice, once in the field and again on the computer at home, aided my memory of data already collected. Several adolescents and adults were pleased at my memory of our conversations, because they felt I was really 'listening' to them. Finally, the information already saved on disk was readily available for later use, especially at the stage of data analysis and writing.

However, this modern technology, that was supposed to make work easier, sometimes turned out to be burdensome. The daily word processing of fieldnotes actually doubled the task. As a result, the enormous amount of data recording curtailed my nightly sleep and at times deprived me of the joy of returning to the field the next day. Toward the end of my fieldwork, I often made a conscious effort to make more legible notes in the field, instead of processing notes once more on the computer, so that I could use the saved time to contact more informants.

Collecting Other Types of Data

In addition to fieldnotes from participant observation and interview transcripts, I collected multiple sorts of data. In my field journal, I recorded my feelings and concerns in the field. Even though the journal was not kept regularly, it provided invaluable information about myself, as a human being as well as ethnographer. Photographs of events in school and in the community captured the vitality of school activities (See Chapters 3, 4 and 10).

Other indispensable data came from works produced by students: classroom journals that students wrote on given topics in English classes, personal journals that individual students wrote for me, essays, homework, the annual school literary magazine, school news-papers, yearbooks, posters for school functions, election campaign posters, and personal memos addressed to me. Significant information and insight were gained through a questionnaire survey with thirty-one open-ended questions administered to all seniors in the class of 1987. (The questionnaire survey form is included in the Appendix.)

Information was also collected through documents and handouts distributed by the school and the school district: the student handbook (distributed annually) that listed general rules with respect to student affairs; daily bulletins, a typed page with daily announcements issued by the administrators for teachers and students; weekly bulletins, a typed page with a weekly activity schedule of the school and the school district, that was distributed to staff; monthly calendars, typed pages containing a schedule for each month, that were distributed to staff and sent to students' homes with a monthly lunch menu; memos from administrators and staff to teachers, students, and their parents/guardians; district and school athletic policies; school lunch menus; and school board agendas and minutes. The final source of data included the Green Lake newspaper, handouts produced by local community groups, and articles from the Riverville newspaper.

Data Analysis and Cultural Interpretation

As an initial step in data analysis, I reviewed the collected data re-peatedly. In the process several categories emerged as of particular importance. Examples of the categories include peer interaction, cars and driving, and employment. After classifying the information according to the topics, I undertook organizational 'cutting and past-ing' in the computer in two ways. After all data were stored on disk, I had freedom to reorganize pieces of information. I broke blocks of information from each day of notes according to topics and printed them on separate five-by-eight-inch cards. Each card was labeled with a topical category, the date, and the page number corres-ponding to that of the original fieldnotes. The second way allowed me to do both cutting and pasting on the computer by using Clipboard.[4] Bits of information pertaining to a specific topic were copied (cut) from their original files, collected (pasted) in a new file via Clipboard, and printed as a single file. The printout of the new file contained pieces of data from all the fieldnote files regarding a specific topic.

Repeatedly I reviewed pieces of information both in a chronological format and within the topical framework. I began this process of data review and analysis while I was still conducting the fieldwork, and continued during the writing. In the summer of 1987, I analyzed the responses of the senior survey administered in May 1987. Responses to each item were collected in one file. At the same time, I prepared a paper to present at the American Anthropological Association annual meeting scheduled in November 1987. These intensive endeavors during the summer helped me organize my thoughts and narrowed down the focus of the fieldwork in the fall. Through reviewing my fieldnotes and undertaking the 'mini' analyses, I tried to make sense out of the details of adolescent life and to discover intuitively underlying themes throughout the data.

In the process of data analysis, I constantly reminded myself of wisdom shared by many ethnographers. The wisdom was condensed in Geertz's statements: 'ethnographic description is interpretive' and 'cultural analysis is (or should be) guessing at meanings, assessing the guesses, and drawing explanatory conclusions from the better guesses' (Geertz, 1973:20). Wolcott (1982) also emphasized that what makes a study 'ethnographic' depends more upon data interpretation than data collection techniques.

The interpretation process cannot be independent from interpreters because they act as research instruments. The cultural interpretation of this ethnography was constructed by a Korean female ethnographer in her late twenties who observed, participated in American adolescent life, and tried to make unfamiliar phenomena familiar to herself. This interpretation was also born in dialogues between science and art; observed facts and the ethnographer as a research 'instrument'; pieces of information and their contexts; and self and others.

Writing Up an Ethnography

As in other stages of the research, I encountered many challenges regarding data reduction, organization, and presentation. One difference at this stage was that the consequences of every decision had a direct impact on the final product. Thus I felt increasing pressure to make 'right decisions' — ethnographic, academic, and ethical.

Reduction of Data

In ethnographic research, the process of reducing data is as consuming as collecting data. One of my colleagues in graduate school confided that data reduction had proven even more difficult than data collection. I speculate on at least two factors that aggravate the reduction process. The first is a human tendency that leaves one unwilling to let go of anything obtained through extraordinary effort. Thus, every detail of the collected data seems of special significance to the ethnographer. The second factor is the massive quantity of data to be processed. Differing from many short-term research projects, ethnographic studies produce more data than could ever fit in a single monograph. As a result, ethnographers face the painstaking task of excluding large amounts of data from the final ethnography with a hope of using them for other writing. My study generated approximately 800 pages of single-spaced typed fieldnotes and many handwritten notes; 100 pages of single-spaced typed interview transcripts; two volumes of senior survey responses; a large file-drawer full of documents; two notebooks of field journals; and an album of photos, in addition to other memorabilia. Only a fraction of the data found its way into the dissertation and, ultimately, into this book.

The first step in data reduction began with sorting, which I initiated at an early stage of fieldwork. There was always the temptation to throw loose data — especially documents — into a box, with a thought of organizing them later. I was glad I had resisted that temptation as I watched such data grow to an enormous volume. I kept different kinds of data in different files so that I could readily identify the sources later. My fieldnotes were bound chronologically in three-hole filebooks. Separate documents were filed in file cabinet folders. All files were clearly labeled by data, source, and/or type.

The second step in data reduction was to select appropriate data for the final product. Although all data were precious and interesting, I deliberately considered only a portion of them for inclusion. The selection process was well thought through and carefully planned. A preliminary table of contents served as a guideline for this process. In addition, the following questions shaped the decision-making: Do I have enough data for any given topic? Do any data present a risk of disclosing the identity of individuals or the community? Do any data deal with sensitive issues that may cause discomfort to students, school staff, and community members? Do I properly observe any requests concerning off-record information? Do I adhere to ethical principles in ethnographic research?

Through these steps I was able to select relevant vignettes and details to be included in my discussion of identified topics and themes.

Organization of Selected Data

Organizing data was neither independent of nor sequential in the reduction process described above. Rather, these two steps were interactive. Using an organizational guideline — in this case, a preliminary table of contents — helped me select relevant data and test their appropriateness for each topic or section. The selected data, in turn, helped to refine the guideline.

I first laid out headings of the table of contents hierarchically in a chart: parts, chapters, subsections, and topics to be include in each subsection. The headings were coded numerically. I literally posted the chart on my wall, leaving a large blank space under each heading. I pulled out index cards (see the section on Data Analysis and Cultural Interpretation, pp. 18–19) containing relevant information for each heading and labeled the cards with the matching codes of the headings. I filled in blanks on the chart with the codes of the cards and sorted out the selected ones separately from the main body of cards. This visual layout allowed me to transfer selected data from one spot to the other and therefore to reorganize the format with ease.

This organizational style sometimes suggested modification of the chart when too much or too little information was yielded for a certain blank. In cases of too much data, the section was broken into subsections; in cases of too little data, the section was either merged with another or dropped.

During this organization process, I constantly made notes of alternative tables of contents and headings, possible ideas to develop in writing, and missing information to be added. While the organization chart gave a concise overview of the developing ethnography, the organization notes helped me to organize material within each chapter.

Presentation of Organized Data

The first consideration of writing was to define the primary readership of the ethnography. In originally preparing the material in the form of a dissertation, the audience was obvious. Committee members already familiar with ethnographic research were the primary readers. Thus I spent minimal time explaining the methods or defending my approach.[5] Beyond my 'ivory tower' audience, I was also conscious of Greenfielders as potential readers. In the presentation of data I wanted to reassure informants of my efforts to maintain the confidentiality of individuals, the school, and the community. In order to keep the identity of the school and community from outsiders, I used pseudonyms for all locations and landmarks within and around the community. Maps of the school and the community (Figures 1 and 2) were rotated in random directions. To protect the privacy of individuals among other insiders, I used pseudonyms for all individuals; sometimes I used more than one pseudonym for a single individual, if I felt that compounded information might contribute to disclosure of an individual or a sensitive issue. In addition, generic titles such as 'administrator' were replaced for too obvious roles like principal or vice principal.

Many ethnographic scholars emphasized the need to write early in the process. They have stressed the importance of starting early in actually *drafting* a study, in addition to the obvious need to keep up with writing fieldnotes. For those who recommended early writing — how early is early? Wolcott advises one to start as early as possible, even 'before ever venturing into the field to begin observations or interviews' (Wolcott, 1990:20). Drafting an ethnographic study without having started fieldwork may sound absurd. However, the truth is that ethnographers have already begun their studies before entering the field, which means they can start writing about their preparation for the fieldwork, their expectations about what they will find, their personal biases, and their intended research methods. It is striking, even enviable, that Norbeck took only a few weeks to finish a 400-page ethnography based on a one-year fieldwork among Japanese farmers (Norbeck, 1986:258). This accomplishment was certainly not a miracle; rather, it resulted from his determination to start writing while still in the field.

Despite this often-offered advice, many ethnographers have experienced difficulties in trying to begin to write early, especially during the primary data collection phase. I was one of them. My rationale for not writing at the time was that I was so occupied with collecting data that I had insufficient time or energy to do any sophisticated organization or analysis. However, my concern about writing grew more serious as the process of organizing data advanced. Keeping the organizational notes, mentioned earlier, helped me start writing.

The purpose of early writing is not to finish up an ethnography quickly; rather, it is to make intermediate assessments of one's own research efforts, possibly to include a need to redirect the focus or to narrow the focus onto specific issues, in what Agar describes as the 'funnel approach' (Agar, 1980:136). Writing, it has often been pointed out, is a form of thinking (e.g., Wolcott, 1990:21). Although I was not seriously engaged in writing a complete draft while collecting and analyzing my data, I had opportunities to write about facets of the study for papers presented at professional conferences (Chang, 1987; 1988). I also had several invitations to give presentations on ethnographic research techniques and processes in graduate classes. These opportunities forced me to 'work on writing' while data were still being collected and analyzed. I am grateful about both the self-imposed and the external opportunities that forced me to begin to process data and start writing. Although neither the papers nor the presentations themselves were included in the finished ethnography as originally prepared, the thinking process helped me narrow my research focus and fill in gaps between my informants' reality and my understanding of that reality as a researcher.

I am not a linear thinker who develops ideas sequentially. Rather, my thoughts often swivel freely from one topic to the other. At one point, I was working on several chapters at the same time. A word processor served me well, allowing me to add, delete, and transfer pieces of data to any location. While I was using a word processor to write a draft, I kept handy the organization chart and notes, in addition to a file box that contained topically classified data cards. This work environment suited my multi-dimensional thinking and writing style.

Once the first draft was finished, I began editing at various levels. I had the primary responsibility to check the accuracy of my accounts and to improve the writing. My informants also read parts of the draft and the principal read the complete draft to verify the details. My proofreaders corrected the errors of a non-native speaker of English; my mentor and my colleagues assisted me with reexamining the analysis and interpretation and polishing my writing. Although I believe that revising and editing are never-ending tasks, repeatedly reworking on the draft helped the final account.

So far in this chapter, I have described several steps of doing ethnographic research — locating a research site, establishing rapport with informants, data collection and recording, data analysis and interpretation, and writing up an ethnography. Ethnographers may adopt different strategies to complete each step, although I believe that the tasks I have identified are the common set that must be addressed in doing ethnographic research.

Notes

1 Names of the school, the community, and all the individuals were replaced with pseudonyms to protect their privacy.
2 During fieldwork in Korea, I did not reveal my age and marital status to the youngsters, because these factors could easily prevent establishing rapport with them. My strategy worked initially, but made it more difficult for me to maintain subsequent contact with them, because of my guilt feelings at deceiving them.
3 Spindler and Spindler also used their car advantageously for conducting private interviews (1986).
4 A clipboard refers to a temporary storage place within the memory capacity of a word processing program. It is reserved for temporarily storing a piece of information to be moved from one file (cutting) to another (pasting).
5 While subsequently revising the dissertation for a wider readership including international readers, I became more fully conscious of numerous cultural 'assumptions' still unexplained in the text.

Part 2

Adolescent Life

Chapter 2

Introduction to a Greenfield Teenager

When I was first aware of Marylinn, who sang in a trio in the 1987 school talent show at Greenfield High School, she was a 15-year-old sophomore. Since then I had often noticed her as a front runner in many activities. My first impression of active students like her had kept me from approaching her, because they seemed to be so involved in their own lives and not particularly interested in meeting new people.

I finally met Marylinn two months after my fieldwork began. During lunch hour on a sunny day in March, I sat in a courtyard talking with Donna, a sophomore, who was sitting next to me. Our sitting together might have encouraged some of her friends to approach me. One of Donna's friends, Marylinn, stopped to speak to me: 'I thought at first you were one of the students. I'm surprised to know you're doing research,' she said. When it was time for the girls to go to class, I asked both Donna and Marylinn if I could talk with them again. I did not realize at that time how much this encounter with Marylinn would affect my research on US adolescents. In about a week, another meeting with Marylinn convinced me that she would make a good informant: she was easy to talk to, articulate, informative, open-minded, and personable. Along with several other Greenfield adolescents, she became an important contributor to my research.

This chapter introduces Marylinn as a likable human being, an embodiment of US culture, a defender of ideals, and a vulnerable teenager. Although mentioned throughout the book, she will be treated as a prototype of Greenfield adolescents rather than as a main character. Marylinn shared many common characteristics with her peers: her concern with grades, social life, independence, and activities. However, I do not attempt to present her as a 'typical' US teenager because I found it impossible to typify US teenagers. The stereotypical image of US adolescents might misrepresent reality. To borrow Max Weber's concept of 'ideal type', the image of typical adolescents is a mere 'logically precise conception' constructed with certain elements of reality (Gerth and Mills, 1958:59). Therefore, the ideal type could not be actually present in the real world where Marylinn existed. However, Marylinn was not an atypical adolescent: she had been reared by American parents in the United States and had studied in American schools.

Growing Up Close to Nature

Marylinn was born about twenty-five miles away from where she lived at the time of fieldwork. When she was 2 years old, her family moved to a small city in Idaho, where her mother had grown up and her grandparents still live. A highlight of her childhood was living in a 'little and tiny caretaker's cabin' on the edge of a lake about fifteen miles away from the small city. While her father worked away from home most of the time as a log truck driver and later as a ski instructor, Marylinn lived in the cabin with her mother and a dog for a year and a half. They lived rent-free in exchange for taking care of the property and a boat owned by a retired couple who stayed there only in the summer. Marylinn recalled that the cabin was greenish, which she did not like, and remarkably small with 'a little kitchen, small living room, small bedroom and tiny, tiny bathroom'. In winter, water pipes were often frozen and the family was snowed in.

Nevertheless, life there was remembered and discussed with excitement and nostalgia by both Marylinn and her mother. When they described their life there, they vigorously interjected their opinions to make the description vivid, even poetic:

> It was very rustic, very small, very crowded, but it was beautiful...out there because we were away from the city and you could...look across the lake and see the lights of town. And winter time, we were just surrounded by snow and we could see elk and moose walk by our place.

Since the cabin was remote, their only neighbors were the landowners during the summer. Marylinn spent a lot of time with her mother, going swimming in the lake, taking walks, and listening to music on the radio. Her dog was a constant companion, and a tiny yellow swing was a source of entertainment. That eighteen month period, before moving to the city where her grandparents lived, gave Marylinn ample opportunities to enjoy nature.

After living in her grandparents' hometown for eighteen months, Marylinn's family, now including a newborn brother, moved to a 'single-wide' house-trailer on private property in Woodland, Oregon. Woodland was the smallest of several little towns encompassed by the Green Lake School District. Since then, her family has lived in this same house-trailer, surrounded by woods, with a small pond formerly inhabited by wild ducks. Woodland was sparsely populated, with less than a hundred residents, and its area was largely forested. Her house was located about fifteen miles away from Peaceland (the center city of about 2,500 residents in the Green Lake community) and about thirty miles from Riverville, the closest middle-sized city. The house was not as isolated as the caretaker's cabin in Idaho, but her neighbor houses were so surrounded by woods as to be out of sight.

In all directions from their house, Marylinn and Dan, her younger brother, found woods to explore, trees to climb, trails to hike, and streams to fish or just paddle in. These natural resources were always there to entertain them, especially on weekends or during vacations when indoor activities were running short. In the eighth and ninth grade, she had opportunities to learn how to ride a horse in exchange for cleaning out horse stalls for her neighbors. Since horseback riding is more feasible in a rural community than in a city, Marylinn took advantage of her rural life.

Marylinn expressed contentment with living close to nature. Although she sometimes missed living in a city where much action took place, she objected to her friends' pity of her 'isolated' life:

> Sometimes I hate when people make it sound as if I'm deprived because of where I live. Randy [a school friend] makes it sound as if I probably don't (or can't) have any fun unless we go out and do something...I do have an imagination. I can come up with things to do outside like taking walks, riding my bike, or going down to the river.

During the summer of 1987 when she was sixteen, Marylinn wrote in her journal that she and her brother often enjoyed hiking on the hill behind their house and going fishing in the stream across the highway in front of her house.

This nature-loving life-style was nourished by her family's way of vacationing. Their favorite vacation spots were beaches along the

Pacific Coast. They took frequent trips to the coast, as well as to inland lakes for weekends or summer vacations. Almost every summer, the family visited her grandparents in Idaho, camping along the way. These frequent outings had enhanced Marylinn's familiarity with nature. Her remarkable knowledge of animals and vegetation on high school biology field trips was truly impressive.

Family Dynamics

Marylinn's family represented a typical United States nuclear family of four including her parents, a younger brother five years her junior, and herself. Marylinn's father had worked at different jobs such as log-truck driver, ski instructor, commercial fisherman, and welder since Marylinn's birth. He went wherever jobs were available, which kept him away from home for lengthy periods of time. He worked as far away as Alaska, coming home only once every couple of months during my fieldwork. Despite her husband's frequent absences, Marylinn's mother observed that he tried to keep his presence at home alive by writing, telephoning, and making visits as often as possible. Marylinn's mother had been a homemaker for most of the time since her marriage. She said that she liked to be at home with her children. It was almost inevitable that she did not have a job, because once her children began school she had to take them to extracurricular activities. Most of the time, Marylinn got along with her brother, Dan, who appeared intelligent and mature for his age. They were not, however, immune to sibling quarrels, especially when Dan tagged along too often when Marylinn's friends were visiting, or when Dan felt Marylinn took charge too much. Despite their conflicts, Marylinn and her 'little' brother often attended each other's activities as supporters.

Marylinn had a close bond with her family. The family had many activities together, but most of them were not extravagant. On weekends, the whole family drove ninety miles to visit her father's mother, or perhaps rented home video movies and ate popcorn while watching them. Marylinn's mother attributed their family-oriented activities partly to their isolated living situation, because they had to create their own entertainment. She insisted that their close family tie was embedded in her husband's vision of 'a good family life'. According to her, he liked to spend time with his family, even after his long work trips. They preferred to do things with their children rather than go by themselves to adult-only functions. Marylinn also contributed to keeping this family-centeredness alive by choosing family activities over competing social interactions with her peers.

Another way of keeping family ties close was communication. Marylinn said that she spent much time sitting down and talking with her mother about everything from school to friends. When Marylinn brought up her problems, her cheerful mother became a good listener and counselor. Marylinn said that it was fun to talk with her mother, and Marylinn's friends sometimes liked to become part of the conversations. Her mother appreciated Marylinn's willingness to communicate and was convinced that family communication was a key to their good relationships.

Marylinn's parents showed their interest in what was going on in their children's lives. Her father remarked:

> We've been involved in the kids' development. We've been involved in schooling. . . . We've been in their schools. We know their teachers. We've been actively involved in their friends. Their friends are welcome here [at our home]. We want to know who the people are.

The parents demonstrated interest by attending their daughter's activities, sports, award ceremonies, Honor Society banquets, and the Homecoming parade. Despite his frequent absence from home, Marylinn's father attended all the children's activities whenever he was in town. Both parents considered sharing activities with their children as a privilege that would last only until the children left home. Therefore, they liked to take advantage of it while they still had their children at home.

Marylinn's parents felt proud of their daughter. They openly expressed their pleasure at being parents of a teenager and did not look forward to seeing their daughter leave home in the near future. They had reasons to be proud of Marylinn. She had close to a 4.0 grade point average (GPA) — a straight 'A', participated in sports, was a member of the Honor Society, and was voted Homecoming princess in her freshman year. She did not take drugs, drink alcohol, or have problems with boys. It seemed that she was a pleasant teenage girl for any parents.

What made Marylinn's parents proud of their daughter was more than her merits. They commented on her mature character as 'a good person'. One element of her maturity was identified as her conscientiousness. According to her parents she consciously made judgments they saw as correct and abided by them, although she sometimes became 'too straight-laced'. The second element of her maturity, as noted by her father, was her sensitivity to the shortcomings of her peers: 'She's surprisingly adept at identifying her friends' weaknesses and trying to help them with them rather than being judgmental.' She tried to compensate for her best friend's hearing problem by consciously raising her voice and directing conversation to her 'better' ear. On separate occasions, I also noticed Marylinn's sensitivity when she attempted to protect a 'special education' boy and an 'unpopular' volleyball player from their peers' unfair treatment. (pp. 37–8) Thirdly, as Marylinn's mother pointed out, she showed her maturity by her ability to 'get along with adults as well as children of her age'. These qualities — conscientiousness, sensitivity, and the ability to get along with others — reflected Marylinn's family values as well as the ideals of the adult society.

Marylinn's parents transmitted their values to their children in an allegedly democratic way: 'You have choices to make and then have to face the consequences.' They also verbalized their trust in her judgment: 'She is at the "young adult" stage....I can find very little fault with most of her judgments. Some of them show extremely good insight.' On many occasions, her parents put their trust into practice by allowing her to drive the family car to Riverville or to participate in social functions with her peers.

In general, though, they were not laissez-faire parents; rather, they readily revealed their firm ideas of how their children should grow up. They only expressed their messages in 'we wish' statements rather than 'you should' commands. For example, in respect to smoking, drinking, 'doping' (using drugs), and driving with excessive speed (all considered common teenage problems), they observed, 'We certainly hope that you never do.' In order to make their case strong against smoking, her father said, 'Our example is extremely poor in that matter.' Her parents also encouraged Marylinn to have high expectations of herself and expressed pride at her being more and doing more than what they had accomplished during their adolescence.

At the same time, Marylinn's parents suggested that she not take her achievements for granted or boast about them. They explained that success in school came easily to some people because of their background: the 'haves' get more and the 'have-nots' get less. Referring to her achievements and awards in the eighth grade when she was active as class president, her father expressed his view of social inequality as follows:

There is a tendency.... When you've been there several years, you...got a relationship with your instructors...administrators. They often choose those to receive the awards.... It's not always based purely on an achievement.... A lot of them are based on a personal preference. And that's what life's all about. So when you don't receive, quite often you can see the unfairness. If you're a recipient of an award, quite often you take it for granted.

Her parents told her that things came easier for her than others. According to them, many more things 'go for her' than for themselves in their high school days. To remind her of ordinary students in school, her mother used herself as an example: 'I was perfectly happy with 'C' grades and was never voted a Homecoming princess in my high school.' Marylinn's parents' way of putting across their values was subtle but powerful. It did not appear imposing, yet Marylinn knew what her parents expected of her and she voluntarily tried to live up to their expectations. Their message of humbleness may have shaped her character: she tried not to judge her peers on the basis of academic status or social popularity, and she was humble about her success.

This style of value-transmission, however, seemed to have put her on a 'guilt trip' about outperforming her parents and her peers. She expressed guilt that she received such good grades, thinking that she did not work as hard as others. Marylinn's ambivalence between the expectation and the guilt of success seemed to prevent her from making career plans to allow her to transcend her parents' socioeconomic status. Thus, despite her academic standing, excellent activity record, leadership skills, and personal abilities, her future aspiration reached as far as attending a community college.[1] She also said that she did not yet know what she wanted to do with her life.

Different Dimensions of Friendship

Marylinn associated with a wide range of peers, from active 'socialites' to shy 'nerds'. Among her peers, she identified Amanda as her best friend. She spent a lot of time with Amanda in school as well as out. On school days, they rode the same bus, shared a locker, took some of the same classes, and spent their noon hour together eating lunch or doing homework. Both of them also participated in track and field together. Both had a common interest in school and grades; school-related topics frequently surfaced in their conversation. Outside school, they visited or telephoned each other at home, and did many 'fun' activities together. Shopping, visiting the county fair, and going to movies were on their list of the 'fun' things. After Marylinn got her driver's license, Amanda was the first friend to be driven to Riverville. The following vignette was taken from Marylinn's journal about their outing:

> I had a really fun time with Amanda today. First, I drove to her house and picked her up. We decided to go to Grand Shopping Center and to shop and eat lunch there.... We both had McDonald's hamburgers at the shopping center. We looked at almost every store there before we decided to drive to the Riverville Mall. At the mall, we went to our favorite store and to the picture booth.... When we were done looking around at the mall we drove home.... I drove by the Peaceland pool. I saw [several school friends].... We had a lot of fun!

The journal illustrates Marylinn's and Amanda's way of enjoying each other's company. Just being together and giggling about trivia seemed to support their friendship.

Despite their close friendship, Marylinn said that she and Amanda were different in many ways. Their personalities contrasted: Marylinn was outgoing and social; Amanda appeared introverted and reserved. Their life interests also had little in common: Amanda was much more interested in boyfriends and clothes. One day, Marylinn and Amanda counted the number of boyfriends each had had throughout their lives. Marylinn had a total of three; they were able to enumerate twenty-two boyfriends (not necessarily all serious ones) for Amanda. On the average, Marylinn spent less than fifty dollars each fall on her school clothes, which were bought at thrift clothing stores. Amanda usually bought hers in fashion stores, spending several times as much as Marylinn. Marylinn and Amanda sometimes had conversations about more serious topics than boyfriends and clothes, but most of the time they just had 'fun'. Marylinn felt that their relationship became superficial at times; she missed conversations on serious matters such as politics and religion.

These differences did not interfere with the two girls' friendship, however, because they fully trusted each other. This trust had built up since they were 10-year-olds in the fifth grade, when both Marylinn and Amanda felt that they did not have any friends in school. When Marylinn's mother suggested for the first time that she become friends with Amanda, Marylinn was not so thrilled, because Amanda appeared to be shy and even 'weird'. But they got to know each other better and slowly became friends. Since then, Marylinn had realized that Amanda depended on their friendship and appreciated her as her best friend. Marylinn said, instead of feeling burdened, 'I felt important because I knew that somebody would always meet me there [at school]...to talk to. That made me feel that actually I have a friend.' Their mutual trust was strengthened when Marylinn was undergoing a heart-wrenching breakup with her boyfriend, Brandt. After that happened, Brandt intentionally ignored Marylinn, and her circle of friends sided with Brandt. Only Amanda stayed with Marylinn throughout her emotional turmoil. Marylinn's mother added, 'Marylinn and Amanda are a lot different, but Marylinn knows Amanda is loyal to her.' Marylinn agreed with her mother that Amanda was a faithful friend.

Linda was another good friend of Marylinn's. Marylinn enjoyed Linda's company and spent much time with her. They visited each other's homes (but probably not as often as Marylinn visited Amanda) and Linda felt comfortable in the company of Marylinn's parents. One day, instead of asking her own mother, Linda telephoned Marylinn's mother to ask how to iron a shirt efficiently. Since Linda felt comfortable around Marylinn's family and could deal with Marylinn's father's humor, she was easily included in Marylinn's family conversations.

To many of their peers, Marylinn and Linda appeared to be very close, since they participated in visible activities like school dances. When they got together, they became loud and enjoyed doing 'crazy' things. Since Linda generally gave an impression of a quiet and reserved person in school, this change usually surprised her teachers. Marylinn said that being with Linda triggered her creative, crazy mood. Marylinn's mother recalled a light-hearted incident that Marylinn and Linda created with another friend, Mary. One night in the eighth grade when they were thirteen, these girls stayed at Marylinn's house. They kept the family out of her room. When they finally called the family to come in the room, these girls were lying on their backs with their heads hanging off the edge of Marylinn's high bed, so that their heads were upside down. They had scarves from their noses up, covering their eyes. They painted two little eyes under their lower lips, taped paper hair on their chins, and lipsynched a song on a record. It appeared that three little eccentric faces dangling off the bed were cheerfully singing. As later recounted, the family stood and roared with laughter.

Marylinn also found Linda more compatible for talk about serious issues, which she found lacking in her friendship with Amanda. When she was with Linda, they usually talked with each other or improvised something to do at home. Comparing the two types of friendship, Marylinn said, 'Amanda is a person that I talk to about more fun things…We go into town and do things. Linda and I usually sit down and talk.'

However, Marylinn hesitated to call Linda her best friend because full trust was lacking; instead, a certain degree of competition existed between them. Her somehow uneasy feeling with Linda dated back to the sixth grade when Marylinn, age 11, had her first 'boyfriend' for a week. Marylinn sensed that Linda, who was his friend, 'was jealous because [he] was paying more attention to me than to her'. Another incident took place when Marylinn began going out with Brandt in her high school freshman year. Since Marylinn 'hung out' with Amanda, Linda, and a few more friends during lunch, Brandt was automatically included in this circle. Marylinn said that Linda seemed to be interested in Brandt and behaved in an unusually outgoing manner in his presence. When Marylinn broke up with him after a month, she could not stand Brandt's 'cold shoulder' and left the group; Amanda joined her, while others maintained friendship with Brandt.

Marylinn argued, 'As soon as we broke up, she [Linda] was kind of waiting so that she could go in and try to get to know him better.' While Marylinn was suffering from the aftermath, Linda kept her friendship with Brandt and began dating him a half year later. Marylinn thought that it was at least considerate of her not to go out with him right away. After a few months of courtship, Linda and Brandt broke up. By that time, Marylinn renewed her friendship with Brandt and became good friends with Brandt's friend, Randy. Brandt treated Linda 'worse' than he had treated Marylinn. As a result, Linda underwent even more emotional distress than Marylinn and held a grudge against Randy whom she viewed partly responsible for their breakup. On the one hand, Marylinn sympathized with Linda and tried to help her; on the other hand, she did not deny that she gloated over her breaking up.

Their competition was also subtly manifested over cars. Marylinn's parents bought her her first car at the beginning of her junior year and Marylinn enthusiastically shared the news with Linda. Linda said, 'Yeah?' as if it was 'no big deal'. After having complained for awhile that she had no money, Linda finally got a car of her own. Marylinn was upset by the fact that Linda did not tell her the big news (owning a first car was always thrilling news among teenagers).

In addition to Amanda and Linda, Marylinn spent time in school with a circle of friends including a few girls from the rally squad (cheerleaders), plus Brandt and Randy. Her friendship with the cheerleaders began in her middle school days (11–13 years) when they used to invite each other to their homes often. Her friendship with Brandt and Randy was relatively new and had grown steadily after the year of the 'cold war' with Brandt. Her circle of friends was actively involved in leadership, the music program, and sports. Marylinn enthusiastically participated with them in junior class activities such as making a Homecoming float or decorating dance halls. Her circle of friends also took school work seriously and they were academically successful, keeping their grades over a 3.5 GPA (a 'B$^+$' average). During lunch hour, they clustered next to their lockers on the hall floor to visit and do homework.

Marylinn's association with cheerleaders and her involvement might give an impression that she was an outgoing and 'in-crowd' girl and, in turn, more likely to be 'stuck-up'. Rather, she actually criticized some 'stuck-up' peers who acted as though they were 'the greatest' and ignored other people. She recounted one incident when she and Linda encountered a couple of self-centered peers. One spring afternoon, Marylinn and Linda decided to go out to play hackeysack (a game in which two or more people toss a ping-pong-ball-sized leather sack filled with sand to each other with their feet) with a group of people who generally hung out close to a smoking area and were considered unpopular in school. The girls did not have a particularly close friendship with them, but did not want to enslave themselves to their own prejudices against them. The hackeysack players were surprised at their approach, but not as much as those in the girls' social group. When Marylinn and Linda finished playing, a couple of so-called 'in-crowd' peers reproached them, 'You played hackeysack with them? How gross! Those guys are scums.' Their criticism immediately evoked Marylinn's response, 'You're so superficial.'

While Marylinn spent much of her time with close friends, she tried to be friendly with a wide range of people in her school. She showed particular sympathy with 'underdogs'. One day, I was sitting with her on a hall floor during lunch. A crowd of boys and girls rushed into the hall with a freshman, John, who suffered mild brain damage. A boy from the crowd asked John to mimic 'He Man' (a cartoon movie character) and John proudly acted, with slightly uncoordinated body movements. When the crowd asked him to repeat his performance, Marylinn appeared uncomfortable watching him make a fool of himself. She told the crowd to stop urging him on and also reminded John, 'You don't have to do it if you don't want to.'

On another occasion, she became furious with her peers who cursed and yelled at her 'unpopular' volleyball teammate, Grace. After a volleyball practice, girls were changing their clothes in the locker room while some of them went out, leaving the door open. Grace expressed her annoyance, telling her peers to close the door behind them. It prompted another girl's verbal attack, 'Shut your mouth.' Marylinn mentioned that had anyone else said the same thing they would not have responded in that way. This seeming injustice upset Marylinn and she ended up yelling at her peers, 'You are hypocrites.' Although this might have cost friendship with some, it certainly helped her gain a good reputation among others.

School as a Source of Fun and Stress

For Marylinn, school was a place for learning but also for many other activities as well. On school days, she participated in sport teams until 5 pm after finishing seven hours of classes. Her off-campus activities were limited to occasional volunteer help in community functions. Therefore, school, family, and friends were the major source of activities in Marylinn's life. Marylinn had always been active in school functions in academics, sports, and leadership. Instead of overloading herself, she distributed her time among one sport per season, daily homework from most classes, choir, a leadership position, and several field trips a term.

In communities where various formally organized sources of entertainment are rarely found, school often plays an important role in producing something for adolescents to do (Peshkin, 1978:147). At Greenfield High School, sports events certainly offered entertainment opportunities for the young people. Especially during the football season, the sole reason for many students to come to athletic games was to meet their friends. Going to football games was Marylinn's favorite activity, because it created a festive mood where people from the school and the community gathered to support the school and to socialize. She was often accompanied by her mother, her father, if he was in town, her brother, and her friend Amanda.

After the games, she usually went to dances with her circle of friends without first bothering to find a date. She said that it was more fun to dance with her friends as a group because she did not constantly have to worry about her date. In addition to regular school dances, she usually attended Homecoming and Prom dances. In her junior year, however, Marylinn could not go to the Homecoming dance because most of her friends found dates and those without did not want to accompany her. Yet, the following spring, she managed to go to the Prom with a group of girls. She explained that she was more interested in having fun than in being concerned about what other people thought of her.

Marylinn also enjoyed opportunities to dress up in costumes during the Homecoming and Prom 'spirit' weeks and for Halloween. Referring to the 'spirit' weeks, she said that she liked them because they are 'not like school days'. For each day of the week, the student government assigned a theme for dress-up, for example, Peace Day, Cowboy/girl Day, and Disneyland Day. Every morning in the weeks, she got up earlier than usual to dress according to the day's theme. She equally enjoyed Halloween. These special occasions offered entertainment not usually associated with normal school activities.

Although some activities attracted adolescent interest, school often became a source of stress. For instance, the fall term of her junior year was almost a nightmare to Marylinn. She had many homework assignments from Math, Honors Humanities, Field Biology, and English classes. She participated in volleyball practice every day, with games scheduled every week. When she had games played at other schools, she did not come home until 9 pm or later.

As stress built up, she almost considered quitting volleyball, her favorite sport. Since she took her school work seriously, she could not imagine slighting her homework schedule. Her years of athletic involvement seemed to have provided a routine in her life. Her active involvement in other school activities was of importance and her outgoing, active nature did not allow her to slow down with social activities. For example, she did not like to miss school dances. They provided entertainment and social contact with her peers in the community where 'there's nothing' for teenagers. Hence, she found nothing to give up. Rather, she chose to cope with stress accompanying the dilemma of being a really active, yet serious and academic-minded adolescent.

A Successful Balance-Keeper

Like many adolescents, Marylinn lived in a complicated web of cultural ideals, messages, and values that were emphasized by parents, teachers, and peers. They often presented her with dilemmas. For example, Marylinn's parents wanted her to make decisions on her own; nevertheless, they set limits. The adults tried to get across the importance of self-assurance and independence from peer pressure. Like other teenagers, however, she knew that friends were needed for everyday survival, and standing for her ideals might result in losing her reputation as an easy-to-get-along-with person. Marylinn tried to be friendly with a wide range of peers; however, she was aware that frequent association with so-called unpopular people could cost her friendship with other types of friends. She also knew she was expected to share time with her family and got along with her parents; often, though, her peers teased her for being a 'mama's girl' or a 'daddy's brat'. Marylinn had been brought up to relate well to adults; now, her peers sometimes accused her of being a 'goody goody' (one who tries to be overly friendly to everyone) or 'brown-noser' (one who curries favors from teachers). The school staff taught patriotism, but Marylinn's parents criticized the injustices in the society. She said that she did not feel patriotic on the Fourth of July, nor did she feel proud of her country's government; at the same time, she said she felt guilty for not feeling patriotic.

How could she successfully survive in this seemingly contradictory world? She might have learned that close adherance to one extreme ideal would not please either her peers, parents, or school staff. It seemed impossible to remain at a mid-point on each continuum of contrasting ideals.[2] Who would have a practical idea of where to locate the mid-point for every situation?

United States adolescents, including Marylinn, reminded me of acrobats who walk on tightropes strung high in the air. They may often lean to either direction to keep balance, but they never lean too far. Likewise, if the adolescents wanted to keep balance successfully amidst multi-dimensional pressures, they needed to avoid troubling any party among their 'significant others', parents, peers, and school staff, if not actively pleasing them. If they accomplished this balance, they might be considered successful and, at least, acceptable among them. If they were not able to do so, they might be viewed as losers, at least in the eyes of one or more of their significant others.

Notes

1 In the second half of her senior year, she applied for admission to a local university instead of a community college and received acceptance as an

undeclared major (an option given to incoming freshmen, who could explore different subjects before deciding on their majors). In the middle of her sophomore year in 1990, she decided to become an elementary school teacher.

2 This idea is further discussed in Chapter 10.

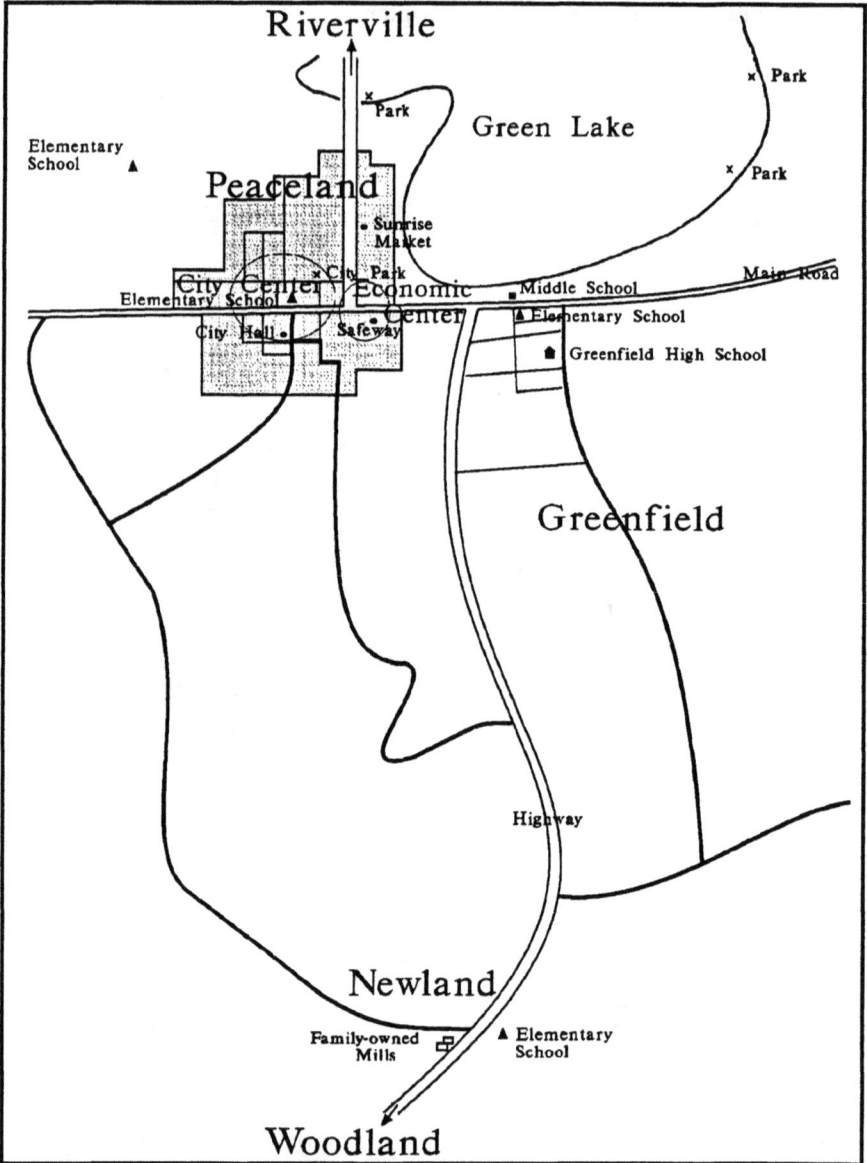

Figure 1. A sketch map of the Green Lake community (not to scale).

Chapter 3

Green Lake Community

The Green Lake community was conterminous with the Green Lake School District, where high school adolescents, the focus of my study, resided. I conducted fieldwork among the adolescents in the high school and the community during calendar year 1987. In this chapter, the community is portrayed as the cultural milieu of adolescent lives. After describing the local economy and the population makeup of the community, I discuss adolescent activities and employment opportunities in the community and its support of the young people. I remind readers that this is not a study of the community, but of its adolescents.

The School District as a Community

The Green Lake community consisted of a small city, called Peaceland, and three semi-rural adjacent towns — Greenfield, Newland, and Woodland (see Figure 1). The territory encompassed about 500 square miles; its population was estimated[1] by a high school administrator at 7,000–10,000. The ratio of population to territory indicated that the community was sparsely populated. The wide distribution of the population seemed to contribute to a lower sense of community among residents in the combined area than would exist in an area of greater population density. Most people (approximately 2,500–3,000) resided in Peaceland; the next largest number lived in Greenfield, followed by Newland and Woodland.

A local history book reported that westward-moving pioneers first settled the region during the late 1800s. In a more recent historical event occurring in 1962, Peaceland was incorporated as a city. Since then, unsuccessful attempts had been made to annex adjacent towns to the city. The three towns were administratively independent of Peaceland, although remaining economically and culturally related to the city. Arterial roads gave the areas a unified appearance to outsiders. Main Road connected Peaceland and Greenfield, which, in turn, were linked with Newland and Woodland by a highway. This highway also ran between the Green Lake community and Riverville, a nearby middle-sized city.

The Green Lake community was viewed as a unity in this study because the Green Lake School District served the whole area. Each subcommunity had its own elementary school. One middle school and one high school drew sixth through eighth (generally aged 12–14 years) and ninth through twelfth graders (generally aged 14–18 years) respectively from the combined community. Enrollment at these six schools in 1987 totaled almost 1,800 students. The high school as well as the middle school knitted the subcommunities together through school activities.

The Community Economy

Farming used to be the major occupation of the Green Lake community and still played an important role in the community. Crops included fruits, vegetables, Christmas trees, and wine grapes. These farms provided city residents with opportunities to self-pick fresh agricultural products. Hay, firewood and Christmas trees were common sale items. Raising livestock was also a typical practice for cash, domestic use, or simply as a hobby: rabbits, chickens, and cows for food or cash; and horses, sheep, goats, and rabbits for fun or trade.

In addition to farming and raising livestock, this area had been known for logging; forest resources abounded. A national corporation had established a large lumber mill in the vicinity of Peaceland two decades earlier, and two family-owned local mills operated in Newland. These mills employed residents from Peaceland and Newland and attracted laborers from outside of this community. The logging opportunities thus engendered had stimulated logging-related construction businesses as well. It was said that a majority of the population worked for the mills when the logging industry had been in full swing in the 1960s and 1970s. Although this was no longer true, a few smaller mills continued their operation.

Since the incorporation of Peaceland as a city, the economy of the area had diverged from farming and logging. The variety of employment opportunities was enlarged by civil and public service agencies such as the city government, fire department, post office, public library, and city park; financial institutions such as two banks, local business offices, and stores; and a local newspaper. The economic center of the community was at the intersection of Main Road and the highway between Peaceland and Greenfield. This area was conspicuously marked with a shopping complex, a few restaurants, and a cluster of shops. The Green Lake shopping complex included a large chain grocery store (I will refer to it as Safeway) and various kinds of small-scale shops. Two locally-owned restaurants and a fast-food outlet stood in the vicinity of the complex. Growing public services and stores had improved local business prospects and expanded the spectrum of employment. The business area also played a significant role in teenagers' lives because it provided a place to 'hang out' during lunch hour and part-time jobs to earn pocket money. Recently, the Peaceland city government had formed a task force to assess ways of boosting economy in this business district.

Compared to Peaceland, other towns contained fewer business activities. For example, the center of Greenfield, the next largest town, had a post office, several stores along Main Road, and a cluster of schools, the elementary, middle, and high school. The center of Newland was barely noticeable, comprised as it was of an elementary school, two family-owned lumber mills, and several smaller stores. A single store with multiple functions of a gas station, food store, book and video rental store, and post office marked Woodland, the smallest town in the community. The limited variety of businesses in the small towns made the residents dependent on Peaceland for grocery and household shopping needs.

The economy of the Green Lake community was also partially dependent on a nearby middle-sized city, Riverville, for sources of income and consumption. The relatively short driving distance (about fifteen miles from Peaceland, and thirty-five miles from the Woodland store) allowed many Green Lake residents to commute to Riverville for professional, manual, or clerical jobs. The proximity to Riverville also attracted a low-income population into some sections of the Green Lake community where housing was more affordable than in the city. As an administrator of Greenfield High School observed, the area was a 'bedroom community' for commuters to Riverville. Green Lake residents not only brought income from Riverville but also spent money there when dining out or shopping. The Green Lake community provided limited kinds of merchandise, but was lacking in clothing stores, a variety of restaurants, an automobile dealership, and other amenities. As a result, many families went to Riverville for major shopping. Some local merchants complained that patrons of the community did not support local businesses.

The dependency on Riverville may have also been attributed to the recent arrivals of 'city folks' who moved into the Green Lake community to seek a pleasant, natural environment. These people enjoyed living in comfortable, well-furnished residences in remote environments, wooded areas at the edge of Peaceland or around Green Lake, while still holding their jobs in Riverville. They tended to associate largely with the social and cultural life in the city, which also accounted for a 'low' sense of community in Green Lake.

The Population Makeup

The composition of the community's population reflected the local economy's reliance upon farming, livestock raising, logging, small businesses, and the nearby city. The desirable characteristics of the area, such as nature, space, and independent-living, also attracted alternative-living advocates and environmentalists to the community. The diverse population ranged from old-timers to newcomers; and included farmers, blue-collar laborers, and white-collar professionals; the poor and the well-off; political liberals and conservatives; illicit drug dealers and ordained clergy; and loyalists, critics, and indifferent residents. Although some cherished the 'rural' character of the community, several school administrators, students, and community members seemed to welcome an image change under way from a poor country 'hick' area to a modern and progressive region.

Despite its vocational diversity, the racial composition of the community was predominantly white. I identified only a small number of racial and ethnic minorities in the whole student body, including one Black, a few Asians, a few Hispanics, and several self-identified Native Americans. A well-published racist incident in the community reflected prejudice among a small segment of the population against racial and ethnic minorities. Personally, however, I do not recall any unpleasant incidents directed toward me during the study.

Five family portraits provided below represent something of the diversity of the Green Lake population. They include families of a well-off self-employed professional; an owner of a Christmas tree farm; a politically active, local business owner; a modest-living, retired mill-worker; and a city commuter with an alternative life-style. All of these families contained one or two high school adolescents.

Except for the fifth family, all of the children attended Greenfield High School. These families represented not only a variety of life-styles, but also varying degrees of involvement in community matters.

The first family, the Walters, was one of the wealthier families in the area. Father and mother were in their forties and college-educated. Mr. Walters was an active attorney before the family moved to Greenfield about five years ago; his wife had been a homemaker. Mr. and Mrs. Walters operated a few businesses in Riverville and in the Green Lake Community while being active in their church. Having five children ranging from 9 to 23 years of age, both parents strongly believed in the value of a good education for all their children. Their children had had private lessons in piano, dance, and voice, unlike most of local youngsters. Mrs. Walter showed her support for their children by attending almost all of their activities in school and in the community. The Walters' participation in other community functions, however, seemed minimal, except for church activities. Their affluence was reflected in their residence; an spacious mansion in the woods complete with a well-mowed, small-scale golf course, a swimming pool, a jacuzzi, and a large trampoline. Indoors, one finds a pool table and a few up-right video-game machines, as well as other entertainment devices. Their style of recreation was obvious from their motor vehicles: two recreational vehicles for the use of ten people (one for sale), two Yamaha three-wheelers, a Honda motorcycle, several smaller-sized motorcycles, and a four-wheeler. Mr. Walter stated, 'One for everyone in the family'.

The second family, who owned and managed a Christmas tree farm next to their modest but comfortable house-trailer, was extremely active in the community. The Wilsons were not natives to the community, but had been living in the area for more than ten years. Mr. and Mrs. Wilson were college-educated and Mrs. Wilson had once taught in a local preschool. They operated the farm almost alone, hiring temporary help only during the Christmas season. Besides the family business, Mr. Wilson had volunteered as a fireman for the past nine years. In addition to her housekeeping responsibilities, Mrs. Wilson spent considerable time participating in a variety of community committees and parents' meetings, coaching children's sport teams, and volunteering as a special education tutor. She sometimes spoke out about her concerns and criticisms in order to realize her vision of improving the community as a safe and healthy environment for young people. The Wilsons actively showed interest in their children's lives by attending their children's school and community activities. They also encouraged their sons and daughter to improve their academic and musical abilities, often using monetary rewards. They paid the children five dollars for a 4.0 GPA (straight 'A'), fifty cents for one-hour of piano practice, twenty cents for learning a new piano piece by heart, and ten cents for retaining an already memorized piece.

The third family, the Martins, operated a local welding shop in the community. Despite a moderate income, the Martins had sent three children to a parochial high school in Riverville. In exchange for reducing their high educational cost, Mr. and Mrs. Martin volunteered to help the school as a part-time maintenance worker and a bookkeeper respectively.[2] Having carried through their activism as 'flower children' in the 1960s, the Martins still maintained their political stand in favor of international peace and a nuclear-free world. Mr. Martin's political beliefs and religious convictions led him to participate in a sit-in protest against nuclear testing sites. The parents' activism had been transmitted to their children. Their two girls were involved in a political form of 'punk culture' concerning the peace movement.

The fourth family, the Tylers, had lived in the community for over twenty years. They had four grown-up children (one in high school), one from Mr. Tyler's previous marriage and three from his present one. Two youngest children — a son and a daughter — lived with their parents. Before retiring, Mr. Tyler worked at a local mill, a branch of a national lumber company, for ten years. A leg injury received on the job allowed him to take an early retirement benefit. Now in his sixties, he and his family depended mainly on his disability retirement pension and Social Security benefits. The family also raised rabbits for cash; in the spring of 1987, they had more than forty rabbits. The children shared the responsibility for feeding them. Mrs. Tyler, a housewife, was proud of her Native American heritage and tried to instill her pride in her only daughter. Among the children of the second marriage, the youngest child — the only daughter — would be the only one who graduated from a high school. The oldest son, who lived nearby with his family, had been looking for work, but found it difficult to land a good job without a high school diploma. The second son, who lived with his parents, earned pocket money by selling plasma. None of the family members seemed to be particularly concerned about community issues.

Like many other families, the fifth family, the Gibsons, lived in the area but had nothing to do with the community. Mr. and Mrs. Gibson, in their forties and college-educated, were pursuing their ideal of a rustic life. On their property, which lay at the edge of Peaceland, they grew vegetables, berries, and fruits for private use. As professional gardeners, they designed an exotic wildflower and rock garden around their renovated farm house; they also raised goats for milk, sheep for wool, peacocks for a hobby, ducks and turkeys for food, and bees for honey. Their daily life was spent in Riverville; they took care of their clients' gardens, participated in the city's social and cultural life, and attended church in that city. The Gibsons, distrusting the quality of education at Greenfield High School, sent their two children to a parochial school where they paid high tuition. They were uninterested in local matters and identified with the Riverville community instead.

The five brief portraits describe families I observed and with whom I developed friendships, in varying degrees. In most cases, the families volunteered to open their homes to me, a complete stranger. Therefore, the reader should not assume that I present random samples from the community. The cases do, however, provide a glimpse of the diversity of the community's population.

Youth Participation in Community Activities

'There is nothing for teenagers to do in this community' was an oft-repeated remark among adults as well as teenagers. The community was lacking in such opportunities for youth social activities by not having movie theaters, department stores, a variety of fast-food stores, drive-ins, roller-skating rinks, a 'gut' (a section of a street open for teenagers' weekend motorcade), and dance halls. Adolescents went to find such entertainment in Riverville. In addition, teenagers drove to the city for private lessons in dance, gymnastics, and other activities.

Despite the paucity of such opportunities, Green Lake teenagers enjoyed a natural environment for many other kinds of activities. Outdoor space at home allowed some adolescents to grow their own gardens or raise animals. Through participating in the 4-H Club, they learned 'hands-on' skills and competency in horticulture and livestock raising. In addition, some teenagers raised horses to ride, trained them for show or to enter rodeos, and 'doctored' the animals when sick. They were exceedingly competent in their knowledge and skill in caring for horses. The natural environment, characterized by ample woods, creeks, and beautiful scenery, also beckoned the young people toward outdoor activities. Hunting and fishing were popular sports among teenagers as well as adults in the community. In their journals, a few boys expressed their pleasurable anticipation of hunting and fishing seasons. Adolescents also took advantage of rustic roads for mountain biking, three-wheeling, and motorcycle trail-riding without worrying about bothering their neighbors. Green Lake itself offered other possibilities for recreation. From late spring through summer vacation, many local residents were engaged in motorboating, water-skiing, sailing, wind-surfing, and swimming. Especially during summers, parks around the lake (see Figure 1) created natural meeting grounds for teenagers to hang out for sun-bathing, swimming, and socializing.

Furthermore, the limited variety of urban entertainment turned teenagers' attention to self-created activities. Sewing provided an activity for some girls and helped them cut down their clothing expenses. Working on cars was popular among boys; their time outside school was occupied with renovating or repairing cars — their own or those of their friends. Since the car was a symbol of independence and gave freedom to 'get around', especially in case of going to Riverville, teenagers developed special attachments to their cars. Watching rented video movies was another way of spending spare time, especially on weekends. Many families owned home video machines as almost a necessity of life. A few local stores added video tape rental services. To many Green Lake teenagers, a home video became a substitute to driving many miles to movie theaters in Riverville.

A large portion of the student body were involved in organized activities in school as well as in the community. Turnouts for evening sport games were high, particularly for football, basketball, and track and field events. Campus Life (a non-denominational Christian youth organization) enjoyed high attendance at its weekly meetings which drew, on average, over fifty high school students, almost 10 per cent of the student body (see Chapter 9). The young people volunteered to help with community functions as individuals or members of high school organizations. Their activities also included participating in the city celebration parade, picking up litter on a clean-up campaign throughout the community, serving refreshments at community meetings, and guiding crowds at the health fair.

Although the statement, 'There is nothing to do in the community', may have proven to be true for certain types of activities, Green Lake adolescents adjusted their social life to their geographical and economic circumstances. They turned their attention from ready-made entertainment to self-created projects; private lessons to school-and-community-related activities; and indoor fun to outdoor pastimes.

The school band, led by two cheerleaders, is participating in Peaceland's 25th Anniversary Celebration Parade.

Youth Employment Opportunities

Youth employment reflected the pattern of adult employment, relying partly on the local economy and partly on Riverville (see Chapter 8). Some students were employed by local businesses, the Safeway super-market, local restaurants, Dairy Queen (a fast-food franchise), Christmas tree farms, hay fields, fruit and vegetable farms, and logging businesses. Teenagers approached possible job opportunities and sub-mitted applications in person. Some agricultural or babysitting jobs came through the school job counseling office when employers re-quested juvenile workers. A number of teenagers located jobs such as yard work and babysitting through their neighbors. While the com-munity thus supplied some employment to the young people, the demand for jobs outnumbered the supply. Many teenagers found jobs in fast-food outlets, restaurants, pizza parlors, shopping centers, and gas stations in Riverville. The scarcity of local jobs for young people added to the Green Lake community's dependency upon Riverville. Youth employment is discussed in detail in Chapter 8.

Support from the Community

Several segments of the Green Lake community played a significant role in supporting the high school and, in turn, the life of adolescents. For example, the newspaper reported on high school sports every week. The sports section editor attended almost every home and away game, wrote separate articles on each sport as well as a general commentary, and reported the total results at the end of each season. For his 'fair and extensive' coverage of high school sports, he was given an appreciation award from the Greenfield Booster Club during half-time at the Homecoming football game. The newspaper also printed honor rolls, announcements of school events, and district news. It sometimes carried feature articles regarding teenagers. An article about a drop-out of the Greenfield High School presented a portrait of the boy, including his reasons for dropping out, his subsequent resentment, and his uncertainty about his future. The article neither condoned nor condemned his decision to drop out; rather, it tried to shed a fair light on the life of an 'at-risk' teenager.

Some community groups showed their support of the high school teenagers in the form of awards. For example, the Peaceland City Council awarded a plaque of appreciation to the high school student body for their services in picking up litter along streets prior to the city celebration. In addition, the Chamber of Commerce granted a Future First Citizen Award to a high school senior each year at the Annual Community Awards Banquet. Local chapters of nation-wide clubs also provided scholarships for the high school students. These supportive gestures showed the community's interest in the high school and adolescents.

Parents' groups crystallized community support for the high school and teenagers. The groups included four organizations: the Booster Club, the Green Lake Parent Network, the 'Grad Nite' Committee, and the Drama Club Committee. The Booster Club, the most active group, was organized to help the athletic program at the high school. The membership of the club was open to anyone over 18 years of age, but most of the active members had children involved in the high school athletic program. Throughout the year, club members raised funds through sales from a food stand during athletic games and an annual spaghetti dinner and auction. With the funds, the club purchased athletic equipment for the high school. The club's major contributions to the school included the establishment of the weight room and the baseball scoreboard.

Unlike the Booster Club, that concentrated its assistance on the athletic program, the Green Lake Parent Network sought to better the lives of children at all levels in the school district. The group was launched in 1985 by two enthusiastic parents who were interested in improving the community as a safe, healthy environment for young people. The main purposes of the group were to identify problems in the lives of children, disseminate accurate information about solving these problems, and prevent their causes. Problem areas identified included alcohol and drug abuse, teen pregnancy and sexuality, low self-esteem, and peer pressure. In spite of its limited human resources — only three to six members for two years — the group's activities were impressive. They held a monthly meeting to discuss the problems and remedies, sponsored numerous talks and workshops given by invited guests, assisted in the organization of the community health fair, distributed brochures containing information on the issues, and expressed the group's goals and activities through the local newspaper.

Like the Booster Club, the Grad Nite Committee and the Drama Club Committee directly supported high school matters. In contrast to the Booster Club and the Parent Network, however, these groups were oriented toward specific, short-term goals. The Grad Nite Committee was organized by parents (mothers mostly) of several high school seniors. The chief purpose of the group was to hold a 'substance-free' all-night party for the seniors at a designated place on graduation night. The parents claimed that the endeavor would be their last 'fun' gift to their graduating children and would reduce the hazard of drunk driving on that night. In order to raise money[3] for the party, the committee members planned fund-raising projects and implemented the plans throughout a year. The fund-raising projects included dances, sales of balloons at sports games, a car bash (part of a celebration in which people pay to strike a derelict automobile with a violent blow for amusement) during Homecoming Week, food booths, bottle drives, and telephone requests for donations.

The Drama Club was abolished for the 1986–87 school year due to the lack of an advisor and funds. The Drama Club Committee, a temporary group of parents, was organized to express their long-term interest in a more balanced activity program in the high school. Parents of students interested in drama started the committee to revive the club, offering to help the high school search for a volunteer drama coach from the community and to repair drama equipment, the stage curtain and lights. The committee disbanded as soon as the club was reinstated at the high school.

Many individual families actively showed support for their

Car Bash on the day of the Homecoming game.

children's education. They participated in school functions and expressed their concerns in parents' meetings. A student teacher commented that she was surprised to see that many parents were eager to express their concerns about the quality of education in the high school. An administrator reminded me, however, that community members generally spoke out more with complaints than with praise. He considered the absence of complaints as a positive evaluation of the school.

The community also served as a critical financial source for adolescent activities. Many students supported their activities of school, churches, and clubs through fund raising. They turned to their neighbors to raise money. Some community members complained that too many young people came to their doors for money, but many others willingly donated for the young people's fund-raising projects. This financial support actually played an important role in the adolescent life.

In this chapter, the Green Lake community, conterminous with the Green Lake School District, has been portrayed not only as a physical haven, but also as a cultural 'home base' for Greenfield teenagers. The environmental features of the community were described as semi-rural, school-centered, and partly dependent upon the nearby middle-sized city. These features were reflected in daily adolescent activities and actively influenced them. Greenfield teenage life also revolved around school-centered extracurricular activities, particularly sports, due to the limited availability of urban entertainment. The young people's employment patterns, like those of adults, reflected the community's economic dependence upon the nearby city of Riverville. The close ties between school and community were mutually reinforcing. Greenfield high school students participated in the community life through employment, volunteer activities, and community functions; community members supported high school activities emotionally and financially. The close contact appeared to reinforce the cultural values of Greenfield teenagers. In the next chapter, the school will be discussed as another intimate cultural home base for Greenfield students.

Notes

1 This estimate was based on local knowledge. School district personnel informed me that they did not have statistics on the general population in the district. The Peaceland city administration did not keep demographic data on residents of adjacent towns.

2 Two of the children transferred to the Greenfield High School in their junior and sophomore years respectively to look for a 'freer' atmosphere than the parochial school. The older one quit the school in her senior year because it did not provide enough freedom according to her.

3 For the seniors of the 1986 class, the Grad Nite committee raised $4,000 to hold an all-night graduation party at a ski resort. After the project was successfully completed, the committee was dissolved. It was the first year of the 'Grad Nite Party' tradition.

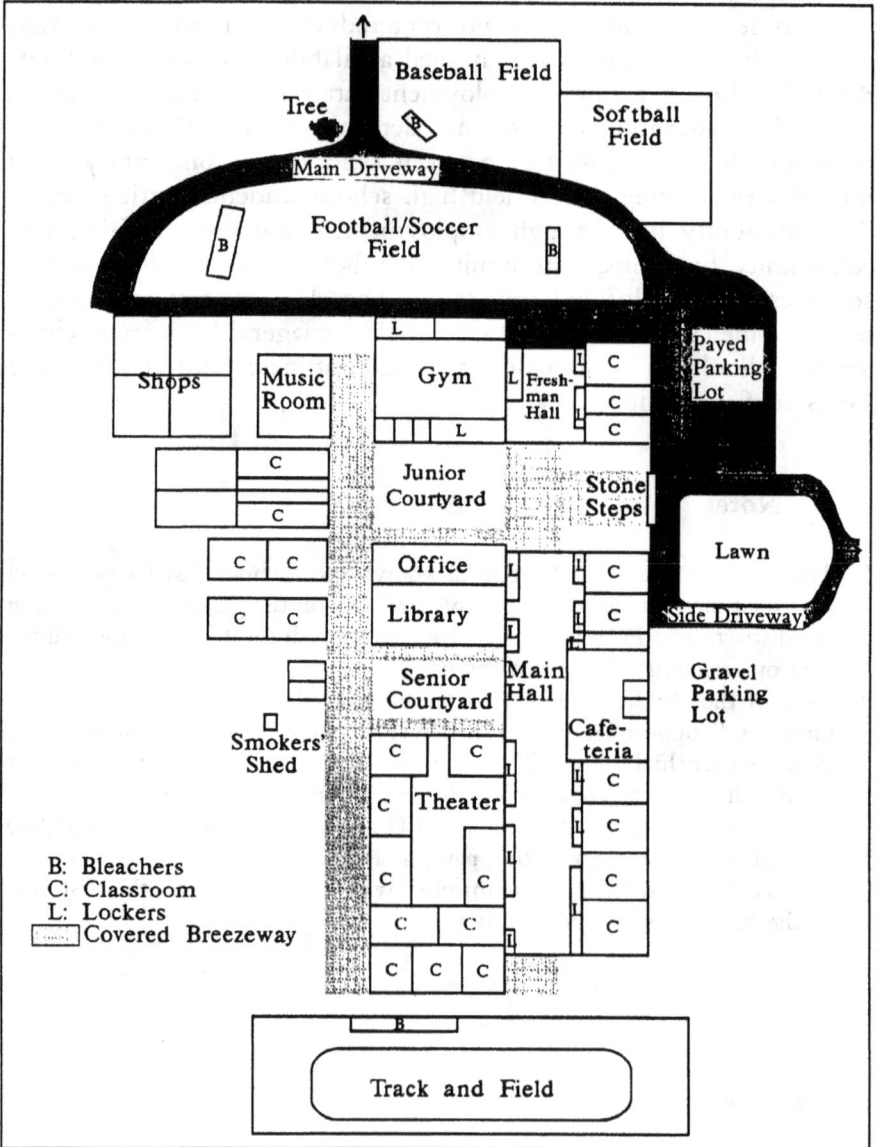

Figure 2. A sketch map of the Greenfield High School (not to scale).

Chapter 4

Greenfield High School

This chapter describes Greenfield High School, focusing on the ecological environment, the students, and roles performed by this institution. The environmental features of the school include subject-oriented classrooms equipped with basic furniture (such as chalkboards, chairs, desks, and a teacher's desk) and wall decorations; special rooms such as library, music and art rooms, science laboratory; hall lockers; student parking lots; and specialized athletic fields. The second section of this chapter presents profiles of three male and three female students selected from all grade levels. The following sections discuss roles that the school played as a place for learning, for discipline, for extracurricular activities, for democratic practices, and for friendship and courtship.

Ecological Environment

Greenfield High School (see Figure 2) is located in Greenfield, the second largest town in the Green Lake community, about one mile from the economic center of Peaceland (see Figure 1). The main driveway to the high school runs from the Main Road which connects Peaceland and Greenfield. Most of the properties abutting the driveway are privately owned. A sign on the right side of the road states that the school gate opens at 6:30 am and closes at 10:30 pm Monday through Friday. The straight 150 yard driveway forks into diverging roads which encircle a football/soccer field. One road leads to a student parking lot, the other to a faculty parking lot. A baseball field is located on the corner of the intersection. A large tree across the field marks an alternative parking area for one or two cars. The space under the tree is favored by students prohibited to drive into the student parking lot because of traffic offenses[1] and those who like to have lunch or to 'make out' with their boy/girlfriend in their cars.

The road to the student parking lot separates the football field from the softball field. The school buildings stand next to the football field, facing the student parking lot. The lot is divided by a lawn into two sections. One section, called 'junior parking lot', is paved and accommodates approximately sixty cars. The other, a gravel section, is larger than the paved one and is called 'senior parking lot'. Since the junior parking lot was paved a few years ago, it has been favored by most students.

From the parking lot, a few stone steps lead to a courtyard, referred to as the 'junior courtyard' or just the 'courtyard'. All the school buses stop in front of the steps. The courtyard provides primary access to the school office, a gym, and classrooms. The other courtyard, called the 'senior courtyard', is surrounded by more classrooms and a library. As with the parking lots, students did not know the origin of the class-specified labels, but they could only speculate juniors and seniors might have had privileged access to these zones at one time. During my fieldwork, however, I noticed that the use of the courtyards was not confined to any specific class. Close to the seniors' courtyard, a small plywood booth had been erected. This front-open building was called the Smokers' Shed and was the only smoking area on campus.[2] The significance of the shed in student life is discussed in Chapter 7.

School buildings are connected with covered breezeways. In two school buildings — the gym and the main hall — on each side of the stone steps, lockers (about six feet tall and one-and-a-half feet wide) stand abreast along the corridors. Most of the lockers are located in the main hall. The locker hall in the other building — the gym — is called the 'freshmen hall'. Main hall lockers were more favored. Two students generally shared one locker, and those who did not have a locker partner were considered lucky.

The Student Handbook clearly pointed out that lockers were *de jure* school property and students were only allowed to *use* them. The lockers were subject to inspection if the school administrators decided it was necessary. However, the lockers created *de facto* private space for individual students. Therefore, the students liked to share a locker with their best friend, sometimes a boyfriend or a girlfriend, because it engendered intimacy. Students added a personal touch by decorating inside their locker doors. The decorations varied from photographs of friends or family to posters of pop stars, from fashion magazine cut-outs to Playboy pin-ups, and from memo pads to mirrors.

Classrooms, science labs, vocational education shops, and athletic facilities tend to be clustered according to subject areas. In addition, the school has special facilities including an art room with a dark-room; a music room for band and choir classes; a home economics room equipped with four kitchens and several sewing machines; a library that seats about fifty and provides both books and audio-visual instructional aids; a theater with approximately 200 seats; and a school cafeteria that sells hot lunches and snacks and is also used for dances or meetings.

The offices, clustered in one area, handled various student affairs. Two secretaries took care of 'nuts and bolts' business such as parental permission forms and locker problems. Among many responsibilities, two full-time counselors helped individual students arrange their class schedules and gave personal, academic, and career counselling. One part-time counselor focused on student employment matters. The attendance secretary recorded students' absences. A bookkeeper sold lunch tickets and received all student fees. An athletic director sched-uled athletic games and attended to individual athletes' concerns. A vice principal was responsible for student discipline. A principal, as his office 'hidden' in the back might symbolize, had the fewest direct contacts with individual students.[3]

The high school has four athletic fields. The football field is equipped with covered bleachers seating approximately 800 home fans and open bleachers reserved for guest team fans. This field is shared by boys' and girls' soccer teams in fall. The baseball field boasts a scoreboard, and open bleachers are shared by home and guest team fans. The adjacent softball field was recently renovated. The field for track and field events has bleachers open to both home and guest rooters. The fields and bleachers were well used by athletes and audiences.

Profiles of Greenfielders

Greenfield High School had 513 students, aged 14 to 18, (I refer to them as Greenfielders) in ninth through twelfth grades on the rolls in April 1987. The numbers of male and female students were about the same. The enrollment of tenth and eleventh graders remained relative-ly stable; ninth and twelfth grades varied noticeably between October 1986 and September 1987 as shown in Table 1:

Table 1. *Greenfield High School Student Enrollment in 1986–87*

Grade	Oct. '86	Dec. '86	Apr. '87	Sept. '87[4]
9th	113	135	134	155
10th	153	156	156	143
11th	138	138	130	137
12th	109	104	93	122
Total	513	533	513	557

A district administrator commented that the district experienced a relatively high student turnover every year. He attributed this tendency to the location of the community. Since the community was near Riverville, it provided low-income housing for temporary residents while they looked for jobs in the city. In some cases, children from single-parent families increased the mobile student population as they moved in or out of the district to live with their other parent. Some of them alternated schools yearly as they lived with one parent and then the other. By contrast, many students had lived in the school district since elementary school. One senior boy reported that he had attended the same schools since elementary school with approximately 20 per cent of his high school classmates.

In order to personalize Greenfielders, let me present brief profiles of six students. David, a senior, had a wide range of cross-cultural experiences as a result of his father's service in the US Army. He exaggerated his international experience saying, 'I was all over the world except Moscow.' He was born in England and had lived in fourteen different countries in Europe and Asia. When he had come to the United States at the age of fourteen, he said he had known more about world geography than his social studies teacher. He had felt that he was repeating the same materials in other subjects as well, because he had already learned them overseas. School had become so 'boring' that he had dropped out of the tenth grade in California. He had looked for jobs, but without a high school diploma he had found only low-paying, 'dull' ones. So he had returned to school in California.

Because family problems had made it hard for him to live at home, he had transferred to Greenfield High School in his junior year when he had come to live with his grandparents. Being a little older than his peers, this 18-year-old junior had felt out of place. David's unique overseas experiences might also have set him apart psychologically from his little travelled peers. In the first year in Greenfield, he had not had close friends and been classified by his peers as a 'jerk', which he defined as 'one who does not get along with others'. He tried to change the negative image in his senior year. Eventually he made some friends, although he said he did not feel close to them. He also became involved in school activities as a yearbook photographer and took school work more seriously. As a result of raising his grades from 1.0 (a 'D' average) to over 3.0 (a 'B' average) during high school years, he received the Most Improved Senior Award. Although unsure about his future, he considered visiting his friends and relatives in Europe and going to a university in California after graduation.

Beth, a senior, had chosen to become legally emancipated at the age of sixteen in order to lead a life independent from her 'abusing' mother. She had moved in with a middle-aged couple with an agreement to pay monthly room and board. She had been smoking since the age of ten and had frequented the Smokers' Shed at the high school. In the summer of her junior year, she stopped smoking with the help of both her job supervisor and her boyfriend. Even after that, however, she continued to advocate smokers' rights in school. She became involved in 'mainstream' school activities, playing clarinet in the stage band and editing the school newspaper. Her grades improved continuously from the middle of her junior year. Her outgoing personality made her visible not only to her smoking peers but also to the general crowd of students. In her senior year, she was voted the Girl of the Month for Dependability.

Dan, a junior (age 17), was a versatile athlete who participated in varsity football in fall, varsity basketball in winter, and track and field in spring. Awards he had received in all three sports recognized his enthusiastic involvement and distinguished ability. Although he attended after-school practices lasting as late as 5:00 or 6:00 pm, he maintained a GPA of over 3.0 ('B'). He was known to have kept up a romantic relationship with one girl for over a half year (considered long for a high school relationship). Like Dan, she was also a well-rounded athlete, participating in volleyball, basketball, and track. Some of Dan's peers thought that he was 'fun to be around'; others criticized him for having a 'big mouth' and frequently embarrassing others.

Mary, a junior, was another active and ambitious teenager. She had been a cheerleader for three years since her freshman year and exercised leadership in the rally squad. She appeared to be 'stuck-up' to some of her peers but was described as cheerful and personable by others. She had maintained a 4.0 GPA (a straight 'A') throughout her high school years. While many Greenfielders considered going to community colleges or small colleges in the state, if she was to go to college at all, her ambition was to attend a prestigious private university out of state. Since her working-class parents could not support her college education, she would have to find financial sources to support herself. Despite the financial obstacles, she was determined to succeed in the future.

Jim, a sophomore, had attended Greenfield High School for a year following his move to a local group home for troubled juveniles. This home was sponsored by the Children's Services Division of the state. He lived in the home with eight other boys and their foster parents. He did not like to discuss his past; yet, he talked about his mother and his girlfriend living in a large city about 130 miles away. He was not particularly interested in studying, and he usually got low grades. The house rules required him to study for a few hours every school evening in order to improve his grades. His major interest was in playing classical guitar. Although his playing annoyed his foster parents and his school work suffered, Jim practiced his guitar diligently with the hope of becoming a professional musician. His individualistic life-style conflicted with the house parents' style of discipline. Before he finished his junior year, he was 'kicked out' of the house.

Kyla was a cheerful and warm-hearted freshman enrolled in the special education program. She was one of the first students who approached me at the beginning of my study. She stated, 'When I came to high school as a freshman, I did not know anybody. I was lost. I like to help new students because I understand how they feel.' In spite of her lively and personable attributes, her visibility was mainly limited to her special education rooms. She was doing well in the special education classes, language arts, mathematics, social studies, and science. She participated in the girls' choir and had sung a few solos. In addition to choir, she helped the school's Special Olympics (athletic events for physically and/or mentally handicapped students) basketball team as a manager. She subscribed to the mainstream social rule of gaining popularity by means of academic excellence and appearance, financing her stylish appearance with assistance from her mother and the sale of animals that she raised.

The adolescents portrayed above describe a variety of Greenfielders ranging from outgoing to shy; academic to party-loving; warm and personable to aloof; popular to unpopular; and fashionable to unstylish. Each of the students contributed to the diversified atmosphere in school.

Multiple Roles of High School

Greenfield High School played multiple functions in adolescent life. In addition to the 'conventional' roles in instruction and discipline, the school assumed responsibilities of providing citizenship education, non-academic activities, and socializing opportunities. Students, school staff, and parents considered the school as an important socializing institution in the community.

A Place for Theoretical and Practical Learning

The curriculum at Greenfield High was designed to integrate theoretical and practical learning. Theoretical learning refers to acquiring cognitive knowledge from written texts or didactic lessons and was considered the basis of formal education and further schooling. Practical learning refers to gaining applicable knowledge and 'how-to' skills by 'doing'. While some subjects emphasized one type of learning more than the other, every subject combined both to a certain degree.

The high school offered a variety of academic classes[5] at different grade and individual performance level. All students were required to take a certain minimum number of hours in the following areas in order to graduate from the high school:

- language arts (English and foreign languages) — four years
- mathematics (math and computer) — two years
- social studies (global studies, history, political process, and economics) — four years
- natural science (biology, chemistry, and physics) — two years
- physical education — two years
- health — one year.

The choice of specific courses in each area depended primarily on students, their parents, and counselors. Beyond these requirements, students could take additional academic courses if they planned to go to college or were merely interested in them. While these academic courses stressed book learning, they also promoted practical learning through field trips, experiments, and other applied projects.

Elective courses were available in which students could obtain skills and knowledge in the areas of industrial arts, business, home economics, and clerical work. These areas were designed to prepare students for the 'real' world, either for everyday life or job situations. Industrial arts included metal, auto-mechanics, and wood shops; the business curriculum encompassed typing, accounting, business machine skills, and communication; and home economics focused on sewing, cooking, crafts, and childcare. Such courses emphasized acquisition of 'hands-on' skills, such as how to handle the machinery in the industrial art workshops, how to type, and how to care for children. Several students gained competency and a variety of skills in these areas. For example, a senior boy in the auto-mechanic class changed the oil and oil filter in my car. A junior boy taught me the names and functions of over ten different electric saws furnished in the wood shop. Some girls made their prom dresses in the sewing class.

In addition to these vocational courses, the school created work places where students could provide service and gain 'experience' by assisting in the library, offices, individual classrooms, and in resource rooms (special education). The student aides took these 'working opportunities' for a half credit a year (as opposed to one credit a year for other courses). The courses assigned a variety of responsibilities, depending on the position. Media aides working in the library assisted in the process of checking books and media apparatus in and out; aides in the main office answered the phone, delivered courier mail, and made photocopies; attendance aides posted and delivered messages to students and teachers; classroom aides assisted teachers in preparing some instructional materials and grading; and peer tutors in the resource room administered individual tests and assisted teachers with projects. Through these experiences, students said they learned to take attendance, to be punctual, to finish jobs on time and as directed, and to get along with co-workers, whether staff or peers.

Arts — music and fine arts — were other areas that emphasized practical learning, although theoretical learning was not neglected. In the music program, practical learning — singing and playing — was integrated in choir and band courses. The school district provided percussion and wind instruments to students who wished to participate in band but did not own an instrument. Band and choir classes allowed students to learn new instruments or refine their playing and singing skills. In fine arts, the photography course provided students experiences in taking pictures, developing film, and enlarging or reducing photos. Some students found opportunities to apply these skills to 'real' situations by participating in the yearbook and school newspaper production courses. Other fine art courses invited students to learn and practice a variety of art forms such as drawing, water color and oil painting, ceramics, crafts, printmaking, graphic designs, and calligraphy.

A Place for Discipline: Awards and Punishments

The disciplinary mode of Greenfield High School appeared to reflect the behaviorist philosophy of education, in which rewards and punishment were used to modify student behavior.

Awards and honors
Awards and honors in the high school were granted to recognize scholastic and athletic achievement and desirable social skills. Scholarship-based awards included the honor roll, decided on the basis of a quarterly GPA above 3.0 ('B' average); Student of the Month, established and granted by individual teachers of some subject areas for students of academic excellence and good classroom conduct; and Student of the Year, chosen in each subject area by teachers and awarded at the Annual Academic Award Banquet.

Seasonal athletic awards were given to students on the basis of length of participation, service to the team, spirit and attitude, and behavior both on and off the playing field/court in a particular sport that season. Despite the variation in different sports, the Letter Award was commonly given to varsity athletes in all sports. According to the Green Lake School District Athletic Policy, 'an athlete who earns a varsity athletic award shall receive the chenille school letter [the first letter of the school name cut out from gold-colored fuzzy fabric] and a certificate'. Students who received the award sewed the 'school letter' on the left side of a 'letterman's jacket' that they purchased separately. The 'lettered' athletes — girls and boys alike — wore the jackets, in particular on game days, to show their school spirit. Some boys lent jackets to their girlfriends, symbolically announcing a relationship. In addition to the Letter Award, several athletes in each sport were either selected by coaches or voted by their teammates for awards. The awards such as 'Most Valuable Player', 'Most Inspirational', and 'Most Improved' were given in all sports and some titles ('Best Defense' for football) were oriented to specific sports. These awards were given at their award ceremonies following the conclusion of each season.

The third kind of award was called the 'Chance Award', invented in 1986 and directed by a teacher. The purpose of the award was to

Annual Academic Award Banquet

encourage students to exhibit 'good behavior'.[6] The procedures were as follows:

1 Staff members identified students who exhibited good academic or social behavior and gave them slips bearing their names and the reasons for nomination;
2 Students put the Chance Award slips into a box set up in the main office;
3 The directing teacher picked out a specified number of slips from the box (the number changed each week);
4 He posted the list of recipients, who came in his classroom to get their prizes: a coupon for a free McDonald's hamburger and french fries, a calculator, a candy bar, a six-pack of soft drink, or an opportunity to have lunch with one's favorite staff member or teacher.

An article from the student newspaper assessed its function positively by quoting from some students and staff:

It has really helped the students here at Greenfield High School to become more polite and thoughtful.

> The Chance Awards system seems to boost the students' positive efforts which make a difference at school.

Other students and staff, however, doubted the effect of the award because of the haphazard selection process.

Rules and punishment

Punishment was another mode of discipline and was used in case of violating rules. The Student Handbook, distributed at the beginning of every school year, delineated rules, regulations, and guidelines regarding academic, social, and physical aspects of student life. According to the book, disciplinary matters included truancies and 'tardies', physical violence, vandalism, and misconducts in classrooms. Of these, my interviews with both old and new vice-principals suggested that attendance problems demanded most of their time. A faculty-appointed task force also identified attendance as one of the focal areas to improve the quality of education at the Greenfield. The school philosophy of attendance was expressed in the Student Handbook as follows:

> The staff at Greenfield High School along with the Green Lake School Board of Directors strongly endorse the philosophy that attendance in school is essential for the educational process of the student. While we strongly encourage regular attendance, we feel parents should determine when their children have permission and consent to miss school.

Attendance-related offenses included tardiness and truancy. Tardiness was defined as coming to a class more than five minutes late after a bell rang. Truancy was defined in the Handbook as follows:

> the absence of a student from school or a class without the prior consent or knowledge of the parents, guardian, or school authorities and/or...with...reasons unacceptable to the school authorities.

It also included leaving a class with a hall pass for longer than the expected length of time.

Attendance problems were associated with the following structural characteristics of Greenfield High School: classroom changes for each period, four-minute breaks between periods, the use of hall passes, an open-campus policy for lunch, and accessibility to cars during school. These structural characteristics presented more freedom to students but, at the same time, more possibilities to 'get out'. School administrators were forced to adopt a complicated tardy/truancy control system[7] while allowing students a certain degree of freedom which democratic ideology prescribed to the system.

The next most disciplinary attention was paid to drug and substance abuse. Some students readily recognized that Greenfield High School was not free from these problems,[8] although they insisted that the situation at their school was not as serious as that of 'big city' schools. An advisory committee of four faculty members collaborated with the counselor in order to eradicate these offenses on campus.

In addition to the school-wide rules, each classroom teacher also set rules for desirable student conduct in their classroom. For example, the following list was posted on the wall of the art room:

- This room and supplies are for your use. Take responsibility in their care.
- Respect your fellow students' right to work; don't disrupt the class!
- Keep your hands off others' artwork!
- No horseplay!
- No obscene language.
- Clean up your work area completely.
- Don't sit on the tables.
- Don't write on any classroom furniture.
- Only photo students are allowed in the darkroom.
- The teacher's desk and files are off-limits. [The underlines are original.]

The student handbook set guidelines for the school's disciplinary acts, stating that if students violated rules and their behaviors were regarded as endangering a safe learning environment, they would be punished by one of the 'disciplinary tools' on the basis of the severity of their violation. The handbook delineated the tools as follows:

(1) admonish students, (2) conference with students, (3) conference with parent, (4) mail letters home, (5) telephone parents, (6) place student on probation, (7) detain student after school hours, [place students in the Saturday School][9] (8) suspend the student, and (9) recommend the student for expulsion.

A Place for Extracurricular Activities

For most students, Greenfield was a center for activities such as sports, arts, clubs and organizations, fund-raising projects, and social events. Students' participation was strongly encouraged by the school staff and students themselves.

Sports

The Greenfield High School supported eleven seasonal sports. In the fall four regular sports were offered in football (men), volleyball (women), soccer (men/women), and cross-country running (men/women). Winter sports were basketball (men/women), wrestling (men), and snow-skiing (men/women). In the spring, students could participate in baseball (men), softball (women), track and field (men/women), and golf (men/women). Administrators claimed that athletic participation was not a right but a privilege, given only to physically and academically eligible students. In order to be physically eligible students had to present a medical record, showing their physical fitness for a particular sport, and proof of a health insurance policy. Academically, students had to pass at least five out of seven courses in the previous semester and be passing the same number of courses in the present semester.

While the official sports program was limited to qualified athletes, single-game sports and intramural sport activities were open to everyone. A tag football game (women) and a weight lifting competition (men) were held once a year. Although regular athletes participated in these events, non-athletes were often involved in them. The intramural program was also designed and coordinated by a counselor to give all students opportunities to get involved in some-thing during lunch time. The program had drawn many non-athletes into a variety of sports such as football, volleyball, basketball, ping pong, badminton, and soccer. Events changed monthly to attract a larger group of students.

Clubs and organizations

In addition to the athletic program, a large number of students were affiliated with club or organization activities. The following were officially recognized organizations: language clubs (French, German, Russian, Spanish), music clubs (choir and band), athletic clubs (weight lifting, ski, track, boys basketball, girls basketball, baseball), cheering clubs (rally, pep club, dance team), journalism clubs (yearbook, student newspaper), Field Biology Club, Chess Club, FBLA (Future

Business Leaders of America), National Honor Society, Girls' League, and Associated Student Body Government. Some clubs were linked to academic classes, while others were totally independent from them. Students of language, music, journalism, and biology classes became members of academic clubs. These clubs had a certain amount of autonomy from classes in that non-class students could belong and several out-of-class activities were offered. For instance, language clubs had social events such as a Christmas party and additional field trips; the journalism club included newspaper staff as well as some photographers from yearbook staff, who spent extra time reporting, photographing, and laying out articles. In addition, members of the music clubs participated in off-campus competitions and concerts. The athletic clubs included players and supporters of specific sports teams, as described earlier. In contrast to clubs related to existing classes or sports teams, some clubs were independent organizations such as National Honor Society, Girls' League, Chess Club, FBLA, Dance Team, and Rally Squad. These groups had their own agenda for goals and activities.

Among club and organizations' activities, fund-raising projects were of critical importance because they brought funds for further activities. Most of the club and organization functions were not financially supported by the school or school district. As a result, the groups had to raise money to carry out their activities or to buy necessary equipment. Fund raising is discussed in detail in Chapter 8.

A Place for 'Democratic' Practices

The school system attempted to incorporate a democratic ideology into its curriculum by allowing students to practice freedom of choice, freedom of expression, and self-government in limited settings. Students exercised their freedom of choice by voting and by choosing elective courses; they expressed their opinions through the student newspaper; and they elected student leaders who would organize student activities.

Freedom of choice
Students were given opportunities to exercise their freedom of choice by voting. One kind of voting concerned the election of Associated Student Body leaders (president, vice president, manager, secretary, and treasurer) and class officers (president, vice president, secretary,

and treasurer). Before every May election, student leaders of that year nominated candidates for each position of the following year, and candidates then campaigned for election. The campaign process resembled elections in adult society, as candidates organized a campaign staff, who recruited campaign managers and workers among their friends. They, in turn, attempted to persuade voters, particularly freshmen and sophomores who could be readily influenced. The teams also put up campaign posters, with captions as simple as candidates' names and running positions. Others presented elaborate captions with pictures and puns.

Voting was also a common practice in determining Homecoming, Prom, and Valentine Court, and Girl of the Month. For the Homecoming Court, seven princesses were chosen, one each from freshman and sophomore classes, two from junior class, and three from senior class. Among the three senior princesses, a queen was elected. The Prom was set up for juniors and seniors. Two junior princesses and three senior princesses were chosen first and then a queen was elected from the senior princesses. The Valentine Court sponsored by the Girls League was not as formal as the other courts organized by the Associated Student Body. The Valentine Court consisted of a prince and a princess from each class, from whom a king and a queen were determined. Students called these practices 'popularity votes' because judgment was felt to be based on individuals' reputation among their peers. As long as their popularity was sustained, the same people could be selected for any court repeatedly.

The Girl of the Month award, sponsored by Girls' League, was administered by and for girls on the basis of different qualities specified each month. The qualities included citizenship (September), friendliness (October), cooperation (November), leadership (December), scholarship (January), sportsmanship (February), dependability (March), sense of humor (April), and school spirit (May). In order to give equal opportunities to every girl, those already chosen were omitted from the vote roster.

Students' freedom of choice was not limited to casting votes. Students also exercised freedom in choosing elective courses. This choice was not as free as voting, because factors such as graduation requirements and enrollment limitation for each class affected ones' decisions. However, students were given choices from a variety of courses within limits. This freedom allowed them to choose which periods they wanted to take specific classes and to take courses with their friends.

Freedom of expression

Freedom of expression was exercised in the form of school journalism. Students of the course produced their own monthly newspaper, for which they planned the coverage, chose editorial topics, collected information, wrote editorials and articles, took pictures, sold advertisement space, laid out pages, edited pages, and distributed the papers. Except for printing, they completed all procedures by themselves under an English teacher's guidance. In the process of planning and organizing, student journalists determined their stand on certain issues and decided how to present their opinions. The newspaper also enabled other students to channel their thoughts by means of letters to the editor and interviews. According to the Student Handbook, student journalism was supposed to reflect the democratic ideology applied in school:

> One of the basic purposes of schooling is to prepare students for responsible self-expression in a democratic society. Citizens in our democracy are permitted free expression under the First and Fourteen Amendments of the US Constitution.

Student staff believed that the constitutional protection should be guaranteed for school journalism. However, the handbook added that freedom of expression should be understood in the context of learning; namely, students' right to express themselves could be controlled if it was assumed to disturb the instructional environment:

> Since schooling is a learning experience, the matter of free expression must also be viewed as part of the learning process. School officials or their representatives...may find it necessary to review publications and speeches to be given by students and to advise on matters of libel, slander, journalistic ethics, and the probable effect...on the orderly operation of the school.

An incident showed a tug-of-war between students' understanding of freedom of expression and the administrators' concern about education. The February issue carried a few letters to 'Dear Jack' (an advisory column like 'Dear Abby') pertaining to pregnancy. One of them reads:

Dear Jack,

I'm pregnant and don't know who the father is. I have it narrowed down to five guys. I'd feel stupid telling one of them if it wasn't theirs. What should I do? I don't have enough money for an abortion.

Signed,
Hopelessly pregnant

In a memo to the journalism class an administrator raised suspicion of the accuracy of the letter and expressed his concern about harming the image of the school. A reporter disagreed with the administrator's letter in the March issue, defending students' freedom of expression:

I feel that the recent letter sent to the journalism class from Mr. Administrator about the 'Dear Jack' column is rude and unnecessary. The Eagle Flashes [the name of the newspaper] is trying to provide a service to the students of Greenfield.... I feel that the letters sent to us by Mr. Administrator and petitioners are sincere in their effort to keep our school clean.... Where is our freedom to print the letters we feel are important?

Although students did not have the upper hand after all, they strongly expressed their sense of freedom of expression.

Student government
Greenfield High School formed the Associated Student Body, defined in the Student Handbook as follows:

The students of Greenfield High School are organized as the Associated Student Body (ASB) of Greenfield High School. Upon entering high school every student automatically becomes a member of the ASB. The administration has delegated certain privileges and responsibilities to the ASB. Students will be permitted to keep these and enlarge on them as they demonstrate ability to handle them.

The ASB elected their officers. Some students criticized this election as a popularity vote just like the Homecoming and Prom Courts. But others were convinced that students cast more serious and thoughtful votes for student leaders. The ASB officers made up the Student Leadership class along with four officers from each class, two representatives from the rally squad and the dance team, and two managers of the student store on campus. The Student Leadership class was a working organization that met every day for one period to plan and prepare for student activities, such as Homecoming, Prom, school dances, assemblies, and fund-raising projects. The Student Leadership class allowed students to make decisions about preferred student activities and procedures to carry them out. Student Leadership granted its participants valuable experiences in self-governing, decision-making, and cooperating with others.

A Place for Friendship and Courtship

In addition to the instructional functions, school was viewed as a social institution in which friendship and courtship grew. Students constantly interacted with their peers of the same and opposite genders on campus. Some students claimed that they came to school to socialize with friends. Several students mentioned that they 'hated to be suspended', because their friends remained in school while they were bored at home.

Some students carried their friendships through from lower grades to the high school; others developed new friends at Greenfield. Many students observed that this high school was not as 'bad' in forming cliques as large schools or even as Green Lake Middle School. It was still difficult for all but outgoing newcomers to get into established groups. Social events such as school dances, sports games, and field trips provided students with good opportunities to make friends of the same or both genders.

Once they made friends, students nourished the friendships in various ways: telephoning homes, exchanging notes, spending free time together in school, and visiting each others' homes. Many teenagers said that they spent an average of one hour on the phone every day talking with their friends. Some parents complained that their telephone was busy all the time because of their teenage children. Therefore, forfeiting the privilege of using the phone as a mean of 'grounding' (restricting a child's after-school activities to home with reduced privileges) was considered a terrible punishment by the young people.

Exchanging notes was a common practice among students. The notes ranged from a short apologies to long romantic confessions. Some were mailed to their friends' homes and others were personally delivered in school. I frequently observed note exchanges in class. In addition, students had extensive interactions with their friends by taking classes together and sitting next to each other, spending morning break and lunch together, participating in the same sports or activities, and visiting each others' homes. For example, three junior boys managed to arrange the same class schedules throughout the high school years and, consequently, did both class-related and out-of-school activities together. Many boy/girlfriends were often seen taking the same classes.

While both friendship and courtship were important in adolescent life, they were different in two ways. First, friendship with the same people tended to last longer, whereas courtship partners frequently changed. Groups of close friends seemed to remain consistent for years, even when vacations interrupted their regular interactions. Many friends stayed in contact during long vacations and were likely to get back together even after infrequent contacts. Many students had kept special friendship with a few selected peers — often, if not always, of the same sex — for many years. In some cases, these went back to friendships formed in kindergarten.

In contrast, courtship was not as stable as friendship. Partners changed frequently and the changes were conspicuous. The length of courtship ranged from a few days to longer than a year. An over-a-year relationship was rather rare, and even the long-lasting ones were liable eventually to break up. The frequent reorganization of courtship increased contacts between opposite-gender peers. A couple of girls exaggerated this phenomenon: 'All girls will probably have gone out with every boy in Greenfield by the end of their senior year.'

The second difference between friendship and courtship is the degree of intensity. Friendship might not be as intense as courtship in terms of frequency of contacts and emotional attachment. When a boy and girl started going out, all of a sudden they were seen together frequently. This new relationship often resulted in redirecting their attention from their best friends of the same sex to their boy/girlfriend. The tension between an old friend and a new one could disturb old friendships and rearrange interaction patterns.

Once a girl and boy were courting, their emotional attachment was strong. I observed that many students 'doodled' about their love relationships on their notebooks in class. Graffiti on restroom walls were classic examples. In journal writing, many students also readily described their boy/girlfriends. Responding to a theme question, for example, several students wrote that they would even go to a confinement camp in place of their boy/girlfriends for forty days, although they would not do the same thing for their close same-sex friends.

When the initial excitement was not sustained, they felt the entrapment of routine from spending too much time together in and out of school. When no compensation for waning novelty was found, many youngsters found increasing boredom with each other, and breaking-up became a reasonable solution. Regardless of the differences between friendship and courtship, both types of relationship were an essential part of adolescent culture.

In this chapter, I have examined the ecological, demographic, and functional dimensions of Greenfield High School. The school was equipped with the conventional academic facilities such as classrooms, vocational facilities such as workshops, and sports areas. The student population reflected the population makeup in the community, ranging from affluent to poor, from 'straight-laced' to 'at-risk', from involved to indifferent, and from high-achieving to low-achieving. Embracing the range of teenagers who attended it, the school was designed to play, or claimed to play, at least five major roles: a place to achieve academic learning, to experience discipline, to participate in extracurricular activities, to practice democratic principles, and to develop both casual and intimate personal relationships. Through these roles, Greenfield High School actively participated in a circle of socializing institutions.

In the next chapter, I will take a glimpse at Greenfielders' daily lives on a typical school day by accompanying a 'composite' student from morning to evening.

Notes

1 The school rule prohibited students who did not properly observe driving regulations from using the student parking lot. The rule also discouraged students from loitering in or around cars parked on the school grounds.
2 Smoking on campus was banned as of fall 1988. Some students initiated the campaign and received support from the student government and the School District Board.
3 In order to increase personal contacts with students, the principal taught a foreign language class and regularly supervised students in the lunch room.
4 Note that this was a new school year. Thus, each class had advanced one grade.
5 The Curriculum Guide 1987–88 issued by the school administration listed courses available in the academic areas: eighteen courses in language arts (English); seven courses in foreign languages (two in German, three in Spanish, and two in Russian); nine courses in general social studies (five

in social studies, two in citizenship/government, and two in personal finance); seven courses in science; and one health course.

6   The 'good behaviors' were subjectively judged by participating teachers and staff members. Therefore, 'good behaviors' ranged from getting a good score on an exam, delivering a message for a staff member, volunteering assistance in an office during busy time, to dressing 'properly'.

7   Attendance matters were handled by a full-time secretary assisted by student aides for each period. For each class, attendance was checked at two levels. First, teachers called the roll at the beginning of each period and recorded absentees' names on a slip to be placed in a paper pocket attached inside of their classroom door. Second, within the first fifteen minutes of each period, an attendance office aide (a student) picked up the attendance slip. The slips were compiled at the attendance office to check if the absentees had legitimate reasons and, if not, to track the absences in individual students' records.

8   School administrators and some community members complained that the community fed the drug problem into the school. The local and Riverville newspapers reported a few incidents of police raids on marijuana farms and methamphetamine manufacturing labs in the community.

9   The 'Saturday School' should be included as an intermediate step between after-school detention and suspension. The Saturday School refers to an extended detention lasting from 8:00 am until 2:00 pm on Saturdays. During the session, students were required to do homework or to read under the supervision of a teacher. They were not allowed to get up from their seats except for a half-hour lunch break.

Chapter 5

A Typical School Day

Some students insisted that no day was typical, and others readily described their typical day. The story presented in this chapter based on interviews, observations, and student journals, allows readers a look at student life through the course of one school day. 'Ann's' day was chosen for description because more information was collected from girls. However, this story is not exclusively about girls.

Before the School Bell Rings

Hectic Morning

Ann is awakened at 6:30 am as usual by her alarm clock, but she finds it more difficult to get up today, because she stayed up until one o'clock in the morning to finish her geometry homework. She is half awake, lingering in bed until 6:50 am. She finally drags herself out of bed, telling herself that she will be late unless she gets up right away.

The curtained windows keep the still tranquil house dim. No one else seems to be awake. Still trying to wake up, Ann leisurely takes a shower. There is no doubt that the noise of water is audible in her mother's room. She gets out of the shower, her wet hair making her feel fresh. Ann goes into her tiny room to dry her hair and to put on her make-up, and make her bed. She began using make-up in the eighth grade but has never liked it too much. A little eye shadow, mascara, eye liner, cheek blush, and lipstick seem enough. The reason she uses make up is that her friends remark: 'Are you sick?' or 'You look pale' if she does not do it.

Her mother usually gets up by this time and wakes up Michelle, Ann's 11 year-old sister. Ann is trying to get her things together for school: track clothes and shoes, notebooks, pens and pencils, math homework and textbook, and her purse with a little emergency money. Miscellaneous items find their place in her duffel bag. Most of the time her mother packs her lunch either on the evening before or in the morning. The lunch usually sits atop all the other things in her bag, but this morning her mother did not make her lunch, because she got up late. Since Ann is late herself, she has no time to make a sandwich.

Socializing on the School Bus

At 7:50 am, Ann takes her first spoonful of cereal, just as the school bus approaches. Her mother, looking through the kitchen window, yells that the bus is coming. Knowing that the bus driver will wait, Ann brushes her teeth in a hurry and runs out the door. Little time to hug and kiss her mom! Her sister follows her. The driver has known these sisters for several years. Since she had to wait for them for a few minutes, the driver is annoyed and reprimands them, 'Tomorrow, be on time.' Ann loves to dream about the day when she will drive her own car to school.

The bus stops in front of Michelle's elementary school at about 7:55 am. Within the next five minutes, Jane, Ann's best friend, gets on the bus. During the ten minute ride to school, they bring each other up-to-date about what has happened since yesterday evening. They discuss television programs watched the previous evening, homework problems, and a phone call from Jane's boyfriend. On board are several more friends who have gone to school together since kindergarten. Ann and Jane greet them, then quickly turn to each other to continue conversation. A few students keep their eyes on homework due today. Most of the pupils from elementary, middle, and high school are socializing with their peers. When the noise level becomes unbearable by the driver's standards, she reminds her passengers to quiet down. Her comments are sometimes ignored, but are most often observed, at least temporarily.

The bus cruises through the main gate of the high school and stops at the front stone steps at 8:05 am (See Figure 3 to accompany Ann's movements in school from this moment). The high school is the last stop for the bus. A few buses have already unloaded students, and some juniors and seniors are arriving by car. The student parking lot is about half filled with passenger cars, pick-up trucks, and a few motorcycles.

Before 'First Period'

Dragging her bag out of the bus, she thanks the driver. As usual, her heavy bag indicates the amount of homework assigned yesterday. Mr. Kay, today's supervising teacher, is standing at the top of the steps and is being greeted by students.

Ann and Jane go to the locker room at the gym to leave their track clothes and shoes. Then they put the rest of their school materials in the hall locker that they share. Students who have just arrived are rushing into the hall. The sound of slamming locker doors echoes throughout the rather deserted corridor in the morning. Ann feels fortunate to have a locker in this hall, because her friends said that another hall, referred to as the 'freshman hall', is 'smelly, unclean, and full of rowdy, immature freshmen'.

Now Ann and Jane go to the library. The library is the only well-lit and well-heated place in the chilly morning. Their other friends, whom they usually meet at the library in the morning, are already there. The air hums with activities; some students are finishing their homework, reading books from the rack of paperback romantic novels, copying another's assignment, or chatting. Ann tries to finish her English homework, occasionally raising her head to interject her opinions to her friends' conversation. The noise level increases as more people enter the library. A librarian comes over to a few students sitting at a table next to Ann's; she orders them to leave, adding that the library is a place for studying, not for talking. Ann and her friends are well aware of the consequence of their dismissal. In order to be neither sitting out in the chilly hall nor walking around the empty campus, Ann and her friends try to keep their voices down.

Morning Classes

First Period (8:35–9:19 am): Biology

The preparatory bell rings at 8:30 am, five minutes before the first period. In no time the library is emptied. Now halls are packed with students trying to get to their lockers as quickly as possible, calling each other, shrieking, and jostling. This seeming 'chaos' is abruptly replaced by quiet order when the first period bell rings. Only a few students are still hurrying to their classrooms.

Ann walks into the biology lab, the walls of which are brilliantly

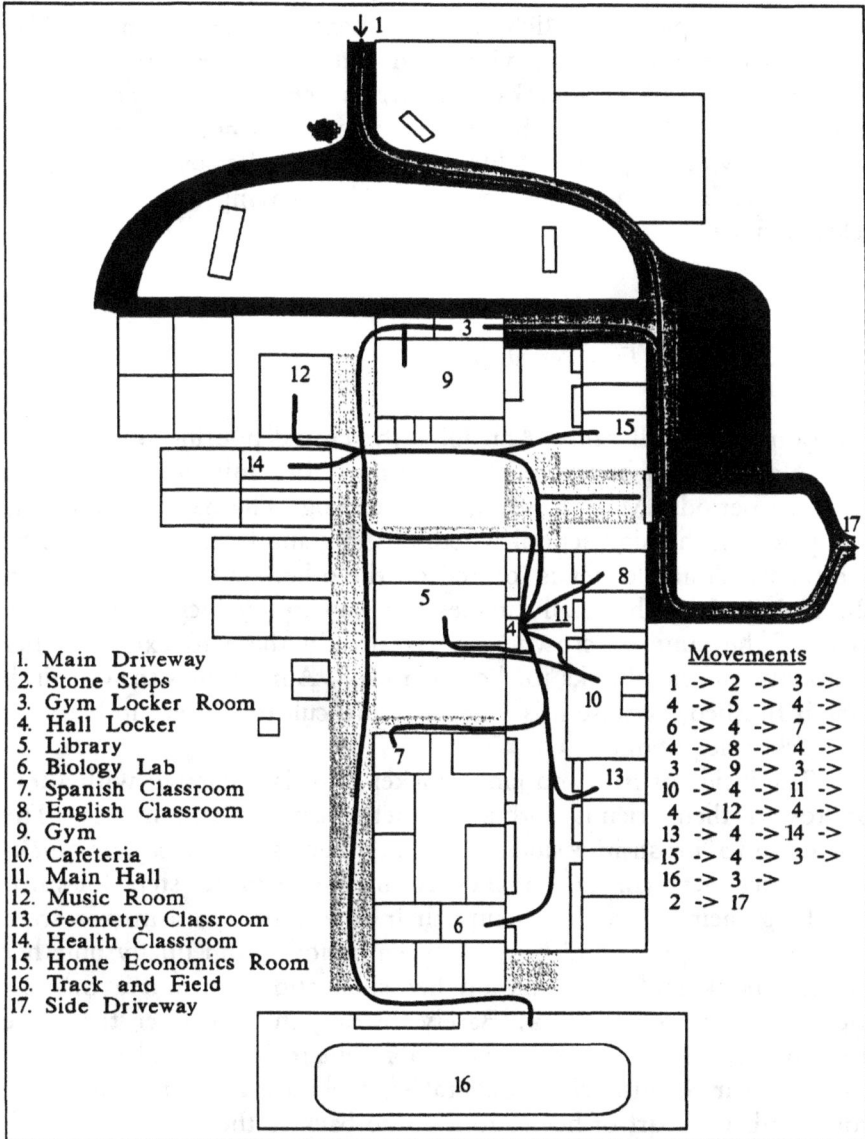

1. Main Driveway
2. Stone Steps
3. Gym Locker Room
4. Hall Locker
5. Library
6. Biology Lab
7. Spanish Classroom
8. English Classroom
9. Gym
10. Cafeteria
11. Main Hall
12. Music Room
13. Geometry Classroom
14. Health Classroom
15. Home Economics Room
16. Track and Field
17. Side Driveway

Movements

1 -> 2 -> 3 ->
4 -> 5 -> 4 ->
6 -> 4 -> 7 ->
4 -> 8 -> 4 ->
3 -> 9 -> 3 ->
10 -> 4 -> 11 ->
4 ->12 -> 4 ->
13 -> 4 ->14 ->
15 -> 4 -> 3 ->
16 -> 3 ->
2 -> 17

Figure 3.   A sketch map of Ann's movements in school (not to scale).

decorated with posters, visual instruction aids, and class rules. The counters around the three walls are covered with aquariums and collections of sea shells, stones, animal bones, and countless objects for different biology classes. She sits at the assigned table with her three male lab partners, Michael usually next to her, and Jon and Alan behind her. Ann gets along with them, but sometimes complains that the boys tell her 'sick jokes' to embarrass her. The jokes annoy her, but she finds it fun when she can return one in kind. While the class watches a video tape about life and ecology, Michael talks to Ann every once in a while. She responds while paying attention to the television screen.

Break After First Period

As soon as the bell rings, Ann joins the crowd pouring out into the hall. No time can be wasted because only four minutes are allowed between periods. More hustling and bustling! The hall is one of the few places in the high school where pushing and bumping seem to be acceptable. Ann's locker is located on the other side of the hall from the biology lab. She finally makes her way to her locker against the flow of the jammed crowd. Jane is already there to exchange her textbooks and notebooks for her next class. Ann decides to wait until Jane is finished, because it is extremely difficult to squeeze in between her locker neighbors.

The inside of Ann and Jane's locker door is decorated with a few photos of their friends and a magnetic handbag-size mirror. The mirror and a 'brush-in-residence' are their necessary items. Jane quickly brushes her hair and makes room for Ann to step forward. Brushing their hair and checking their appearances in a mirror are a ritual for many girls and boys between periods. Ann finally puts her biology book and notebook on her shelf and takes out a Spanish workbook and a notebook. Barely hearing the bell over the noise around her, she bangs her locker door shut to lock it and runs with Jane to their Spanish class. Several students are also running in the courtyard. It is part of her routine to go back to the locker after each class. Such chaos in the hall between periods is sometimes bothersome, but Ann views lockers as indispensable: without lockers students would have to carry their stuff around or stay in one classroom 'like seventh graders', which is not 'cool'.

Second Period (9:23–10:07 am): Spanish

Ann is almost late for her second period, but she is never actually tardy for any class. She runs if she thinks she is getting late. She likes second-year Spanish and plans to take it again next year, especially since the advanced Spanish classes will take a trip to Mexico during spring break. Spanish is one of the three classes that Ann and Jane are taking together this year. It was possible for them to choose all classes together at the fall registration, but they decided not to, because they might grow tired of each other if they saw each other all the time.

At the beginning of the class, the teacher tells the students to turn in their notebooks at the end of class. Students check their notebooks to see if everything is there. Then the teacher asks students questions in Spanish from the workbook and they are told to answer in Spanish. Most of them try, but they speak softly and hesitantly in Spanish. The teacher also makes the students repeat some Spanish words after him. Some students giggle about unusual pronunciations.

David (Ann's ex-boyfriend) and John sit behind Ann and Jane. During the time to do seat work, Ann asks Jane, 'Did you watch *Family Ties* last night?' Television soap operas are typical conversation topics between Ann and her friends. Their talks continue while they are writing down answers in a workbook exercise. Every few minutes, David interjects some jokes. According to Ann, David has a strange sense of humor, but he's fun to listen to. Ann and Jane listen to David's puns and joke around with the boys for the rest of the free time.

'Morning Break' after Second Period

After the second period, what is called 'morning break' allows students a ten-minute recess. Ann does not have to hurry as much as during the first break. Ann and Jane stop on the way to their locker to chat with their friends. Members of Future Business Leaders of America are selling doughnuts from the cafeteria window to raise funds for their club activities. About five people are standing in the line to buy them. While walking to their locker, Ann and Jane encounter Jeff who is holding a partially eaten maple bar. He asks them, 'Do you want a bite?' Ann answers, 'Sure!', and rips off a piece, but Jane politely declines. Ann and Jane pick up materials and go separately to their next classes. Ann usually goes to the empty classroom early and sets out her materials on her desk. When Ann walks in today, her English teacher is working at her desk and exchanges a friendly greeting with her.

Third Period (10:17–11:01 am): Advanced English II

English is one of Ann's favorite subjects because she likes to read and write. She studies hard for other subjects but 'extra hard' for this English class. This is an Advanced English class for sophomores. She took Advanced English I the previous year, so it was an automatic transition for her to take Advanced English II this year. When she began high school, she was assigned to Advanced English I because she took English in the Talented and Gifted Program in her middle school. Ann does not like the label of 'talented and gifted' student because she is concerned about being perceived as arrogant by her peers.

Today, as the class is supposed to do the second session of library research, they move to the library where students search for sources of information pertaining to their self-chosen topics. Ann chose to write a paper about the difference between American and Asian education. She has been inspired by a current news magazine article praising Japanese education. Among the three required references, Ann has already collected information from a newspaper and an encyclopedia. Today, she looks for pertinent articles from magazines.

Fourth Period (11:05–11:49 am): Physical Education

After her English class, Ann is reluctant to go to the physical education (PE) class. She does not enjoy running around in circles in the gym at the beginning of the class. Thinking, 'No choice', she enters the girls' locker room in the gym building. Her locker is in the slightly secluded and spacious area designated for athletes. Her classmates who do not participate in sports have baskets in the area close to the door.

Soon Jane walks into the locker room. Ann likes to have her best friend in this class. Last year she did not have close friends in the PE class, and it made her feel miserable at times. Especially during pair activities, she often ended up with a boy partner, because most girls had their best friends in the class. Ann changes her jeans to a pair of flower-printed shorts, and her pastel-color blue shirt to a baggy short-sleeved tee-shirt. She pulls the shirt down over the shorts. Although disdaining the overly-fashion-conscious crowd, she knows it is not a fad to tuck shirts in pants or skirts. Today she does not have to change shoes because she is wearing soft-soled ones.

By the time Ann and Jane finish changing and closing their lockers, the bell rings. They hastily run out to the gym to be on time in roll call line. Some students show up for the roll call but are not dressed for gym class. They will observe the class but are excused from participation in today's activity. The teacher checks any absence by 'eye-balling'; she knows most students by sight and name. Students address her by her first name. She attributes her casualness with students to having been born in the community and having attended this high school with some of her students' parents.

After the roll call, the class runs around the gym in circles for about five minutes, which Ann thinks is boring. Chatting with Jane makes running at least bearable. A Boys PE class joins the girls for running. A few of her classmates are allowed to walk instead of run because of their health problems. After running, students are paired up to play badminton, which this class has been doing for two weeks. The teacher is walking around to help students individually with their skills. Giggles are heard here and there but some pairs are seriously engaged in playing. The class will be devoted to volleyball during the next two weeks.

The 'shower bell' rings five minutes before the class actually ends. Ann and Jane quickly stop playing and rush to the locker room with other girls. Ann's classmates do not conspicuously show themselves in their undergarments but express no embarrassment at changing clothes in the presence of their peers. No one takes a shower because, unlike at middle school, it is not required at high school. Ann washes her face when she perspires a lot. After dressing, Ann brushes her hair. Several girls are trying to peek into mirrors to check their appearances. Jane curls her hair and does her make-up again. A few girls bring their electric hair curlers to school; some keep theirs in the gym lockers. Others borrow one from a friend for a few touches. Ann and Jane continue dressing in the locker room for about the first five minutes of the lunch period.

Lunch Time

Lunch begins at 11:49 am and lasts for thirty-nine minutes. Yesterday, Ann and Jane got a ride from Duane to Sunrise Market, a small chain store, for lunch. Greenfield High School has an open campus policy: only students, who submitted written parental permission at the beginning of the school year, are allowed to leave the school ground during the lunch period. Since the written permission is rarely checked, however, many students freely go off campus during this time. Some students go to Dairy Queen, to Safeway, or to other local stores; several go home for lunch or drive around the community. Many go to the Sunrise Market, which sells three hot dogs for a dollar, a hamburger for fifty cents, and various kinds of soft drinks. The store also has a few small tables where students may sit. Yesterday, while Ann was sitting at a table with her companion, about thirty Greenfielders came in and out.

Today Ann and Jane decide to remain on campus because they have to prepare for a unit test in the Health class. If they go out, they know they will waste the whole time by driving out and back, 'sitting around', and socializing with friends. By the time Ann and Jane walk into the cafeteria, three long lines have already formed for hot lunch, hamburgers, or snacks. Half of the lunch room tables are occupied. The principal, today's supervisor of the lunch room, is standing against the main window and talking with students.

Today's hot lunch includes pizza or super submarine sandwich, carrot sticks or onion rings, chilled pears or fresh fruit, and regular or chocolate milk, in addition to cookies. One can instead get a chef's salad with assorted vegetables, cheese, and ham strips. From the hamburger line, one can get a cheeseburger with pickles, ketchup, and mayonnaise, and side dishes from the hot lunch menu. These three options — a hot meal, a cheeseburger meal, and a chef salad — are purchased for one dollar and five cents at the regular price. The same meal is available at a reduced price, or free, to students from lower income households. Ann is not eligible for either benefit. From the snack line, students can also get plain cheeseburgers, delicatessen sandwiches, chips, cookies, ice cream bars, fruit juice, milk, hot pretzels, or cakes with icing for various prices.

Most of the time, Ann brings her own lunch. Even when she does not, she rarely buys a hot lunch, because if she is late for the lunch line, only limited choices are left. Today Ann and Jane stand at the tail of the snack line. A few girls and boys come from the back and squeeze in in front of Ann. This 'cutting in' behavior is commonly seen on campus and it does not bother her any more. Ann buys a hamburger for sixty-five cents with a chocolate milk for twenty-five cents; Jane purchases two chocolate chip cookies and a carton of regular milk.

On days when they want to be able to glance at a certain boy who sparks their interest, they go to a table close to him. Today Ann and Jane find seats against a wall, where they usually sit. Even though seating is not restricted, most students sit in the same area every day. Eric, whom they know well but do not consider as their close friend, has already occupied the table where Ann and Jane usually sit. Since Ann gets along with many of her peers, she does not object to sitting with him. They are soon joined by two junior girls. For his lunch, Eric has bought two large pieces of pizza. One of the girls has a plate of chef's salad, the other has a piece of white cake. Eric calls pizza a 'dirty carpet' and the girl with the cake agrees by saying that the cafeteria food tastes like plastic. Complaining about the school lunch is quite common in this school; a student-initiated lunch committee has spoken out to improve the quality of school lunch.

As soon as they finish lunch, Ann and Jane leave the cafeteria. This room is usually emptied within the first twenty-five minutes. A cleaning crew of several students with a janitor move students out of the cafeteria when they begin to wipe and fold lunch tables and sweep the floor. Ann and Jane go to their locker and take out their Health textbooks and notebooks to prepare for today's test. They sit against their locker and spread their books on the worn carpeted hall floor. Their friends — David, Duane, John, Mary, and Lynn — come and join them, some studying and others bantering with each other. A few passing peers stop and strike up conversation with some from this group; those who bend their heads over books are usually left alone. Ann feels comfortable studying in the hall, if she does not go to the library during lunch time. Lunch period is also a good time for her to catch up with some homework or study for tests.

Afternoon Classes

Fifth Period (12:31–1:15 pm): Eagle[1] Tones

As soon as the preparatory bell rings, Ann puts away her health book in the locker and heads to the music room for the stage choir class. She looks forward to the next hour because they sing and dance throughout the period. Recently, they have been practicing choreography for a Broadway show tune medley. It will be performed on the choir trip to Canada in the spring term, as well as at the school spring concert.

Eagle Tones is the only one among three school choirs that

accepts students through annual auditions. Despite the music teacher's de-emphasis on the hierarchy among the choirs, Eagle Tones is recognized as a small group of 'elite' singers. When her parents encouraged her to try out for the audition at the end of her freshman year, Ann was quite doubtful of her success. When she actually did audition and was accepted, Ann was pleasantly surprised. Six of the twelve members (eight girls and four boys) are sophomores who were selected at the same time as Ann. The Eagle Tones are unique at Greenfield as they add choreography to many songs. For performances, choir members wear special outfits: girls wear a knee-length black skirts white long-sleeved blouses with black bow ties, black vests with a front made of blue sparkling fabric, and black dressy shoes; boys wear black trousers and shoes and white shirts with black bow ties.

When Ann walks through a side door to the music room, several classmates are already there. Some are practicing their musical instruments, singing, or having lunch in this room. Ann exchanges greetings with them and joins their conversation. Choir members have a close relationship because the enrollment is small and they have stayed together for a year or longer.

When the teacher enters, students are bantering with their neighbors at their chairs arranged on the carpeted amphitheater floor. The teacher looks around quickly to informally check the roll, because he knows everybody well. Now class members step down to the bottom floor to face the piano. Ann helps some boys with folding and moving away the chairs from the floor to make more room for dancing. As the choir has almost mastered the singing part, the class is today synchronizing choreographic movements. Students dance to the music that the teacher plays on the piano. Sometimes, the teacher stops the students and corrects some moves. Some students freely interject their opinions on how some moves should be modified. Ann confidently takes steps and enjoys herself. She likes most music chosen for this class, Broadway show tunes, hits of the fifties and sixties, jazz, and theme songs from films.

Sixth Period (1:19–2:03 pm): Geometry

After the excitement in the choir, Ann has her least favorite class, Geometry. She finds mathematics generally difficult. From a door at the back of the classroom, she walks all the way up to a front seat. She used to sit in the middle row in the first part of the year when she found the work easier; once the class began the topic geometric constructions, in which she was to identify and construct two-dimensional shapes using a ruler and compass, she found it less comprehensible. The different teaching style of a student teacher made the lessons more difficult to follow. In addition, students who sat in the back of the class 'goofed off' and sometimes distracted her. She figured that it would be better to sit in front to pay attention. She is still struggling with the subject, but she feels that changing seats has helped her concentration.

Today, the student teacher explains how to find the center of a circle geometrically and demonstrates the procedure on an overhead projector. She distributes compasses, rulers, and worksheets to have students practice the same steps. During the seatwork, Ann sometimes turns to her neighbor to ask questions, but mostly she concentrates on the work. At the end of the class, Ann turns in her completed worksheet; those who have not finished are allowed to complete it at home and bring it back the next day. A few minutes before the bell rings, the student teacher hands out assignments to students who complain that she gives too much homework. Ann tries to finish her seatwork in class so that she does not have to take home both seatwork and assignments.

Seventh Period (2:07–2:51 pm): Health

After exchanging class materials at her locker, Ann walks with Jane to their health class. This is the last period of the day, the third one they take together. They decided to take health at the end of a day because it was expected to be the easiest class of all — the one with the least pressure. Ann and Jane also decided to take this class together because they thought they might have some free time in class to socialize with each other.

Since the teacher is easily approachable and lively, Ann likes him. She thinks, however, some classmates abuse his relaxed style and are unruly. The situation was worse until a month ago. Many students talked back to the teacher, teased him, or conversed among themselves while the teacher was talking. Being the last class of the day did not help the situation at all. Ann became resentful that students who usually sat in the back called those in the front 'brown nosers'. Since the teacher switched students from the back to the front and vice versa, Ann has been pleased. Now she feels that her seventh period class is better.

For a few weeks the class has been focusing on sex education. A couple of Ann's classmates were excused from this unit because they and their parents believed the topic conflicts with their religious conviction. Ann feels comfortable with class discussions about sex and presumes that most of her classmates do not feel embarrassed about the subject either. She assumes that some of her classmates have a 'personal interest' in this unit.

Homeroom (2:55–3:15 pm)

Ann usually goes to her homeroom directly from her health class. She was assigned to Mrs. Anderson's homeroom in her freshman year and will stay with the same teacher until she graduates. Jane was assigned to another homeroom, because students were alphabetically grouped on the basis of students' last names.

When Ann walks in the home economics room, Mrs. Anderson is writing notes at her desk. As usual, some students have already congregated around a stove and the microwave oven in the back of the classroom, making popcorn or grilled cheese sandwiches. The teacher allows them to do it, because they do nothing in the homeroom but sit around and chat. Ann sits alone at a table most of the time, as she does not have close friends in this homeroom; she does not enjoy this solitary twenty minutes. She has already looked through the pattern books furnished in the sewing section from cover to cover countless times, so she sometimes reads a romance novel or does homework.

Ann does not see the value of the homeroom, and many of her peers agree with her. Some teachers argue that students should be able to use it for productive activities, catching up with studying, doing homework, or reading. Yet Ann is aware that some other teachers would share with her the same view of the homeroom. The skeptical crowd thinks that the homeroom only works to keep students under supervision until school buses arrive.[2]

After the School Bell Rings

Track Practice (3:30–5:00 pm)

After school, Ann has about fifteen minutes before a track practice. She likes the sports she considers 'hers' — the 400m hurdle and the high jump, but she also feel lethargic and regrets not being able to go home to relax after such a long day. Ann and Jane try to take as much time as possible in packing their bags in the hall, moving the bags to the gym locker, and dressing in track clothes. While Ann and Jane walk to the track field, some of her friends are waiting for their late buses. They are either standing in a circle talking, sitting on benches, or chasing friends for fun in the courtyard. Ann and Jane stop briefly to greet them but soon run to the field because their track coach is strict about being tardy.

Some athletes are already jogging on the track, and others are stretching muscles before beginning individual training. After briefly stretching out, Ann and Jane begin warming up on the track. Once she begins to run, Ann says that she forgets the lethargic feeling and enjoys the practice. All participants are supposed to run for four laps (one mile) before beginning practices in their specialties. She is encouraged because her record continuously improves. The practice is finished at 4:50 pm. Ann remains on the field for awhile, assessing today's training result with her coach and socializing with her peers.

Ann and Jane stroll back to the gym with other girls. Some girls go home directly after the practice; others shower in the girls' locker room. Today Ann and Jane decide to go home without showering, because Ann's mother will pick them up soon. Their mothers take turns in transporting the girls home after sport practices. They wait for their ride in front of the stone steps, their heavy bags filled with textbooks and notebooks for tonight's homework.

At Home in the Evening

The brown van cruises along the main driveway and stops in front of the steps. Ann's sister is riding next to her mother. Ann and Jane quickly slip into the middle seat. Ann's mother suggests stopping at Safeway for grocery shopping. Ann was extremely tired after the practice, but now feels a 'second wind' as she gets out of the van, and she follows her mother. After purchasing a few items, they head home. Jane's house is on the way from the school to Ann's. Ann's mother drives the van carefully along Jane's long, narrow, steep driveway. Jane's mother, a good friend of Ann's mother for many years, is preparing dinner. These mothers immediately strike up a conversation about families and neighbors. Ann is anxious to go home to take a shower and relax as soon as possible.

By the time they come home, it is already 6:30 pm. Ann's appetite is soaring; she fills her stomach with a couple of bowls of chili, salad, and bread. After the meal, she sits in front of the television as usual. She does not feel like doing anything but just being a 'couch potato'. The time passes quickly and, at 9:30 pm, her mother finally reminds her of doing homework. This time, Ann does not protest against her mother's command-like suggestion, because she knows that otherwise she will have to stay up late again tonight.

The first thing she does in her room is to turn on her portable radio; easy-listening music seems appropriate now. She sits at her desk and makes a list of what she should do tonight: a workbook exercise for Spanish, a short paper for English, and a geometry worksheet. Starting the Spanish assignment, Ann works diligently on the assignment, which takes only half an hour. Ann has already prepared an outline for the English paper she needs to write, but by the time she finishes her English paper, it is almost midnight. All of the sudden, she feels too tired to keep her eyes open, and her eyelids become heavier and heavier. Since she slept for less than six hours last night, Ann decides to do the geometry homework during lunch-time tomorrow and to go to bed now. She realizes that she cannot help appearing a 'nerd' against her will, because she spends almost every lunch-time completing assignments. However, what else can she do? She takes her grades seriously, but does not have enough time to do homework in the evening after sport practices. By the time she is ready to sleep, the house has become quiet, just as in the morning when she gets up. Her mother and sister are already in bed.

Notes

1 The eagle (pseudonym) was the mascot of the high school. Many school organizations such as the student newspaper, the dance team, and the performing choir carried this name.
2 Homeroom was discontinued beginning fall 1988. Under the new policy, the seventh period was the last class of the day on Monday through Thursday and the homeroom time on Friday was designated for school-wide activities such as assemblies or club meetings. Since the bus schedule had not been adjusted to the new policy, students who did not drive had about twenty to thirty minutes of free time before the school bus arrived.

Chapter 6

Life Outside School

What goes on in teenagers' lives when they are not at school? What do they do? Where do they go? With whom do they 'hang out'? What do they think? I found these questions intriguing but not easy to answer as an ethnographer, because I could not observe adolescents in their incredibly varied settings. This sort of frustration always accompanied my field research, although I did not dream of observing and understanding the whole spectrum of a teenager's life. Just as Hermes, the god of messages in Greek mythology, 'promised to tell no lies but did not promise to tell the whole truth' (Crapanzano 1986:76), my participant observations and interviews allowed me to tell the story of teenagers only on the basis of what I had experienced and heard.

As an attempt to overcome the limitedness of researchers in space and time, Csikszentmihalyi and Larson (1984) used technological assistance. They asked a selected group of adolescents to carry an electronic pager and a pad of self-report forms. The forms had three large categories — location, activities, and companions — and subcategories. The adolescents were instructed that, whenever the pager beeped, they were to fill out the form indicating where they were, what they were doing, and with whom.

In my research, I utilized personal journals in order to gain insight into adolescent life out of sight. These accounts added more dimensions to what I could observe and hear personally. The students' thoughts and personal lives were reflected in essays, journals, and responses to a survey with open-ended questions. In this chapter, I let the young people talk about some aspects of their lives — what they did, what they thought, and what they valued — in their own voices.[1]

Weekends

Most teenagers looked forward to weekends. The weekends broke the routine of weekdays such as waking up early to get ready for school, taking the same seven classes every day, having lunch basically at the same place, participating in after-school activities, doing household chores, eating dinner, watching television, doing homework, and going to bed. Instead, many teenagers reported doing a variety of different activities during weekends which they could not usually do during the week: going on family outings, working in part-time jobs, 'sleeping in', visiting with friends, cruising the 'gut', shopping, going to church, and pursuing hobbies. To some teenagers, weekends might not have been drastically different from weekdays except for not going to school; they spent weekends socializing with friends and family or catching up on schoolwork. Some adolescents described their activities on specific weekends in their classroom journals:

> Saturday, I went trail riding with some friends of mine. I enjoy trail riding because I love to see God's wonderful creation. I love to see the different trees, hear the birds, and listen to the horse's hooves as we gallop down the long trail. I rode a friend's horse. I don't really like riding other people's horses, especially this one. Blue — which is the name of the horse — has a very stubborn attitude about things. She enjoys doing things her way, (don't we all) but her way is usually either dumping the rider or taking off running. She did, however, take off which scared me to death but I stayed on OK. The next time we started running, I pushed her instead of trying to hold her back. We had fun that day. I wish I could have had my own horse but I still had a lot of fun. One really neat thing I enjoy is getting together and praying for a safe trip when we go horseback riding. [a sophomore girl]

> I just got back from hunting and told my mom where we went and how many deer we saw. That day my dad and I saw twenty-four deer in all and I was surprised because of it being so dry. This next weekend I am going again and I hope I get a buck. The buck must be a forked horn or above. [a sophomore boy]

> My weekend was the greatest. I went out with a friend and we went to the gut. We met a bunch more of our friends and all cruised together. Mellisa knows almost everybody down there so I met lots of new people. I got to know this guy Rob and now I'm going to meet him at Video Games Arcade this weekend. It's gonna be cool. Yeah! [a senior girl]

The following excerpts were taken from senior survey responses to show some typical weekend activities:

We [the family] usually go camping, boating, or fishing. Sometimes I like to stay home and be by myself or go out with friends. [a girl]

I usually sleep in until 11:00, laze (i.e., be lazy) around until 2:00 and then go to work with mom. [a girl]

Worked. Stayed with friends. [a girl]

We usually just stay at my boyfriend's house and watch TV after I get off work. We don't go out much. [a girl]

Went to the hot tubs with my girlfriend and made love. [a boy]

Fri — played Bingo, Sat — babysat, Sun — Went out to dinner and played Bingo. [a girl]

I went out with some friends to [visit] a friend in town, played some sports and went to the speedways — where I watched the car races. [a boy]

Usually I have some big activity planned, so I don't have a 'typical' weekend, like [our] choir Canada trip, humanities field trip, prom, etc. [a girl]

Twice went to church. [a girl]

I worked on my car and went fishing. [a boy]

I usually volunteer at the hospital. [a girl]

In addition to the activities mentioned above, some teenagers were engaged in each of the following weekend activities: studying; skateboarding; school-related activities such as dances, fund-raising projects, and athletic and choir competitions; private parties that involved watching rental videos, drinking alcohol, and smoking; and community-related activities such as helping at community and church functions.

Holidays

Most teenagers reported that they acted or thought differently on holidays than on other days because of the special meanings that holidays had attained in their lives. Their cultural and family traditions made holidays different.

Thanksgiving

Many adolescents celebrated Thanksgiving with their families, relatives, and friends, enjoying the traditional feast. Two girls described their Thanksgiving in classroom journals:

> I am mostly anticipating going to my grandma's house and seeing my cousins and other relatives. My grandma usually makes an enormous dinner and cakes, pies and jello desserts. The younger kids usually sit at card tables or with TV trays. The TV is usually on and the male folk are watching some football game, telling everyone what that player could have or shouldn't have done, or how good so and so is. After dinner grandma tries to convince everyone to try a certain dessert or pie. She usually succeeds. Then everyone says that they shouldn't have eaten so much pie or cake. [a sophomore]

> Thanksgiving is strictly a family day; a time to share. It's the only holiday in which gifts are not exchanged (traditionally). You don't have to think about giving gifts or what you're going to get. It's probably the least expensive holiday of the year. [a freshman]

A sophomore girl ridiculed the excessive association of turkeys with Thanksgiving:

> What was really kinda funny was that all day Wednesday I heard 'Happy Turkey Day!' Not only is it extremely corny but we are not celebrating turkeys. If we were, why would we eat them?

The typical image of Thanksgiving may lead one to assume that all the teenagers celebrated it in the 'typical' way. Some teenagers corrected the stereotype by depicting their unpleasant experience with the holiday:

> I will have to truthfully say I don't anticipate Thanksgiving. Thanksgiving to me is being stuck at home with my sister and my mom. We go somewhere different every year and have only been home twice in my life. We don't decorate or have tradition either. Especially since my step-grandma came, really I don't even know where I'm eating tomorrow. Turkey is not a basic in our meal and I've only eaten it a few times for Thanksgiving. One thing I do look forward to is that Daddy might go on an outing with me Friday if he doesn't work. So now that you know about my Thanksgiving, maybe you can figure out why I don't like it. I don't like it because nothing stays the same. [a sophomore girl]

> My Thanksgiving wasn't all it was cut out to be. Larry [room-mate] was having trouble with his girlfriend. I was still getting over the loss of my girlfriend and my parents weren't talking much. Right when I got off work I went home and didn't eat much. That whole weekend I only ate about one good hot meal. I felt as if my world had come to an end but I'm a survivor. When I got home I took one look at my parents and grabbed Larry and said that we were gonna get drunk. We did. The day after, my head felt like an overripe watermelon. Every word spoken to me made me feel like screaming.... My Thanksgiving was actually a bummer. [a senior boy]

Thanksgiving was not a happy time for these two teenagers. It meant neither a large family gathering nor a bounteous feast. Rather, they viewed Thanksgiving as another weekend with extra free days.

Halloween

Many Greenfield adolescents considered Halloween an exciting event. Along with a few occasions like Homecoming Spirit Week, Halloween allowed teenagers to look different without being ridiculed. They could transform into somebody else or something different. There seemed no limit to what identity one could assume: from a witch to an angel, from a monster to Dorothy in the *Wizard of Oz*, from Native American to a Russian, or from a Disney character to a pumpkin. Why did this superficial transformation bring excitement to teenagers? Did it assure them a temporary escape from boredom? Or did it beguile young people with the momentary realization of a dream?

Halloween was a day of 'trick-or-treating' when younger children roamed the neighborhood 'demanding' treats at each household. The question arose each year as to when one is too old to join in that activity. A junior girl declared that she did not feel too old for trick-or-treating. She would have done it even at the age of sixteen, if she had not had to drive a couple of miles to reach her neighbors. Many high school students wanted to sustain the same kind of spirit. They went in costumes to Halloween dance parties, some sponsored by parental groups and others sponsored by community groups, churches, or individual families. Two youngsters described their pleasant experiences on Halloween:

On Saturday morning I awoke to excitement. My sisters were giggling and screaming things like 'Trick or treat', the phrase so well known to people in America. Although I wasn't spending Halloween with my family, I knew they would have fun going to the party the school was having. I helped to get my sisters ready that evening after a relaxed day for my parents but intense for my little sisters for they wanted to get candy, candy, candy! Jinna's [best girlfriend] sisters...picked me up.... When we got home [Jinna's house] I went upstairs and the whole thing had been transformed. There were Halloween doors and a witch piñata. (It will later only take a couple of taps with the baseball bat to break the fragile thing open.) I went downstairs and we ate dinner and ate some Halloween candy and carved pumpkins, then watched some movies. One of them was so dumb I had to leave the room to keep from crying. By that time we were all kinda sleepy, but we watched Saturday Night Live anyway. We all crawled up to bed and fell asleep at the witching hour — 12:00. [a sophomore girl]

Last Friday I worked in 'Scream in the Dark' [a ghost house built for Halloween in Riverville]. It was really fun. First I worked in the jungle room and we had a springy bridge in there and people kept falling down. One girl fell down and almost got trampled. Another little boy fell down and his dad just dragged him out. I then worked in the chain monster

room where another guy and I were chained to the walls. . . .
[a sophomore boy]

Christmas

Christmas was also regarded as a family time: visiting relatives, sharing a big dinner similar to that for Thanksgiving, and exchanging gifts. A sophomore girl wrote about her anticipation of the holiday:

Christmas is my favorite time of the year. I got to see all my relatives that I haven't seen in months. Everyone (with the exception of a few) gives and enjoys the people's pleasure in what they give. All the food smells good and there are always lots of goodies to eat. I just love Christmas!

Compared to other holidays, gift exchange was regarded as an essence of this holiday. In the society of excessive commercialization they described, the social expectation demanded that teenagers behave accordingly, which put pressure on them. Not meeting the expectations made them feel inadequate. In particular, the stress was more apparent for those who had neither substantial income to buy satisfactory gifts, nor the creativity to construct something for others by themselves. Several adolescents described the pressure of getting presents for the Christmas season:

My Christmas list for others would be something that is rather cheap and inexpensive. Something like a plain old Christmas card. With no money in it of course. But unfortunately I just can't do that. That would be terrible if I only got cards for Christmas. But we all have to remember that it's only the thought that counts. [a junior girl]

I've been thinking Christmas is coming up pretty soon and with five dollars for allowance a week I'm not going to have enough money for my mom, dad, sister, and brother. . . . Things are just too expensive nowadays with a weekly allowance of five dollars. [a sophomore girl]

Christmas just doesn't seem the same anymore. It's become too commercialized. What happened to the old fashioned Christmas that I used to enjoy. . . The pressure of buying gifts and getting the money to buy them is what I really hate. Our society is so materialistic. [a boy]

Memorial Day[2]

Memorial Day weekend (the last weekend in May) was slightly different from other holidays because it included a Monday. Some teenagers took a trip with family or friends. A few students pre-arranged an absence for Friday before the weekend to extend their family vacation. However, most teenagers spent this weekend as they spent other weekends. In the survey, seniors described activities that they participated in on that weekend:

Car shopped, painted the house and watched movies. [a girl]

I went up to a lake in the mountains with my parents and brother. And with a bunch of other people. We had a lot of fun. [a girl]

Friday night I went to a party with Julie, Becky, and Iris, etc. Then to XXX [a local hard-rock band] concert, then to another party. Saturday night I stayed at Julie's and we baby-sat. Sunday night I went to the drive-in with Brian, Julie, and Dan. Then went to Dan's house with them. [a girl]

I worked Friday night. Saturday Sheryl and I went shopping in Riverville. Saturday night I worked. Sunday I did some of my homework and went to work that night. Monday I helped my parents around the house and got my graduation announcements ready to send. [a girl]

I left Thursday night. Went to a camp ground. Laid out in the sun Friday and got a sun burn. Met and talked to three guys. Saturday I went with three friends to the dunes and rode a quad racer all day. Then Sunday and Monday just talked to the three guys I met and went home Monday. [a girl]

I went to [the eastern part of the state] with my family and went hiking and fishing and visited relatives. [a girl]

Help my sister and brother-in-law paint their house. [a boy]

I tried out for the Riverville Pepsi Challenge Baseball team. [a boy]

Sat: I worked all day. Sun: I went to Loveland for a Bible talk and then went to a friend's house for lunch there. Mon: went out in service (witnessing), cleaned the house and went out to town that night with my friends. [a boy]

I went to Blue Lake and went water skiing all weekend. [a boy].

Went to the State track meet. [a senior boy]

First went to swimming at Echo, then went to the lake [Green] with a bunch of friends, cruised the gut, then back home around 2:00 am. [a boy]

The Fourth of July

Since my contact with Greenfielders was limited to a few teenagers and adults during the summer, I did not have many opportunities to observe how they spent the Fourth of July. Among the few, Marylinn wrote in her journal her feelings about the national patriotic holiday:

Since Ridgeport has a big fireworks show on the Fourth of July and we haven't seen my grandma in a while, we decided to go there for the holiday. The fireworks show was a lot of fun to watch. We were down on Newbeach's bay front and we watched the fireworks explode above us. There were a lot of people who were there to watch. The show only lasted for about a half an hour. When the show ended, we went down to the beach and watched some people light off their own fireworks. Even though I did have fun, I wish that I felt more patriotic or something. I felt as if it was just another day, but there were fireworks. I didn't feel a sense of pride or independence at all and in a way that makes me feel guilty.... When I was little, holidays seemed so special and exciting, but as I get older, they aren't such a big deal. I think that most of my friends in my age feel a lot the same way. [Personal Journal]

Summer Vacation

Summer vacation was the longest break from school in the year, beginning mid-June and lasting until Labor Day, the first Monday in September. Therefore, it gave ample opportunities for high school adolescents to do a variety of things: get jobs, travel, make up credits through summer school or independent studies, socialize, or pursue extracurricular interests.

Working during summer was popular among teenagers. Even those youngsters who did not advocate working during the school year strongly supported the idea of working during summer. Seniors identified the benefits of summer jobs as good experience, making money, something to do, something to keep them out of trouble, and a feeling of usefulness. Among those benefits, money was the most important reason for seeking summer employment. This money earned was saved either for a special purpose, such as purchasing a car, or for personal expenses in a coming school year.

The following excerpts taken from the senior survey represent the types of summer jobs and experience that they gained:

I babysat five days a week for my aunt in another town.... I came home on the weekends and did what I wanted. While I babysat we went to the lake. The kids had swim lessons.... [a girl]

I worked on my parents' farm, driving grain trucks and I did yard work also. [a girl]

I went to San Diego and worked at Desert Industries all summer. [a girl]

I sheared or trimmed Christmas trees for a local Christmas tree farm. [a boy]

I worked as a conservation fire fighter. I fight forest fires. [a boy]

I hayed for about one month. Then I worked [the] rest of the summer. [a boy]

Some seniors described other kinds of activities they enjoyed in addition to their jobs:

Mostly worked at a pizza parlor probably about five to six days a week. I took a week vacation to California. Everyday went to swimming and water-skiing, rode my bike, worked on my car, etc. Hung around with my friends. [a boy]

Worked for Peaceland Parks and Recreation Association. Went to...Girls' State — 300 girls from all around Oregon for a week at the university to form a mock state government. Went to Miss Teen of Oregon Scholarship and Recognition Pageant — got fourth runner-up based on school and community participation, personality, poise, general knowledge, etc. Went to week-long church girls' camp — helped run it. [a girl]

Last summer I went to a university track camp for a week. The track coach is really nice. I really enjoyed myself. I also had a job as a summer school tutor at Green Lake Middle School.... Went camping for a week in the mountains on a family vacation, spent the night at my friend's house, went horseback riding on the beach with my friends for my birthday and much much more! [a girl]

Some part of summer, if not all of it, was often used for traveling. Visiting relatives or a divorced parent, sightseeing in the country, and participating in an international Teen Mission project in other countries are noted in these examples:

Went on a vacation to Wisconsin to visit relatives. Also had a friend come from California to visit me. [a senior girl]

Visited my father in Montana. [a senior girl]

I went on a trip with my grandparents all over Oregon on fishing trips and went to Kansas with my mom. I worked a lot with my dad also. [a senior boy]

Went rafting down the Delaware [river] and archery hunting and went to Washington to get my girlfriend. [a senior boy]

Went to Argentina on a Teen Mission trip in July to help local churches, to spread Gospel, and to participate in community development activities. [a sophomore girl]

A few seniors reported that they spent the summer on academic activities: attending summer school to earn extra credits, doing independent studies to make up for credits, taking courses in programs offered at colleges and universities:

Independent study for graduation. [a girl]

Went to school and gained my certificate as an nurse's aide. [a girl]

Some seniors said that summer was also time for 'goofing off' (relaxing), pursuing extracurricular activities, or improving athletic skills:

Partied with XXX almost every night. I was going out with the lead singer. We went to drive-ins, had lake parties, or parties at my boyfriend's (at the time) house. [a girl]

Lay out in the sun. Drove different cars.... Spent a lot of time with Ed [boyfriend] when he was not at work. [a girl]

I rode my horse. I went to a few horse shows. [a girl]

Water-skied a lot at the lake. [a girl]

I played softball for a team. [a girl]

Played eighty-five baseball games for the Pepsi Challenge. [a boy]

Special Occasions

Sixteenth Birthday

The sixteenth birthday seemed to be celebrated specially, probably more by girls than boys. Some guessed that teenagers liked to celebrate this birthday because movies had made a big deal of being 'sweet sixteen'. Others actually thought of it as a special day. Many restrictions disappeared from this specific day. Adolescents were able to apply for a driver's license. Some girls were liberated from parental rules banning dates with boys prior to their sixteenth birthday.

Adolescents over sixteen were legally allowed to work after six o'clock in the evening, which increased their employment options. Many adolescents said that they could hardly wait for their sixteenth birthday.

Parents of many teenagers recognized the significance of this meaningful day and helped their children celebrate it in special ways. Here is an excerpt from Stephanie's seven-page journal entry about her sixteenth birthday:

> There's so much to tell you about [my birthday]!... Yesterday, they [my family] all told me 'Happy Birthday' and gave me hugs and kisses. There were presents sitting on the table from mom and brother, and dad had one in his truck for me. There was also one from my grandma.... I loved all of my presents. Everything fit and the bag was needed!... The plan for the day was to go bowling [with four girl friends] and then go and have pizza afterward.... My dad showed up and surprised me with a bouquet of red roses. That was one of the neatest things! I sure love my dad!...
>
> That night we all ate cake, ice cream, pop, chips, and other junk food. We watched the movie 'Jaws III'. When it got dark we went outside with our sleeping bags.... We had fun talking about boys, people, problems and stuff like that. At 3:00 am we started having running races in our sleeping bags.... This morning...when we got inside, I asked mom and dad if it would be possible to go to the coast.... Today we went to the sand dunes, the beach...and to old town, Ridgeport. We ate at Taco Time in Ridgeport and then drove home (very tired) tonight. I think that this has been the best birthday I've ever had!

Whereas Stephanie included her friends in celebrating her sixteenth birthday, Tricia, a sophomore, celebrated hers with her family and her grandparents. Being shy about sharing her journal on her birthday, Tricia told me about her special day:

> Tricia's mother made her a two-piece long-sleeved dress out of mint-green silky material. She also received a hair dryer and a curling iron from her parents, and a flower-printed paper organizer from her grandparents, in which she found seven five-dollar bills folded in the shape of a shirt and a handmade round-neck collar made of white lace. Then, the whole family

went out for dinner at a high-class restaurant in Riverville; she wore the dress that her mom made. After dinner, Tricia had a surprise. Her father took her to the *Music Man*, a musical performed by a high school drama club. After the play, the whole family went to the best hotel in the city and had cherries jubilee. She stayed out until 12:30 am. It was the greatest birthday for her.

Special Events Related to Cars

Teenagers assigned special meanings to getting a driver's license and getting a car. The following journal entries show their excitement about passing the driving test and owning a car:

I PASSED!!! I am now an official licensed driver! I was pretty nervous at first, but the instructor was very nice and made me feel very comfortable. I passed with a ninety-five per cent! [a sophomore girl]

I was happy to finally own a car of my own and more freedom. A car can give you more freedom to go and see people that I was never able to before. [a sophomore boy]

Dating with an Opposite-sex Friend

Friendship affected teenagers' lives to a great deal, in particular relationships with the opposite-sex friends. When the relationship went smoothly, it enhanced self-worth and satisfaction with their lives. When it did not go well, many teenagers developed negative attitudes toward school, family, or other friends. The following examples show both cases:

It's October twenty-sixth and it's a special date. It marks an anniversary — mine and Tina's. It has been four months now. Gee. We've come along way from that first night we met — a hay ride. She let me sit by her.... On June twenty-sixth we decided to date.... That night we walked together under a starlit sky. A few words, a subtle kiss. How were we to know it would last four months? Well it has — we're hoping for another forty years. [a sophomore boy]

We were first going out as a date to Homecoming.... Then, he asked me, 'Would you go with me?'...After that, we were together all the time at lunch or did things together in school.... [He was] wishy-washy.... I was kind of bored...tired of [being together all the time].... We just kind of say good-bye before a three-day weekend. On Tuesday when I got back, I said 'Hi, John.' He ignored me.... He didn't talk to me for the whole rest of the year.... It ruined my year.... From December on, I didn't feel a part of the high school...didn't go to school dances. [a junior girl]

This chapter has reported teenagers' stories of their own activities and thoughts on weekends, holidays, summer vacation, and special occasions. By quoting directly from what they wrote or spoke, I intended that my readers hear the voices of the 'authors'.

Notes

1 Adolescent life in this chapter was written or spoken in a first-person mode. This collage of stories consists of excerpts from classroom journals, personal journals, interview transcripts, and responses to the senior survey. Minimal editing was done; all names are pseudonyms.
2 I administered a survey to all seniors in Greenfield High School after Memorial Day weekend. As a result, I obtained many responses with respect to their activities on that particular weekend.

Part 3

Adolescent Ethos

Chapter 7

Getting Along with Everyone

Ethos is defined by Kroeber as something that 'deals with qualities that pervade the whole culture' and 'includes the direction in which a culture is oriented, the things it aims at, prizes and endorses, and more or less achieves' (Bock 1979:272). The ethos of Greenfield adolescents involves three major aspects: 'getting along with everyone', 'being independent', and 'getting involved'.

Many Greenfielders regarded 'getting along with everyone', having well-rounded human relationships, as a desirable attribute and stated that their lives were guided by this ethos. This dimension of ethos was particularly emphasized in peer interactions. When adolescents claimed that they 'get along with everyone', it could mean two different things. One group literally meant that they had good relationships with a wide range of peers, regardless of their various levels of academic and socio-economic status, gender, or age difference. The other meant that they did not have apparent conflicts with most of their peers. Whichever they implied by the statement, the young people promoted the idea of good human relationships.

Why did adolescents consider it important to get along with others and particularly with their peers? Why did they criticize those who did not conform to this ethos? In this chapter, I try to seek answers to these questions in the context of teenage social network structure. I first describe the close knit structure in Greenfield School and the social demands involved in interaction. Next, the adolescents' concern about their social image is discussed as a survival strategy. Finally, I point out that the adolescents' inclination toward forming cliques appears contradictory to the ethos of getting along with everyone; yet, I suggest that both of these stem from the similar desire for social security in their peer interactions.

A Close-knit Society

Greenfield adolescents were well acquainted with each other. They often stated, 'Everyone knows everyone here', implying that these young people recognized many of their peers by name and almost all of them by sight. A student teacher who taught at Greenfield for a term confirmed that the students 'never say "Who's that?" to their peers'. She attributed this phenomenon to the fact that most of them had seen or known each other from their earlier school years. Most new students did not fail to notice this mutual familiarity among Greenfielders. This 'everyone-knows-everyone' situation in Greenfield could be attributed to four factors: the small size of the school, the linear transition from middle school to high school in the district, a high proportion of siblings in the student population, and the flexible dynamics of friendship.

Greenfield teenagers got to know each other well because the high school had a small number of students and was physically confined to a limited space. In 1987, approximately 550 students were enrolled, averaging 140 at each class level (See Table 1, Chapter 4). The students also got to know one another through their constant passage in hallways where all the lockers were located. The school buildings surrounded two courtyards and were connected with breezeways. The courtyard-centered building structure (see Figure 2, Chapter 4) increased the 'traffic' among students passing through the central areas. Most students met fellow classmates by taking the same required courses. Greenfield's individualized time scheduling provided students with opportunities to interact with peers of the same and different grades. Each class period involved a different mix of people. In addition, extensive sports programs and other extracurricular activities drew participants from a relatively small student population and, in turn, created overlaps of participants.

The Greenfielders' mutual familiarity seemed to be attributed to the fact that the school district had only one middle and one high school. Obviously, anyone who stayed in this district attended those schools with their peers. Some students had gone to the same elementary school, even kindergarten, with the same peers. For instance, Lynn had followed the same course with 10 per cent of her classmates since the first grade. She could find more people from other classes whom she had known since her elementary school days. Graduates of Peaceland and Greenfield elementary schools (larger schools) had gone through a comparable sequence with more peers.

The large number of siblings in Greenfield helped adolescents extend their friendship across grade levels. More than a quarter of the student population had one or more siblings in the high school.[1] Some Greenfield adolescents identified their siblings as their best friends. They were often seen 'hanging out' together both in and outside school. Siblings often became a means through which adolescents met students from other classes.

Greenfield adolescents got to know each other in the dynamics of breaking up and regrouping with new people in friendship and courtship. Friendship refers to a close relationship between same-sex and cross-sex peers; courtship is usually defined by Greenfield adolescents as a romantic relationship between opposite-sex peers. Friendships and courtships remained continuous among some sets of students. In general, however, membership in other groups of friends was constantly reshuffled when new friends were introduced or conflicts occurred between old friends. New friends, whether opposite-gender or not, affected the dynamics of present friendships either by becoming incorporated harmoniously or by facilitating changes in the old structure. Breaking up and making new friends were common practices among Greenfield adolescents.

Adolescents said that a friendship was liable to break up when friends drifted away to make new friends, perhaps as the result of repeated personality clashes. Courtship tended to be discontinued when partners 'cheated' on their present relationship, became too possessive of their partners, or felt 'tired of' the same relationship. Compared to friendship, courtship appeared to be more unstable, because it demanded more intense involvement between partners and, in turn, soon became 'boring'. A junior girl recalled that her previous boyfriend expected the couple to spend most of their time together during and after school so that it became 'exhausting'. Likewise, a parent pointed to a short life expectancy of her daughter's courtship, saying:

> Sarah stays with a boy for two weeks. It's a record for her. . . .
> The reason why she does not stay with one boy for a long time is that she has a girlfriend. When she meets him every day and every period, she feels restricted. She cannot interact with her girlfriend. Then she thinks, 'I don't want him anymore.'

Several girls and boys agreed with this observation that resentment at being stuck with one partner led them to break up with their boy or girlfriend. Changes in courtship relationships might have also been more noticeable than friendship patterns because the former attracted more attention among teenagers. When a friendship or courtship broke up, adolescents often sought new friends and relationships. The phenomenon of breaking up and building new friendship encouraged teenagers to know a wide range of peers in their school.

In many ways Greenfielders became acquainted with each other and could claim that 'everyone knew everyone' in the school. In this closely knit system, newcomers stood out distinctly and were readily identified by old-timers. The former were often greeted with questions such as 'Are you new?' and 'What grade are you in?' Some inquirers had a genuine interest in the new people; others only allowed themselves to show temporary curiosity. The newcomers regarded the old-timers' initial interest as a sign of Greenfielders' friendliness and openness. A sophomore girl from another state did not have difficulty in adjusting to the new school because 'people were very friendly'. Many other new students shared the same impression of Greenfielders.

Old-timers admitted that they knew most of their peers at the school. This mutual familiarity sometimes meant lack of privacy. A senior girl said, 'Everyone knows your name and practically everything about you', indicating that her recent breakup with her boyfriend quickly became public knowledge among her peers. Greenfielders also implied that no freshness was expected in school because they knew everyone in the school. Thus, newcomers offered a diversion — until their novelty wore out.

In this close-knit society, words spoken about others traveled fast and often had a strong impact on one's public image. Adolescents were aware of the negative consequences that could follow their peers' recognition of anti-social behavior or ill treatment of others. This awareness motivated them to make conscious efforts to get along with others and not to give an unfavorable impression of themselves in this everyone-knows-everyone situation.

Peer Interaction as a Social Necessity

In order to understand the ethos of 'Getting along with everyone', one must probe the nature of social interactions among US adolescents. Young people encountered multiple situations requiring informal and unexpected interaction with their peers. Such situations were often created by an educational structure, perhaps unique to US education, that allowed individual freedom and nourished social activities among adolescents. In this socially-oriented institution, young people were given many opportunities to select specific peers with whom to associate and interact.

For instance, a majority of students commuted to school via school buses. Once they boarded, teenagers had the freedom to choose where to sit and with whom to converse. If their close friends were aboard, they could move next to them; if not, they had to make a choice between sitting alone (if seats were available) or interacting with others. In order to avoid the reputation of being a loner, they might feel compelled to interact with their peers.

When they arrived at school, opportunities for informal inter-actions increased, because students were only required to be in their classrooms during class periods. Outside the structured hours, they were free to choose where to go and with whom to interact before first period, during breaks, during lunch hour, and after school. Few teachers assigned permanent seats in classrooms, at the library, or during assemblies. When students went on field trips, even more free time was granted for informal interactions, such as choosing seat partners on the bus. In the case of frequent outings, this decision-making could be a nuisance. In addition, many students participated in sports events and social activities such as dances and parties. If they wanted to participate to any degree in these informal occasions, adolescents had to decide with whom to interact. Making these deci-sions was not often optional, because most adolescents did not want to be social loners. Peer interactions thus became a necessity in a society in which social activities played such an important part in adolescent life.

Gaining Popularity[2]

Most Greenfield adolescents tried to appear to get along well with others, regardless of their backgrounds. The frequent statement, 'I get along with everyone', reflected Greenfielders' social ideal. A senior girl criticized her peers for clinging to their own group of friends and ignoring others. She insisted, however, 'I get along with basically everyone', denying that she had this partisan tendency.

Like Greenfield adolescents, newcomers soon noticed the positive value of getting along with everyone. Many of them expressed their wish to adhere to the same ethos. For example, Danielle, a junior girl, who transferred from a local Christian school[3] noted:

> At the beginning, I didn't know many people. I'm naturally
> shy. But I decided to break out from my shell of shyness and
> to be nice to people. Friendly and open to others. I want to get
> a reputation of being nice to everyone.

Most new students made obvious efforts to appear friendly to everyone. They initiated greetings with peers and approached even newer
people sooner than old-timers did. Their attempts were sometimes
rewarded by gaining a positive reputation among their peers. Danielle
is an example of a newcomer's success in gaining a good reputation.
When I met Danielle at the beginning of my research, she had been in
Greenfield only a few months. I found her approaching me often and
smiling readily at me, and she appeared to treat others in the same
way. Her efforts to get along with others were explicitly recognized
when seniors voted her as one of the six junior arch bearers in their
graduation ceremony. This recognition was considered a great honor
to those selected, and it reflected a high degree of peer acceptance.

Gaining a good reputation as a result of ones' efforts might have
been easier for newcomers than old-timers, because newcomers were
free of their peers' preconceived notions. Since their past reputations
were not known to their new peers, newcomers could enjoy the thrill
of establishing new images if they wished, though no data suggests
whether or not they actually did so. It was not easy to guess how
many newcomers would actually change in order to gain popularity in
the new environment. I observed that many transfer students gained
recognition for being highly personable, and several were voted into
office as student leaders, a sign of acceptance. Many of them confessed
that it was slightly difficult at the beginning to establish their status
under new circumstances, but that they tried 'extra hard' to get along
with others.

By contrast, the everyone-knows-everyone situation seemed to
present an obstacle for old-timers trying to change their image. Their
peers had known them for years and had developed fixed images
about them. Several adolescents mentioned, 'If you were popular
in middle school, you will be popular in high school. If you were
unpopular in middle school, you will be unpopular in high school.'
Greenfield adolescents sensed the tendency of reputations to endure
over time, but both newcomers and oldtimers subscribed to the view
that if one could be perceived as getting along with others that
perception could pave the way toward popularity.

In a senior survey administered in 1987, 'getting along with
others' was mentioned as one of the traits that made a person popular.

This type of popularity consists of being not only 'well known' but 'well liked' by their peers. Popular people were viewed as those who 'are liked by others', 'have lots of friends', or someone whom 'everyone wants to be like'. Among various attributes identified in the survey responses, the following were related to the personalities of those who had good relationships with others: outgoing, fun, caring, honest, friendly, nice, warm, mature, smiling, easy to get along with, not self-conscious, talking to other people, always saying 'Hi' to others, willing to listen, supportive, and having an understanding character.

Why did adolescents strive for a good reputation and 'popularity'? Gaining a good reputation among peers was a survival strategy of Greenfield adolescents in a society where young people achieved social status mainly through peer interactions. The US high school provided adolescents with ample opportunities to interact informally and socially with their peers. The types of, and partners in, the social interactions were not automatically tailored by the system, but depended rather on individual choices. High school adolescents interacted constantly with their peers in situations such as on the school bus, in hallways and classrooms, on field trips, during extracurricular activities, and at private social events. Unless they did not mind being viewed as people who did not get along with others, and, in turn, were shunned by others, the young people felt pressured to be sociable, or at least appear sociable, by behaving in a friendly and open manner to others.

Social acceptance was highly valued by adolescents because it offered a sense of security in peer relationships that were both an unavoidable and active feature in adolescent culture. Being a socially acceptable person was likely to save young people from many worries, such as wondering whether particular peers would include them at parties, ask them for dates, seek them out for friendship, or be willing to sit next to them. A positive reputation helped them be readily accepted by their peers and eased their approach to others by giving them confidence that they would not be rejected by their peers.

A personal reputation influenced an individual's social status more than did objective parameters. Some adolescents were concerned about the fact that some people were not even acquainted with others whom they accused of being 'stuck-up'. According to them, many teenagers perceived others on the basis of reputation, and not who they 'really' were. Despite some students' awareness and disapproval of this process, this social structure seemingly continued to drive adolescents to subscribe to the value of gaining a good reputation in order to survive and to protect themselves in the web of peer interactions.

Losing a Reputation

While Greenfield adolescents expressed the desire to have a positive reputation for getting along well with others, they were equally concerned about 'losing their reputation', by being perceived as being stuck-up or a jerk, being identified as a smoker, or belonging to a clique. Those so characterized were viewed as self-indulgent, partisan, and unsociable.

Both males and females could be considered to be stuck-up if they 'brag about themselves', 'think they are the best', 'only care about themselves', 'are rude to everyone else', or 'do not associate with others'. A group of five boys expressed the adolescent disrespect of stuck-up peers in a rap (a musical style of fast and rhythmic speaking), 'Don't Be Stuck-up', written for and performed in the school talent show. The song depicted a girl who always boasted about her clothes, grades, and family. Their performance purportedly entertained the high school audience but tacitly underscored a lesson: if you stop being stuck-up, people will like you. The response to the song was a thundering applause.

Another unfavorable classification for individuals was that of a 'jerk'. Jerks were defined as those who did not get along with others, were mean or rude to others, treated friends dishonestly, or had personality clashes with others. Like stuck-up people, jerks were regarded as socially undesirable. However, there were a few differences between these two classifications. While 'stuck-up' was a relatively fixed classification for specific individuals on the basis of their character, 'jerk' was a more general, and often more temporary, label given on the basis of behavior. The other difference was that 'stuck-up' was often used for well-known students and 'jerk' was indiscriminately used for all kinds of adolescents. Teenagers were not shy of stating, 'John is a jerk because he took my friend away.' However, when John changed his behavior, he was not considered to be a jerk anymore. The flexibility of the label also helped people recover from it if they wanted to do so. A senior boy mentioned, 'I was classified as a jerk last year, because I behaved like a jerk. But this year I get along with people.' He was no longer referred to as a jerk by his peers.

The third unfavorable category of individuals was 'smoker'.

'Smoker' was a value-laden social label in Greenfield, equated with 'low class people'. This label included cigarette smokers, tobacco chewers, 'scums' (untidy people) and 'stonies' (drug users). Smokers were referred to as students who allegedly 'hung out' regularly in the smokers' shed and the nearby senior courtyard. This physical-boundary-dependent definition sometimes led to an inaccurate representation of non-smokers and non-drug users who frequented the specified area; the label also missed those who smoked, chewed tobacco, and took drugs in private.

In contrast to the individuality of stuck-up people and jerks, smokers were regarded as people with a shared interest. They were seen as a self-contained group that disassociated from others. On some occasions, this perception proved correct. Several smokers told me that they had a sense of unity, because they had a defined territory and were candid with each other. One girl felt accepted immediately when she walked into the shed and greeted other smokers on the first day of school. Several of them said that their association with each other was limited to school hours. Yet the smokers also organized activities of their own. For example, they selected their own Prom Court princesses and princes, and announced it in the school newspaper. The rationale was that students classified as 'popular' were always elected to the school Prom Court and smokers were excluded from being a part of it. The smokers also arrived at the Prom together in a rented limousine.

Smoking was viewed as 'stupid' and smokers were considered as 'untouchables'[4] among most teenagers. Several students declared that they would never go to the shed, even to talk to people out there. It became a 'public secret' that a Senior Prom and Homecoming Princess smoked in her car or in a restroom because she did not want to be identified with smokers. The rejection of smokers was represented by the comment that Marylinn and Linda received after they played hackeysack with 'smokers' (see Chapter 2). A senior girl who used to smoke complained of some jocks' unfavorable treatment of 'smokers' as follows:

> Yesterday someone put honey on the bench in the smokers' shed. I don't know who did it, but I guess football players. Many yellow jackets buzzed around. I was scared. Two years ago on Superbowl Sunday, some football players took a jeep and literally knocked down the shed. Sports people gang up together against smokers. Smokers didn't do anything to them.

Some Greenfielders did not belittle smokers; yet most believed that being classified as a smoker was one way of losing a reputation. Once one was labeled as a smoker, quitting smoking did not necessarily redeem them from their previous status.

I have explained three unfavorable labels given, based upon what adolescents judged to be self-indulgent and anti-social characteristics: stuck-up, jerk, and smoker. Teenagers also tried to avoid being identified with a particular clique. The young people defined a clique as 'a small group of people, maybe two to four at most, who spend a lot of time exclusively with each other'. A clique might include both males and females, but it typically referred to a group of same-sex friends. Sometimes the term 'clique' was used without value judgment to refer to a pair of best friends who 'hung out' together all the time, but more often this label carried a negative connotation. People in cliques were viewed as violating the principle of getting along with 'everyone'. They got along only with their circle of friends and tended to reject others.

Adolescents' concern about losing their reputations was reflected clearly on a self-versus-other dichotomous rhetoric: 'There are cliques in this school, but I'm not in any of the cliques' or 'Angela is in a clique, but I get along with others.' This self/other opposition indicated that the young people tried to avoid displaying themselves as divisive and to project an image of themselves as cooperative. It represented their attempt to establish a positive reputation as being a socially open and approachable person among their peers.

Between General Friendliness and Close Friendship

On one hand, most Greenfielders tried to gain the reputation of getting along with everyone, and consequently dissociated themselves from socially unfavorable labels such as 'stuck-up', 'jerk', 'smoker', or 'clique' member. On the other hand, the adolescents were often observed passing time with the same few friends. They readily identified one or two peers as 'best friends' and admitted as a fact that they spent most of their time with these friends, both in and outside school. This latter phenomenon might have appeared to conflict with the 'getting-along-with-everyone' ethos. However, both the ethos of getting along with everyone and the practice of clinging to best friends appeared to reflect the young people's longing for a sense of security that was often derived from social acceptance of peers.

Most adolescents acknowledged that they had best friends and also affirmed that they got along with everyone. However, they hesitated to identify themselves with certain cliques; they referred to their circles of close friends only as 'best friends'. Charles offered the following distinction between a clique and a best friend during an interview:

Charles: A 'clique' means a group of people who always hang out with each other. It's not good.

I: Don't you have one person whom you like most and want to be with most?

Charles: That's a 'best friend'.

Whereas this conceptual distinction did not clearly separate a group of best friends from a clique, the term 'best friends' as used here carried a positive connotation compared to the term 'clique'.

Marylinn's story (Chapter 2) shows the coexistence of seemingly contradictory values. She verbalized her belief in the ethos of 'getting along with everyone'. She made efforts to be sociable with a wide range of people and was actually known as a friendly person. At the same time, she spent a substantial amount of time with a circle of close friends, especially her best friend Amanda, both in and outside school. They rode the same school bus daily, shared a locker, took the same classes, spent lunch time together, participated in the same sports teams, telephoned each other at home, and shared activities together after school, on weekends, and during vacations. Although Marylinn did not always share the same values and interests with her best friend, they mutually acknowledged their close friendship. Their closeness gave them a sense of security because they knew they had 'somebody to trust'. She said this mutual trust and loyalty had tied them together since the beginning of their friendship.

Many teenagers identified their best friends for me and did not hesitate to affirm that friendship in front of each other. Most teens underscored the value of close friends. Best friends were viewed as those whom one could trust, talk to, depend on, and feel comfortable around, and who listened to one's problems and concerns. Best friends would be easily available for casual situations, reducing teenagers' concerns about having company. For instance, best friends took the same classes and became partners in cooperative activities. They readily agreed to accompany each other to go shopping, attend school dances, or watch sports events. When life got 'boring', teenagers often telephoned their best friends, in some cases interfering with their studies. Some teenagers identified their boy/girlfriends as their best friends. Many teenagers readily admitted that they could not 'survive' for a day without talking to their friends. Through close friendship young people seemed to gain a sense of security in a society in which they needed constantly to engage in informal interactions with their peers.

Summary

'Getting along with everyone' was part of the pervading ethos of Greenfield adolescents. This aspect of the ethos was embedded in a culture where peer interactions became more important than any other human relationships. Especially in a small, well-acquainted society such as Greenfield, individual 'impression-management' (a concept introduced by Erving Goffman, 1959, and developed by Berreman, 1962) was considered as an important, all-consuming task. The young people subscribed to the ethos in varying degrees, whether or not they wished to conform. Those who chose to comply with the ethos tried to avoid getting a reputation as a stuck-up person, jerk, smoker, or member of a clique and to gain a positive reputation as a sociable person. This concern about making a good impression indicates the interactive characteristic of Greenfield adolescent culture. Adolescents were aware of the risk of being isolated or alienated from their peers, if they chose not to associate with them. In order to be accepted, young people were compelled to choose interaction over solitude. The positive reputation was likely to help them gain a sense of security in the web of interactions. Hence, they tried to project the image of a person who got along well with others and to stay within the conceptual boundaries for mainstream — as opposed to deviant — teenagers.

Although most young people I talked to — including mainstream as well as 'unpopular' individuals — tried to put forth the image of a person who could get along with everyone, they in fact clung to a few friends most of the time. The ethos of getting along with everyone might appear to contradict the spirit of establishing intimate friendship with a few of good friends. However, both the ethos and the inclination toward intimate friendships fell under the general theme of adolescents' longing for social acceptance. The adolescents sought the security of guaranteed friendship in an actively interactive environment. Although some adolescents sacrificed one for the other between general friendliness and intimate friendship, many felt that they could not dispense with either. In order to survive in the social arena of human relationships, adolescents tried to combine these two paradoxical ideas: 'getting along with everyone' and forming close associations with a group of selected friends. I discuss the way that Greenfielders handled the duality of these ideas in Chapter 10.

Notes

1 The number of siblings, defined here as students with the same last name and same home phone number, accounted for sixty-seven sets, involving 133 students in 1987. The total would have increased if those meeting only one of the above criteria were counted.

2 The concept 'popularity' was defined in two ways. First, it referred to the degree to which someone's name and appearance were known by others, actually meaning someone's visibility. Second, popularity referred to a degree of someone's likeableness based on his/her attractive personality. The first and second definitions were conceptually independent of each other, but interchangeably used by many adolescents. Several of the students acknowledged that their indiscriminate use of the term sometimes was confusing.

3 There was one small Christian private school for kindergarteners through ninth graders as well as public schools in the community. All graduating ninth graders (five students) from this school transferred to Greenfield High School.

4 The use of 'untouchable' may be too strong in the sense that Greenfield smokers were not totally severed from contacts with other groups of students. However, its usage is justifiable, because they were segregated as a distinct circle and looked down upon by other social class members in the adolescent society.

Chapter 8

Being Independent

Independence represents another element of Greenfield adolescent ethos, expressed verbally as well as symbolically. Greenfield young people viewed independence as a keystone of adulthood. They thought that adults treated one another with more seriousness and enjoyed more freedom and social privileges. Teenagers claimed that they, by contrast, were treated by adults with less seriousness and were granted less freedom and fewer social privileges. This perception led them to prefer the adult state to that of teenagers or children; they wanted to taste the experiences of 'grown-ups' as early as possible.

In the first section of this chapter, I discuss the adolescent perception of independence that 1) is achieved rather than automatically given; 2) entails being treated as an adult; and 3) accompanies autonomy. Greenfield youth attempted to gain and exhibit independence in two ways: either by acquiring symbolic markers of independence or by defying external authorities. The second section deals with five symbolic markers of independence: getting a job, raising funds for activities, being allowed to drive an automobile, moving away from home, and relying more on peer interactions than on adult authority. Taking on the characteristics of an adult life appears in contrast to rejection of an adult authority; yet, two different strategies are grounded on the same incentive of being treated equally with adults. While adolescents valued autonomy and freedom associated with independence, many of them tended to de-emphasize the increased responsibility that accompanies adulthood. Their acceptance of responsibility often did not equal their claim to freedom. In the last section, I argue that the adolescent perception of independence tends to be one-sided, focusing on freedom but neglecting responsibility.

The Adolescent Perception of Independence

Greenfield adolescents viewed independence as a privileged state characterized by less adult supervision, greater freedom of choice, and more respect from adults. Their striving for independence may not be unique to US adolescents. However, high school adolescents in this society expressed their longing for independence explicitly.

Not Given, but Earned

Independence was perceived as something that adolescents could earn by acquiring the markers of independence, not as something automatically given at a certain age. A sixteenth birthday was a turning point for many Greenfield teenagers, as the special celebration of the birthday symbolized (see Chapter 6). From age sixteen, young people were able to do various things that they had not been able to do, for example, driving an automobile, or obtaining employment. Therefore, this 'magic' number for Greenfielders may appear equivalent to the age for rites of passage in many traditional societies, in which initiation rituals marked the transition point from childhood to adulthood (see, for example, the case of Mende in West Africa as reported by Little, 1970:211). I feel compelled, however, to distinguish the Greenfielder's sixteenth year from an initiation age of some societies in which ceremonies were officially administered by the adults. In those societies, completion of the initiation changed a person's social status from a child to an adult, and, in turn, introduced one to the full privileges and responsibilities of adulthood.

In contrast, age sixteen in the American community only opened possibilities to sample the world of adults, it did not fully transform teenagers from children into adults. In other words, the age factor only activated the transition process into adulthood. In contrast to tribal societies, Greenfield adolescents did not go through a society-wide initiation, a focal moment that would publically proclaim someone's newly given social status. Becoming sixteen neither made a public statement in itself nor did it automatically guarantee adulthood, as an initiation ceremony did.

In this social situation, American adolescents — including Greenfielders — needed to struggle for independence, because it was not automatically given. Once reaching a certain age — in this case, sixteen — young people began to strive for the symbols of independence and to prove their independence. This attitude reflects the conquering spirit of the American society: nothing is given; everything is to be earned; efforts will be rewarded. Independence was granted to those who were actively involved in making money, driving, and moving out. The other side of the coin is that those who do not take steps to pursue this goal would not attain it. In a classroom journal, a 15-year-old expressed her concern about getting behind the desirable time schedule of earning independence:

> I don't think I'm ever going to get my permit in this life time.
> I've been fifteen for three-and-half months now. If I don't read
> that book [Driver's Manual] now, I'll end up like my sister. It
> took her eight months to get her permit after she had her
> fifteenth birthday and now she has to take the test a second
> time because it has already been a year.

In addition, independence required personal initiative. For example, teenagers could apply for a driver's license after they turned 16 years old; actual qualification as a legal driver, however, came only when they passed a behind-the-wheel test. The further freedom that accompanied 'driving around' came only when they had access to a car. Gaining independence by moving away from home worked on the same principle of personal initiative. If they completed proper legal procedures (a school counselor can help), teenagers could become legally emancipated as early as the age of sixteen. This allowed them to live independently from other adults. Only those who actually took the initiative to become emancipated and to move out of their parents' homes could demonstrate this type of independence during their high school days.

Being Treated Like an Adult

Greenfield teenagers also equated independence to being treated like adults, rather than children. They viewed children as incomplete beings who needed to obey adults' commands, who lacked the freedom of making decisions, and who were supervised all the time by adults. By contrast, adults represented freedom, 'the final word', power, and independence. Thus, adolescents preferred adult status to that of the child and favored the label 'young adult'.

The following journal entries show adolescent understanding of independence. To Martha, a senior, becoming an adult meant taking control of her life, independent of her mother's authority:

> If I could be any age and stay there, it would be 21, because then I'm still somewhat of a teenager (young) but then again I'm old enough to be a legal adult. Have more control of my life as far as doing what I want without having to ask for permission from my mother.

Jane appreciated her mother's respect of her judgment:

> When my mom asks my opinion, I feel very important. Whether it's a new shirt or just how to rearrange the living room furniture, I know my opinion matters.

Becky compared a difference between her father and her mother in the way they treated her:

> Daddy was like every other adult. He cheated me as I really was a child [he broke promises to do something for her] but mom had a way of making me feel grown up.

By contrast, Patricia felt comfortable around her father because he allowed her to exercise freedom within limits, if she responsibly observed the latter. She did not enjoy being around her mother, who did not trust Patricia's judgments. She described the situation in her journal as follows:

> This past weekend I went to a gun show with my dad. I had a feeling of freedom. As long as I stayed with the basic rules and asked permission when I wanted out, I could rule my own life. I could eat, sleep, and wander as I wished when my duties were done. This is what it's like with my father.... Now, my mother — I am very subdued around my mother. She yells a lot and everything is my fault.

Adolescents appreciated adults who treated them as equals, with fairness and respect. If the young people sensed an absence of such treatment, they viewed the adults as unfavorable authorities. When adolescents did not feel respected as independent beings, they experienced mental conflicts. Many arguments with adults stemmed from this resentment of childlike treatment by adults. A sophomore girl wrote about her unhappiness as follows:

> My mother and I were fighting. When we fight, all that really happens is she yells and I go into my room and cry. An important thing to bring up about my mother is that she's very judgmental. What I mean is whenever I say or do something she always has the last word.... She makes me feel like a nothing. She puts herself first.

This girl had trouble accepting that her mother always acted as the final authority in determining right and wrong. In addition, she did not feel that her own opinion was respected.

As much as they liked to become independent, teenagers recognized that the process of gaining independence was highly influenced by adults' responsiveness. Ron, a junior, observed that adolescents became independent to the degree that adults expected them to:

> Mother treats me like an adult. She trusts me and my responsibility. If I say, 'Mom, I don't feel like going to school today,' she lets me stay at home and calls school for my sick absence.... Angel's parents are much more strict. They won't do it. So they [Angel and her siblings] are more rebellious. They tell them a lie. But if I'm honest about things, my parents trust me. If parents treat their kids like kids, they behave like kids. If they treat their kids like adults, they behave like adults. I get along with my parents.

More Autonomy

Greenfield adolescents associated independence with gaining more autonomy in their lives. Autonomy meant being able to do certain things without adults' permission or supervision. Youth exercised autonomy by actively making decisions on their own or by defying external forces that hampered self-government.

Many adolescents observed that they preferred to choose their activities and companions without adult consultation or permission. Some asked their parents for approval, but tried to retain control over their own social lives as much as possible. The father of Kris, a junior girl, complained of his daughter's 'modified autonomy'. According to him, his daughter usually volunteered to decorate the school cafeteria for dances before asking permission to attend them. In this way, she knew that her father, who had taught her to keep her word, would not disallow her to participate in the dances. Her father once said that he felt manipulated, because he had no choice but to allow her to go to the dances.

Other adolescents often acted on their own. Dick did not usually tell his parents what he did after school or where he went with his friends on weekends. He was convinced that his parents trusted his judgments. More than that, he seemed to feel that informing his parents of his social life was not 'cool'. He regarded one of his female friends as over-protected because she reported her whereabouts whenever going out with friends.

Many young people felt that their claim for autonomy was legitimate, because they literally 'paid' for it with their own money. When they went out with friends, they drove their own — often self-purchased — cars. When they went to movies or shopping, they spent money that they earned. By securing these resources by themselves, teenagers felt legitimate about voicing their right to autonomy in decision-making.

Another expression of adolescent autonomy took the form of challenging authority figures, existing systems, norms, and rules. Lauri, a senior girl, expressed her independence by adopting a form of 'punk' culture. She identified herself as a 'wavo' whom she defined as 'a prior step to a punk'. She criticized school for being 'real conformist'. According to her, students were forced to take required classes that were not relevant to their career aspirations, to take examinations, and to depend on grades for their future. She added that school perpetuated the *status quo*: those classified as the 'popular' held on to their status, and 'low class' (often unpopular) people did not get a fair share. She demonstrated her individuality by wearing a black, oversized male jacket, black trousers or skirt, black oversized man's leather shoes, black-dyed hairdo, and bright make-up. After receiving unfavorable comments from school staff regarding her 'unique' appearance, she said with resentment, 'They want me to be like them.' Through her newspaper articles she challenged school authorities for their censoring attempts. At home, Lauri objected to her parents' rules: going to church once a month, cleaning her room, and dressing in a more 'acceptable' way. She often argued with them because of their different views, and she contemplated moving out of her parents' home. Her 'non-conformist' mind finally led her, with one semester left in her senior year, to drop out of high school and move to Riverville.

Lauri's outspoken challenge to authority might have been an early signal for her later action of dropping out of the 'conforming' system. By defying the conventional authorities she not only broke away from them, but also struggled for autonomy. Her striving for autonomy was represented by her advocacy of the punk philosophy: in her words, the punk culture endorses 'chaos', referring to 'self-government' in which everyone is encouraged to rule themselves, instead of being governed by higher authorities. Perhaps Lauri presented an especially strong case of adolescent longing for autonomy, but many other teenagers commonly staged acts of 'rebellion', such as arguing with parents or disobeying home and institutional rules imposed by adults.

The three teenagers mentioned above — Kris, Dick, and Lauri — had adopted different ways of obtaining autonomy. All of them, however, consistently believed that being independent meant gaining more autonomy in their everyday lives.

Symbolic Markers of Independence

Adolescent understanding of independence was embodied in such symbolic markers as employment, fund raising, driving, moving away from home, and dependence on peers. These markers were interrelated, representing financial, cognitive, physical, psychological, and social dimensions of independence. Most adolescents exercised these different aspects of independence in the process of socialization.

Employment

The result of a survey administered by a faculty task force[1] showed that slightly over one-third of the student population was employed during the school year of 1987–88, working from two to forty hours a week. According to my senior survey, three quarters of the seniors earned outside income during the 87–88 school year.

What kind of jobs did teenagers hold? While food service, cleaning, and yard work were done by both males and females, some jobs were sex-linked. The female work force concentrated on babysitting, clerical work, and fast food service; males had a broader range of choices, including cooking at restaurants, agricultural work, lumber mill work, gas station service, and warehouse work. The pay scale depended on the job: babysitting for one child usually paid $1.00 to

Table 2. *Employment of Seniors in the Class of 1987**

Respondents[2]	Male 37	Female 35	Total 72
Types of Jobs			
caretaking (child/nurse aide)	1	7	
clerical	0	7	
animal caretaking	0	1	
food service (host/dishwash/cook)	5	11	
cleaning	2	3	
yard work	2	1	
construction	1	1	
warehouse	3	0	
sport (officiating)	2	0	
agricultural service	3	0	
gas station service	3	0	
lumber mill	3	0	
ship deck work	1	0	
Monthly Earning	Male	Female	
below $30	3	9	
$ 31– 50	7	9	
$ 51–100	6	2	
$101–150	4	7	
$151–200	3	3	
$201–300	8	2	
$301–400	2	0	
range	$28–400	$10–270	
median	$115	$50	

* Of the 72 respondents, 27 males and 26 females held jobs. They did not all respond with the type of job they held.

$1.50 per hour; hard physical labor such as moving irrigation pipes or working in a mill usually paid more than the minimum wage ($3.35 per hour). Consequently, the average income for boys was generally higher than for girls. Only one female student responded that she took care of horses for a job. Most students who were involved in animal caretaking did it at home and made money by selling the animals. It was a way of earning money but could not be called a job.

What did teenagers think of working during the school year or summer? A majority of high school students approved of working. More preferred working during the summer to during the school year, because jobs could take too much time away from school work or extracurricular activities. Many said that academic work should have a priority over employment, despite the temptation of extra spending money. If they could keep up with their school work, many young people stated that they would like to be employed even during the school year.

Adolescents identified several advantages associated with employment: earning money, learning responsibility, gaining work experience, and being occupied. Among these advantages, the most openly mentioned incentive was earning money. The employment provided some teenagers with up to a few hundred dollars a month, which most parents could not afford to give to their children. Self-earned money was a mean of 'buying' their own independence, particularly in their social lives, because they could participate in activities that they could not have pursued without money. When they earned their own money, many adolescents did not feel compelled to follow their parents' financial guidelines for its use. They also did not need to 'beg' for extra money for outings with friends. Several working adolescents said that they no longer received an allowance from their parents. Although many parents liked to advise their children about how to spend self-earned money, their offspring made the primary decisions on what to do with their own money, using it to buy personal items, food, and gifts, and to pay for social activities and entertainment. Few students indicated that they contributed any part of their earnings to their families. While their financial freedom might have been incomplete in most cases, adolescents nonetheless enjoyed this newly found independence.

Adolescents described important lessons that could be learned from employment and that might prove beneficial in the future. They learned responsibility, punctuality, and the ability to complete tasks. Melanie, a senior, described two incidents at her work place that impressed upon her the importance of responsibility. She said that her co-worker was fired after failing to show up for her scheduled hours. According to her, such an immediate firing happened only once during her employment at a pizza parlor, but it affected her attitude. On another occasion, a boy who was not making pizza fast enough was demoted from a pizza maker to a weekend dishwasher. This demotion meant a substantial pay cut. Such stories appeared to provide young people with a lesson to manage their time responsibly.

Another advantage of employment was that teenagers gained experience with the real world, learning to deal with human relations smoothly, a critical skill in continuing employment. They also said that they gained practical knowledge and hands-on skills from their jobs. Most adolescents were aware that employers preferred job applicants with experience. Therefore, they thought that work experience during their high school days would help them in later employment. The final advantage of adolescent employment, a way of occupying their time, will be discussed in the next chapter.

Fund Raising

Fund raising represents an important, if not unique, aspect of the adolescent culture. Fund raising refers to activities designed to earn money to support individual and group functions. Some adolescents raised funds for individual causes. Robin, a sophomore who was invited to compete in an international track meet in China, wrote about her efforts to raise traveling money as follows:

> I had a car wash on Saturday to help pay for my trip to China. [Three friends and her sister showed up to help.] After six hours of washing all different kinds, shapes, and colors of cars, I had made $74.01. I was very pleased. So far I have made $474.01 for my trip out of $1,700. Another money raiser I am planning to is sell raffle tickets on twenty-five-inch [Raggedy] Ann and Andy dolls. I am going to make the dolls and hopefully sell tickets at the football games that are left.

Most fund-raising projects were group activities to benefit the school or specific organizations. Whether for individual or group projects, young people underwent similar steps of collecting ideas for possible projects, outlining agendas, and executing the plans. These steps created a set of new activities.

Greenfield fund-raising projects can be categorized into four types: collecting free donations, selling labor, selling merchandise, and providing entertainment. The first category was rarely used for group activities. I observed it only when individual teenagers asked for monetary gifts for good causes. In order to raise funds to attend an international track meet in China, Robin and Holly sent letters to potential sponsors in the community and gave presentations outlining their projects to local organizations. Earl and Tracy also collected monetary donations for their summer Teen Mission trips to the Dominican Republic and England, respectively.

The second type of fund raising involved the sale of labor. With a few exceptions, most adolescent fund-raising projects were direct exchange of labor and cash. For example, the 'car wash' was popular among Greenfielders as a fund-raising activity. Young people set up cleaning equipment with a 'Car Wash' sign in the parking lot of businesses (after first securing permission from the store owners) and waited for customers. Drivers of washed cars paid for the young people's labor. In the direct exchange, both parties — sellers of labor and buyers of service — benefited.

Labor was also sold in a pledge form where labor-provider, service-user, profit-maker, and donors were separate. For example, in a free car wash, teenagers collected pledges from donors and made a profit by washing others' cars (often not the donors) at no charge. Once the activity was completed, they collected the pledges. The Dance-A-Thon presents another example. The Greenfield rally squad organized a dance marathon to raise funds for their new uniforms. Dance participants (not the squad members) collected pledges and danced continuously for eight hours and the rally squad received the pledged money. In both cases, adolescents were labor-providers and profit-makers, but donors were not necessarily service-users.

The third type of fund raising is selling merchandise; I found that students sold various items in school, ranging from food to flowers to coupon books. Teenagers profited in two ways: either by selling merchandise at a profit or by collecting commissions on their sales. In the former case, junior class officers sold doughnuts during morning breaks for a term. They paid the wholesale price for the doughnuts delivered every Tuesday and Thursday mornings and earned the profit as they sold them. In addition, snacks at the student store, Valentine flowers, balloons, and food at dances were sold in this way. By contrast, coupon books were sold under contract with a printing company, which compiled discount coupons from businesses in the Green Lake community and Riverville. The six-dollar coupon books that members of the Honor Society and senior class sold independently yielded a two-dollar return.

The fourth type of fund raising involves sales for entertainment events in the form of admission tickets. Among Greenfield High School activities, admission fees were collected for school dances and certain sports events. School dances usually cost $2.50 for a single admission, $4.00 for a couple. For football, basketball, or volleyball games, non-community members were charged $1.00–$2.00 per event. Admission fees to dances went to the organizing groups of the particular dances; those to sports events went to the student government. The fees made up a substantial amount of student activity funding.

Fund raising reflects the adolescent ethos of independence. By raising funds to finance their activities, young people felt self-sufficient and autonomous. Teachers particularly allowed students to exercise more freedom by planning self-supported activities. Fund raising also helped adolescents to be independent of their parents' financial support.

If funds had not been available for certain activities, their cost would have been passed on to participants. Young people who did not have their own financial resources would have had to either ask their parents for money or not participate in such activities. This lack of self-generated income and consequent dependence on parents' financial resources might thus determine the degree of students' involvement. For example, Christina, who lived with her mother and did not have a job, could not join the choir trip to Canada, which cost $100.00. Even though she made $50.00 by participating in some fund-raising activities, neither she nor her mother could make up the balance.

Except for this expensive type of event, the cost of most student activities was covered by funds that group members raised together. Therefore, fund raising allowed teenagers to feel financially independent because they supported their activities themselves and did not have to depend on their parents' support.

Driving

Becoming a licensed driver thrilled most teenagers, because they considered it an important step toward freedom. Therefore, they were eager to obtain the license and a car as soon as possible and at any cost. They were willing to sacrifice social life, free time, savings and grades. According to the survey administered by a faculty task team, 40.6 per cent of the student body owned a car. It can be correctly assumed that more students acquired a driver's license, since not every driver could afford a car. The team indicated that drivers were concentrated in junior and senior classes because freshmen and sophomores are not generally 'old enough to drive'. My survey revealed that 79 per cent of seniors had a driver's license; 63 per cent had a car of their own; and 54 per cent regularly drove a car to school.

Their exceptional interest in driving and cars frequently surfaced in conversations and classroom journals, both of which devoted attention to acquiring a driver's license, purchasing a car, car accidents, maintenance, and refurbishment. Most adolescents discussed these topics with a certain degree of excitement and boastfulness, including even car accidents.[3]

Once teenagers obtained their drivers' licenses, many of them had access to cars, either their families or their own. If they used the family car, many adolescents paid for their own gas or repairs. If they purchased their own cars, parents' support with car expenses varied: Marylinn's parents paid for everything except for daily fuel consumption; Paul took on his truck payment, insurance, and gas. The common arrangement was that parents paid for the vehicle and the student took on operation costs and insurance.

Adolescents viewed driving and owning a car as a critical means of independence. Once they started driving a car, they immediately noticed increased freedom in several ways. First, they did not have to depend on rides from their parents or guardians. This meant that they could participate in more activities after school, visit friends at their homes, or 'just go out'. The second reason is that they were able to attend teenager attractions without adult company. Cruising 'the gut' (the main street of the nearby city) was a favorite activity for some adolescents when they could drive a car. Third, they could get away from 'confinement' when they wished — leaving campus at lunch gave some young people a sense of freedom. Many students, particularly the upperclasses (juniors and seniors), went off campus during lunch hour. Even when they did not have enough money to eat out, many Greenfielders enjoyed driving off campus just for the sake of going out. Several students brought lunch from home and ate in their cars while driving around. In addition, some teenagers 'drove away' from conflicts at home. Fourth, a car not only increased mobility but created private space for courtship away from adult supervision. It was frequently observed that boys (or girls) took their girlfriends (or boyfriends) for rides. A girl who made her pregnancy public knowledge among her peers said that one of her common weekend activities was driving around with her boyfriend and 'spending time with him' in his parked car. Finally, driving increased employment options: neither distance nor working hours mattered as much in considering possible jobs.

Obtaining driver's licenses changed not only teenagers' life styles but also patterns of family life. Many parents noticed that their teenagers spent more time outside, getting involved in activities, working on jobs, or socializing with friends. The parents also were freed from a fixed schedule of transporting their children to and from activities. Some welcomed this freedom; others felt saddened about increased independence of, and decreased contacts with, their teenage children.

The change in the adolescent life sometimes led adolescents into conflict with their parents. Students without a car of their own obviously had to request parental permission to use family cars, permission that was not always granted. In order to secure more independence, many teenagers were willing to sacrifice other aspects of their lives to own a car. They took jobs at the expense of grades and social life, and saved money in order to purchase a car. Some teenagers reported that they spent as much as a few hundred dollars a month to cover their car payment, gas, insurance, and car accessories. Cynthia saved all her weekly $4.00 allowance for gas and spent most of her birthday gift money to buy seat-covers and a stereo for her car. The adolescent obsession with driving reflects the value that Americans place upon mobility as a symbol of independence.

Moving Away From Home

Moving away from home may be a dramatic way for adolescents to assert their independence. It was infrequently practiced at the high school level, but some Greenfielders chose this alternative. Moving away from home was different from running away from home. Whereas the latter was often accompanied by dropping out of school, the former served as a way to avoid family conflict but to continue with their schooling. In contrast to other symbols of independence, most adolescents considered physical relocation as a very serious step, realizing that it might mean more than a temporary release from an oppressive family situation. Despite the serious consequences, several adolescents at Greenfield selected this way of resolving family conflicts and, in turn, discovered the 'painful' cost of independence.

Most adolescents who moved out turned initially to their relatives or friends. This was quite favored because relatives or friends were more accessible and the move generally entailed less financial and psychological hardship. David, a senior, moved from California to live with his grandparents, because he did not get along with his divorced father. David's parents compensated his grandparents for his expenses. Michelle, a freshman who experienced physical and emotional abuse from her stepfather, ran away from her family to her best friend's house after a violent argument. Under the temporary guardianship of her friend's parents, she was supported for a few months by funds from her natural father before moving to live with him. Some teenagers temporarily stayed with friends until their problems were resolved and they could return home. Others made their move-out permanent, when they found financial resources, such as jobs or welfare funds and alternative living options.

Those who decided to move out permanently tended to rent a room from a family. Living alone in an apartment was rare for Greenfielders for three reasons: (1) not many apartments were available in the community; (2) landlords avoided renting to minors; (3)

renting an apartment from a landlord was too expensive for most adolescents. Young people least favored this third option.

Beth, a junior, was one who chose to live on her own. She moved out of her father's house in her sophomore year because she had continuous arguments with him; she said he did not know how to 'father' a girl. She stayed with her boyfriend and his parents for the first month, before a disagreement about physical involvement broke out. In the meantime, she gained a legal adult status at the age of sixteen. After failing to find a landlord in Peaceland who was willing to rent an apartment to her, Beth settled on an arrangement with a middle-aged couple, to whom she paid $290 a month for room and board. In her senior year, she finally shared a rental apartment with her new boyfriend in Riverville and began to lead a totally independent life.

Adolescents who lived away from their parents experienced considerable independence — freedom of action and choice. A senior boy explained, 'When you do leave home, you gain independence by being able to do whatever you want, with not so many pressures to do anything.' In addition, they gained a more realistic perspective on independence that freedom is accompanied by responsibility. Beth's experience of 'life in the alone zone' was reported in the student newspaper: 'I have to rely upon myself to get up and go to school. I have to pay the rent and stuff.'

Living-out adolescents also tasted the bitter emotional costs of independence. Several teenagers resented the loss of an intimate relationship with family members and a sense of personal security. A senior boy said that he missed his little sister whom he could visit only twice a month. A sophomore girl admitted longing for contact with her younger brother and advice from her mother. A junior girl elaborated on mixed feelings about moving out: 'I was free from my stepmom's possession. But I had left my home where I've lived for sixteen years and I left my dad and two little sisters. I miss them very much but I couldn't take the pressure any more.' A senior boy who moved out for the second time pointed to the lack of security and adult guidance when living alone: 'You may lose security and a sense of family unity and emotional support. Further, you could have a lack of guidelines for making decisions.'

Many living-out teenagers realized that responsibility came with independence and learned to look at their family situations with greater detachment. A detached perspective might have helped them improve their relationships with authority figures with whom they had had problems. The senior boy who came to understand his parents better said, 'Once you are out on your own...you begin to understand what your parents go through.' Kim agreed with him regarding her improved relationship with her mother: 'I think my mom and I both recognize that we've built on our relationship since I moved out.... In a lot of ways, things are better between us.'

Thus, while moving away from home might be the most striking means of acquiring independence available to high school adolescents, such freedom came with a high price. That high price seemed to help them alter romantic notions about unlimited independence.

Orientation Toward Peers

Peer interactions of high school adolescents increased as they spent more time in school and on extracurricular activities. When they began driving, the young people sought — and were able to engage in — more activities with their friends after school or on weekends. In addition, many Greenfielders spent a substantial amount of time talking on the phone with them.

Many adolescents said that they preferred interactions with peers to those with adults, because they felt more comfortable with people of their own age. Teenagers reported that they frequently felt the need to modify their speech and behavior in front of adults, and that, even so, many adults still complained that young people were unruly and did not respect their elders. The adolescents' conscious adjustments to the presence of adults made them feel restricted and unnatural. A freshman girl indicated that she felt more comfortable with her friends than with her family:

> When I am out with my friends, I am happier and more enjoyable to be around than when I am with my family. I'm not saying I don't care for my family's company, but it is easier to talk to my friends.

Varenne explained that this orientation toward peers derived from Americans' upbringing of children. Since they are left out of adult activities from early childhood, they feel not 'wanted' as they grew older and became inclined to seek companionship from their own age group (1977:45).

Teenagers viewed peer interactions as horizontal relationships that involved a great deal of equality. In contrast, relationships with adults symbolized inequality, represented in a hierarchical relationship.

In horizontal relationships, young people related to each other as beings with equal level of privilege and autonomy. No one 'bossed' them around in this relationship. However, young people felt less powerful when they dealt with authority figures such as parents, teachers, and other adults. Although they often related to adults fairly easily, adolescents' dependence on adults for finances, emotional support, and evaluation of performances undermined their sense of autonomy. Adolescents thus searched for the best opportunities for independence through peer interactions. They avoided making contact with adults in informal settings as much as possible, because it often meant no excitement and a restrictive atmosphere.

Mike, who said he got along with his parents, preferred going out for activities with friends — even 'just driving around' — to 'sitting around at home' with his parents. Many young people sought more independent environments with a minimum of adult supervision, although they did not necessarily experiment with prohibited activities such as drug abuse. For example, Mindy's house was favored by her friends to gather for private parties, because her single parent was seldom home during the week. Kelly's house was the second choice of the same group of friends for a similar reason. Mike said that their gathering often meant watching home video movies with popcorn or talking. Their activities would not have raised any adult's eyebrows. They still chose to have peer interaction out of adults' sight, because the absence of adults symbolized a liberation from hierarchical relationships.

From Childhood to Adulthood

While trying to achieve this grown-up status and indicating success with symbolic markers of independence, adolescents expressed ambivalence about moving from childhood into adulthood. In a class journal, a junior girl expressed longing for a carefree child status that did not require full responsibilities:

> If I could be any age and stay there, it would be five, because ...you can play all day and not have many responsibilities. Life then is carefree and fun.... You don't have to pay for anything or go to school. You don't have to abide by social rules.

A freshman, who experienced an intimate relationship with her ex-boyfriend, reported mixed emotions about losing her childhood security and innocence. She felt that her 'daring' grown-up experiences had trapped her in premature adulthood. Caught between adult independence and childhood security, she observed her feelings about the limbo status in two journal entries:

> I feel older than I am because...I've experienced a lot of very 'grown-up' feelings. Sometimes I get scared and lonely and I hate being so far ahead of other people, but sometimes I use it to my advantage.
>
> I realized that guy I ever try to have a relationship with I'm going to (in the end) expect from him what I got from Don, and that scares me. Why did I let myself experience such a serious intimate relationship so young?

Many seniors were apprehensive about graduating, because it meant more independence but less security. They looked forward to graduation because they would enter into new environments with more freedom; simultaneously, they were afraid of this change, because they would miss their long-term friends and security from home.

Greenfield adolescents seemed to emphasize the advantages, privileges, freedom, and autonomy that accompany independence, as long as they did not have to stand alone completely. Some parents observed that adolescents seemed to play a game of switching their association between adulthood (independence) and childhood (security) at their convenience. For example, many adolescents who claimed to be independent financially — making money and spending it on what they wanted — expected their parents to assist them with large expenses, such as Prom costs or class pictures. A school counselor summed up their attitude as follows: 'Eighteen-year-olds want independence but don't want to pay, and want to make up their minds but don't want to take responsibility.'

Some parents complained that the social system perpetuated the adolescents' game. For instance, in the name of medical confidentiality, some parents said that teenagers could take a drug or pregnancy test at the expense of their parents, who were not entitled to know the results: 'Parents just have to pay the bill.' The school counselor, however, did not think adolescents were totally responsible for their mixed feelings about independence. She said that this attitude was partly contributed to by adults' inconsistency: 'Parents have mixed messages. We say, "Be responsible but, by the way, I'll be in charge of it."' Whoever was responsible for the ambivalent attitude toward independence, many young people wanted to see only the benefits (adult-like privileges), but not the hardship of reality (responsibilities of adulthood).

Summary

Greenfield adolescents acquired independence to the degree that they earned it. Independence was also viewed as something that adolescents must obtain with their own efforts, rather than something given at a certain socially-prescribed age. The adolescents tried to enjoy the 'sweet' taste of independence before assuming full responsibilities, which they assumed would happen when they moved away from home after high school graduation. Demonstration of their independence, either by obtaining the symbolic markers of independence or by defying adult authorities became, to some degree, a preoccupation for almost all adolescents.

The symbolic markers that Greenfielders were concerned with included getting a driver's license and owning a car, getting employed to earn spending money, relying on peers' opinions and social life, and leading a physically and emotionally independent life. In pursuing independence, young people tended to emphasize its pleasant aspect, such as having less adult supervision and making more free choices. When they acquired a more realistic understanding of independence, adolescents longed for the carefree status of childhood that did not require so much responsibility. Those who did not — or did not want to — realize the harsh reality of independence concentrated on enjoying the present, intermediate status.

Notes

1   The leadership teams of eight teachers and administrators participated in a state-wide program, *Onward to Excellence*, to improve the quality of education in Greenfied High School. The tasks that they were to accomplish were as follows:

   1   to attend state-wide workshops to gain information on the program;
   2   to organize local staff meetings to identify problems in the areas of academic achievement, social behavior, and student attitudes;
   3   to conduct a survey and document research on specific matters;
   4   to design and implement a program to improve situations;
   5   to evaluate the program;
   6   to adjust the program to gain better results.

As a part of the process, the task force administered a survey to all high school students in the Spring of 1987.

2   All seniors, except two students who attended school on the day of the survey, completed the survey.

3   As many teenagers could drive, tales of car accidents were told off and on, ranging from fatal accidents to minor ones. An example of a minor accident was described in a classroom journal:

> The biggest shock of my life was when I was in a car accident.... One of my friends drove me to his place to pick up some things. On the way, things got pretty wild. He did a three-sixty on a sharp turn at eighty miles per hour and the car flipped over. We got out of the car and put it right-side up. The car started on the first try and went back home. The car had a 'few' scratches here and there, but it was quite a shock to me that it all happened. [a junior boy]

Chapter 9

Getting Involved

Greenfield adolescents appeared to be continuously involved in physical and mental activities both in and outside of school. Before school began in the morning, they gathered in the library or halls to do homework or converse with their peers. Most class activities — group projects, individual seat work, and lectures — demanded physical and mental energy. Following each class, students moved from one classroom to another. During lunch, many drove away from the school grounds, assembled to socialize, or did homework. They were rarely seen sitting alone in contemplation. After school, many participated in sports at school or pursued other activities outside school. Many teenagers said that they got 'bored' if they had nothing to do; some classes were considered boring, because they required minimal involvement other than lecture note-taking or individual seat work. By contrast, 'fun' classes often referred to those that offered a variety of programs or broke away from routines, ranging from simulation activities to field trips.

'Activeness', as displayed by individuals' participation in various physical and social activities and/or staying busy with the multiple involvements, was advocated by school staff, parents, and adolescents, and was reflected in the widely mentioned expression, 'Get involved'. This expression carried somewhat different meanings for adults and adolescents. When adults suggested that teenagers get involved, they usually meant students should acquire 'structured experiences', such as school sports, clubs, or organizations. While adolescents accepted the adult concept of activeness to a certain degree, they also extended its meaning to engagement in informal activities with peers.

One may argue that the idea of 'active involvement' is not unique to Greenfield adolescents. However, it is significant in the adolescent culture, because activeness carried a social value. The degree of activeness was used as a measure of the social maturity of adolescents and of their social success in the future. Greenfield individuals were motivated to become active by the incentives of having something to do, having fun, developing new friendships, becoming well known, and building a good record for the future.

In this chapter, I portray an example of a remarkably active adolescent and discuss the types of adolescent activities. After describing the various incentives for social involvement, I also discuss the social meanings of activeness. In conclusion, I analyze the way that adolescents cope with the action–oriented ideal and the stress that can result from the multiple involvements.

An Active Adolescent

Shirley represents a distinctive example of an active adolescent. She was known as 'a junior version of superwoman' among her teachers, peers, and community members. The label 'superwoman' reflected her competent handling of various and extensive responsibilities at home, in school, and in the community. She had a full schedule from 6:00 am until midnight. Every weekday morning, she attended a religion class beginning at 6:30 at her church. Then, she practiced for a school band at 7:30 before the first class period began. This class was called an 'early bird class'. After a heavy concentration of four classes in the morning, she used her lunch time to take care of business as president of Girls' League and Honor Society, and vice president of the Track Club. Her tasks included organizing activities, writing memos, and making the phone calls. Sometimes she completed homework during lunch hour; only rarely did she find time to eat lunch at the regular time. After her three afternoon classes were over, she participated in sports from 3:30 (cross-country in the fall and track in the spring). She trained with Judy, her best friend, who had similar academic and athletic credentials. After having dinner at home around 6 pm, she had school, church, or community activities to attend almost every night. She began her homework at about 9:30 pm and usually went to bed at midnight.

Shirley's weekend schedule was not any less frantic than that of the school days. She said, 'I usually have somewhere to go. I can't remember the last time I slept in.' For example, on Memorial Day Weekend, she took part in a statewide track meet of intermediate-sized high schools on Friday and Saturday; on Sunday, she went to church, attended the church choir practice, and read some books for pleasure; on Monday, she put up American flags for seventy-five businesses in the community before she joined her family picnic, then took them down in the evening.

Shirley's lengthy activity sheet[1] recorded her extensive involvement in sports, leadership, music, and volunteer work since the ninth grade. Her senior year activities, for example, demonstrated her musical and athletic ability, leadership in clubs and organizations, and volunteer work at school and throughout the community. As a musician, she played flute for the school band; she also accompanied the school choirs, Stage Band, and the church choir as a pianist. As an athlete, she competed as a member of the track and cross country teams, and played girls' tag football. As a leader, she represented Girls' League and Honor Society as president, track club as vice president, and church youth group as music chairperson and Sunday school class president. Besides all the activities at school and church, she volunteered to help in multiple community projects. This busy schedule, however, had not interfered with her academic work; she had maintained a 4.0 GPA (i.e., a straight 'A' grade point average) throughout her high school years.

Shirley's activity record and grades had earned her multiple awards in and outside school. She received a Future First Citizen Award from her community. At the Achievement Awards Banquet in her senior year, she won ten awards, making her the student with the most recognition. These ranged from Presidential Academic Fitness Award to Outstanding English Student Award. She received a total of forty-eight honors and awards during her high school years. At the graduation ceremony at which, with other two students, she gave a valedictorian speech, she received multiple scholarships, amounting to about $3,000, plus half-tuition to a private university she planned to attend. Shirley exemplified the image of the 'successful' adolescent who was active, busy, inexhaustable, and well-rounded. In agreement with the judges who selected her as the recipient of honors and awards, her senior classmates also voted her 'Most Likely to Succeed' and 'Most Talented.'

Types of Activities

Although Shirley may be an extreme example of an active high-achiever, many other adolescents in Greenfield were active in various ways. Adolescent activities fell into five different types: 1) school

activities such as sports, clubs, or organizations; 2) community functions; 3) part-time or full-time jobs; 4) informal interactions with
peers; 5) family activities. Most public recognition was given to those
who were involved simultaneously in several formal school activities,
because this kind of involvement was most visible to those who could
publicly reward it — school staff and peers. However, many adolescents seemed to be more concerned about engaging in enough activities to alleviate boredom, rather than to gain recognition.

School Activities

School activities such as sports, clubs, organizations, and classes were
commonly available to Greenfield adolescents. The Green Lake community, located in a semi-rural area, offered limited options for social
activities for young people (see Chapter 3). As a result, after-school
extracurricular events attracted many Greenfielders who either could
not afford expensive out-of-school involvements or did not want to
bother driving so far.

Sports, popular and relatively inclusive, provided plentiful opportunities. Thirteen different sports were offered throughout the school
year, including ten for men and nine for women (see Chapter 4). An
administrator and some students observed that the qualifications for
prospective athletes were not too strict: basically, applicants were
required to have a GPA of 2.0 or more (a 'C' average) and be willing
to follow the conduct rules, including a specific rule against 'substance
abuse'. As the athletic director noted, a large majority of Greenfield
students participated in the athletic program. Students were restricted
to only one sport per season with the exception of single-event,
intramural sports such as the 'powder puff' (tag football) and a weight
lifting competition. Since athletes were recruited from the small
student population, individuals in Greenfield had a better chance to
participate in sports than did students at large schools. The policy of
one athlete for one sport was seasonal; many students repeated their
athletic involvement throughout the year. For instance, a successful
and 'popular' male student, Jeff, played football in the fall, joined
wrestling in the winter, and participated in track and field in the
spring. Sandy, chosen Girl of the Month for her sportsmanship,
played volleyball, basketball, and softball in their respective seasons.
This full cycle of sports kept many adolescents busy and involved.

In addition to sports, many Greenfield adolescents became affiliated with school clubs and organizations (listed on pp. 69–70). Some

clubs or organizations set out busier activity schedules for members than others. The rally squad and dance team were two of the most visible and active organizations. They coordinated cheerleading at football and basketball games, prepared for off-campus competitions, and executed fund-raising projects throughout the year. In some organizations and clubs, such as Girls' League and language clubs, officers became more active than members, planning activities and carrying them out. In these groups, getting involved was tantamount to becoming an officer; membership alone did not offer much action.

Some classes functioned as clubs because they demanded so much time for out-of-class projects. These included choir, band, journalism, and yearbook. In addition to receiving class instruction, choir and band members performed in on- and off-campus concerts and interscholastic competitions. Beside the busy local performance schedule, choir and band alternated years for a performance trip to Canada in the month of May. The journalism and yearbook classes produced the student newspaper and the annual, respectively. In the production process, members of these classes took photos of school functions and sports events, collected information (through interviews or research), wrote and edited articles or captions, and laid out pages. The class members often stayed after school when their production process came close to a deadline. Another class which functioned as a club was Field Biology. The class included in its curriculum several one-day outings and a major four-day fieldtrip.

Through these classes, even those who might not be involved in other clubs and organizations experienced a high degree of activeness. One sophomore girl described her busy schedule of the spring term filled with numerous trips for her classes: the four-day choir trip to Canada, a few one-day and one four-day Field Biology trips, and two one-day outings for Spanish class. A senior girl, who kept a low profile in school and appeared inactive in areas other than journalism, summarized her perception of activeness as follows: 'Everyone [in the school] is active. I'm active on the newspaper staff.' Her statement suggested that although not everyone was involved in 'popular' or high visibility activities such as sports, they regarded themselves as active in other areas.

Activities in the Community

Young people got involved in community activities through churches, local clubs, and school organizations. Churches offered youth possibilities of social gatherings and activities. The Green Lake community had fifteen Christian churches, including ten in Peaceland with its 2,500 residents. While the number of church-goers was not documented, community members remarked the high ratio of churches to residents in the area. Several churches provided independent or joint youth programs regularly. Peter, a sophomore, went to a youth meeting every Monday evening, where about ten to fifteen high schoolers from three local churches gathered, presumably to receive spiritual nourishment and enjoy companionship through games, discussions, and video movies. Campus Life was another Christian youth group that attracted high schoolers. Since the Christian faith was not a prerequisite for participants, many non-believers regularly attended weekly meetings for a more recreational purpose. Like many other youth programs, Campus Life heavily incorporated 'fun' games (see the section *Incentives for Active Involvement* in this chapter) into their weekly meetings.

The 4-H Club[2] represented another community organization oriented toward youth activities. The 4-H functions were well received in a rural area such as the Green Lake community. Helen, who appeared quiet in school and lived in a remote wooded area, was an active member of the 4-H Club. The club activities included sewing, cooking, making crafts, and taking care of animals. Club members pursued their own projects and entered them into yearly competitions at a county fair. Helen won a ribbon for her fruit jam in the junior canning division. A freshman girl also said that she learned to take care of sheep through the 4-H involvement. She raised several head and sold some of them at the summer fair for $300.

Adolescent school activities extended into the community when campus organizations volunteered services for local functions. This type of involvement was common in Green Lake, because its high school had close public relations with the community. High school dance and rally squads were frequently summoned to assist the Booster Club (see Chapter 3) with fund-raising projects; choirs and bands were frequent entertainers at community ceremonies and fund-raising events. Over a hundred volunteers from the high school participated in a city clean-up campaign for the Peaceland city celebration. They picked up litter along streets, and the Woodshop students repainted picnic tables in the city park.

Some adolescents volunteered individually to assist at community functions. Many high school students helped to serve food and to clean up at the annual community Thanksgiving turkey dinner, serving over 700 people. Several teenagers also worked as guides or aides at a community health fair. A few high schoolers were involved in middle and elementary school functions, as sport officiators, chaperones at dances, or camp counselors. This type of individual, short-term volunteerism often resulted from encouragement by parents or friends who were involved themselves. Some young people made a relatively long-term commitment as volunteers. Every Saturday, Linda volunteered as a nurse's aide at the general hospital in Riverville. After four days of training for two hours each day, she was assigned to tasks such as changing bedpans, giving patients a bath with a washcloth, or taking temperatures. She was initially introduced to this work by her high school friend who had also volunteered at the same hospital.

The community activities mentioned above occupied adolescents' evenings or weekends, and kept them quite busy. They offered young people something to do, as well as opportunities to interact with other teenagers and adults.

Jobs

Jobs occupied many Greenfield teenagers' time out of school. Working hours per week ranged from two to forty-five hours. Debbie, a sophomore, babysat a few hours a week; Adam, a senior, worked both full time (forty hours) and overtime (about five hours per week on average) as a dishwasher and prep-cook. He worked from 4:00 or 5:00 pm until midnight (sometimes after midnight when he cleaned pots and pans) on school days and in a morning shift on weekends. After he started work, Adam quit participating in the track team, which was his main activity in school. He usually left school at 3:30 pm and went home to get ready for work. Since he worked five days, he had two free evenings from work each week. He admitted that sometimes his schedule became too full. He liked the job, however, because it gave him not only financial rewards, but a reason to avoid an older brother at home with whom he did not get along.

Jobs often replaced, rather than supplemented, other activities. Employers did not want to excuse adolescents from their regular working hours. A cheerleader who continued her summer employment through the following term was eventually forced to make a choice between her rally practices and work; both demanded her full commitment after school. A junior boy expressed resentment about not being able to attend his friend's graduation ceremony, because he could not leave his job for that event. Many adolescents said that getting a job could cost them grades, social life, and/or extracurricular activities. Many seniors noted the effects of jobs on their lives: 'It usually — not always — destroys your social life', 'It gives you no free time', 'It makes things hectic', 'You fall behind in school work and you're tired at school', and 'It takes away from the activities that a person would like to do.' Jobs kept adolescents busy; the same jobs kept them from more active participation in the school or community.

Informal Peer Interactions

As mentioned above, phrases like 'get involved' or 'get active' usually meant getting involved in formally organized activities. These types of activities were counted — literally — when adolescents were to be nominated for awards or scholarships. The major criteria, so-called objective parameters, were concerned with the number of activities in which they were involved, leadership experiences, and grades. Leadership within a clique, or membership in a skateboard (informal) group, did not count.

Nevertheless, peer-oriented activities seemed disproportionately significant in adolescent life, because young people spent a lot of time interacting with their peers. Adolescents spent seven to ten hours a day with their schoolmates. After school, many visited others' home, went out together for social life, and telephoned each other frequently. On weekends, many adolescents made plans to 'do something' together. Especially after school or on weekends, socializing became the typical routine for many Greenfielders. Greater mobility gained through being able to drive facilitated socializing. Charlie, a junior, visited Randy's house a few times a week after school and then often went to Mark's house with Randy to talk, skateboard, play frisbee, or watch television. Randy, a junior who owned a car, frequently drove to Riverville after school for window-shopping or cruising in the city. He took every chance to join in these activities with his friends. One day, he overheard his friends Carol and Mindy planning an excursion to buy a birthday present for Carol's father. He asked if he could go with them, and happily joined their trip to the Grand Shopping Center in Riverville.

The following vignette illustrates an example of informal interactions among peers. On a chilly, but sunny afternoon in February, eight male students gathered with skateboards in a church parking lot that had a slight grade. They set up two wooden ramps sloping to a height of approximately three feet, and rode their skateboards between these ramps. A couple of boys came to watch their friends riding skateboards for awhile. The skateboarders demonstrated various skills: some turned around gracefully at the top of the ramps, while others tried to keep balance on their skateboard on the ground. They repeated jumps off the ramps, 180-degree turns, and slides on sidewalks. They sometimes stopped to talk about jumps that one just finished or to exchange remarks with each other. I sensed a feeling of unity among them, based on the fact that they had gathered there for one purpose (skateboarding) and were pursuing it together. Charlie, the boy who invited me to this meeting (he called it a 'skate jam' or 'skate session'), told me that most of the skateboarders regularly showed up at the sessions whenever the weather and their schedules allowed.

Another example of peer activity took place in a student's home. After participating in a community parade on Saturday, Kathy invited Joan and me to her home for lunch. After finishing lunch with the family, we, joined by Kathy's other sister, went swimming in their outdoor pool. Kathy suggested that we take turns jumping off the diving board in any original style. All of us followed her suggestion, amid laughter and splashes. After about an hour of such a 'creative' recreation, we moved to a trampoline to continue our physical activity. Kathy again suggested that one of us begin to create a move, the next person would pick it up and add a new move, and so on. We were engaged in this activity for about half an hour. Then, we went to Kathy's room and looked at her class pictures. (Kathy acted as a sales representative for the photography studio, by showing her portfolio of class pictures; in return she received, from the studio, a free set of photos and credits toward additional copies or another sitting.) Kathy and Joan soon started a conversation exchanging opinions about boys and marriage. As in the first vignette, the teenagers engaged in physical activity that they considered to be 'fun'. Along with the activity, they were engaged in conversations of various subjects such as friendship, courtship, and family life.

Family Activities

Although teenagers spent many hours with their peers, their families were still a significant part of their daily lives as long as they lived together. Despite their love-hate relationships with family members, many students claimed that their families provided security and support they needed.

Participation in family life ranged from house chores to extended family trips. Many adolescents were expected to do housework after school. Household chores included cooking, washing dishes, vacuuming, doing laundry, feeding animals, working in gardens, mowing the lawn, chopping firewood, etc. Some adolescents were expected to do several tasks, whereas others were required to do only minimal chores or were assigned no regular tasks. For example. Dorothy's major household chore was unloading the dishwasher at home. Richard was expected to do all the 'male stuff', such as chopping wood and making repairs around the house, to help his single mother who suffered from a back problem. These activities filled slots in the adolescents' daily schedule. Some teenagers procrastinated in their household chores in favor of other activities, but in many families children were reprimanded or 'grounded' (temporarily restricted to their homes except for attending school, limited peer interactions, reductions of telephone usage and allowance, and forfeiture of certain privileges, if they shirked their duties). Several adolescents complained that they were short of time, due to the combined load of school activities, homework, social life, and household chores.

Some families spent time together 'sitting and talking'. Other families reported involvement in more action-oriented activities: going for walks, driving around town, or taking family trips. In some cases, family activities took priority over school activities. A senior girl from a well-to-do family took a few weeks out of her spring term to travel across the country with her family. A junior boy joined his family's trip to Mexico for two weeks during a fall term. Andy, a sophomore, took a week off to go to a ski resort with his family. Andy also invited a male friend to join the family trip, and Andy's parents paid the friend's expenses.

Incentives for Active Involvement

If Greenfield adolescents appeared to be fond of getting involved, what drove them into the stage of constant activeness? This section discusses incentives for their activeness as follows: having something to do, making friends, having fun, getting popular, and getting ready for the future.

'Having Something to Do'

'Having nothing to do', synonymous with boredom, is a devastating situation for many adolescents in Greenfield. 'Having nothing to do' can be interpreted in two ways: a lack of action, or the seemingly endless repetition of everyday routines. A junior boy who participated in football for the fall season said he felt 'dull' after the season was over. To my question, 'What do you do in your spare time?', he responded unenthusiastically, 'Nothing. Sometimes, I get bored. I'm looking forward to playing again.' To him, 'having nothing to do' did not mean that his life was totally boring, because he was engaged in a budding friendship with a girl, which occupied him in a way. Rather, his tedium derived from not being engaged in action-concentrated activities. In comparison, Paula, a senior, described her life at home as having 'nothing to do'. She could watch TV or do homework, but she did not anticipate any excitement from any unusual event occurring at home.

To avoid the 'have-nothing-to-do' situations, adolescents put themselves in various active situations in school, community, or jobs. Many athletes participated in sports, season after season. They said that they were so accustomed to such activities that they could not imagine living without them. Wanda, a year-round athlete, mentioned that she felt guilty when she even considered the option of taking off a season when pressure built up. She had been involved in sports every season since the sixth grade. Neither long driving (twenty miles one way from home to school) nor inconvenience in arranging transportation kept her from participating in the activities. Even after their divorce, her parents made a relay arrangement for transporting her to sports functions. Wanda lived with her mother, who drove her to a mid-point between the school and their home. Wanda's father, who lived close to the school, picked her up at the mid-point and brought her to athletic events in school. After the activities, she was picked up by her father and the reversed relay was done. In spite of the inconvenience, she said that if she did not participate in sports, she would miss being in action.

Likewise, some students were content with their jobs. They stated, 'Work keeps me busy and gives me something to do.' Getting involved in activities or jobs allowed them to be occupied and stay active, which was much more satisfying than a relaxing schedule with much spare time.

'Making Friends'

Getting involved in activities was considered an excellent means of getting to know people and making friends. By getting involved in activities, many freshmen and newcomers found ways of breaking into established circles of friends and getting socially adjusted to new circumstances. Stacy, a freshman, became a member of the girls' basketball squad and soccer team, where she made friends with many freshmen and other upperclass students. Unlike classes, most sports teams, organizations, and informal circles of friends had cross-class members. Holly, who transferred to Greenfield High School in her junior year, also made many friends through activities. She was more than a year older than most of her classmates, and this age gap could have been an obstacle in making friends, but she became involved in track and field, ran for an office in Girls' League, joined the newspaper staff, and initiated contacts with a various circles of peers.[3] As a new student in a small school where 'everyone knew everyone', her outgoing activeness soon became noticed and her efforts eventually paid off in multiple friendships.

Many adolescents had discovered that getting involved in activities not only helped them make new friends, but also nurtured already established friendships. Shirley and Judy were often seen together. They had maintained a 4.0 GPA (straight A), shared leadership as president and vice-president in clubs, ran competitively in cross-country and track, and were co-valedictorians at graduation. Shirley said that she cherished a deep friendship with Judy, which she gained through their parallel participation in activities.

Needless to say, informal peer activities provided ample opportunities to make new friends and develop friendship. Brenda met her boyfriend while 'cruising the gut' in Riverville and they were a couple for a year. In the gut — a designated section of a major thoroughfare — young people drove up and down at an extremely low speed. Many people often were packed in one car, playing rock-n-roll music at full volume on a car stereo and hailing teenage passengers in other cars, sometimes stopping to talk with them. The gut was a popular place for some Greenfielders to meet new people of different ages and from various high schools in the region.

Birthday parties were another occasion to get acquainted with new people. Grace said that when she was invited to Dayna's birthday party, she met people with whom she was not associated at school. Even though she had participated in many activities with Dayna before, they did not share the same circle of friends. Therefore, she would not have gotten to know some of Dayna's friends without the party. This type of chain reaction was quite common in making new friends through informal activities.

'Having Fun'

Phrases such as 'It's fun' or 'I had fun' were commonly expressed in adolescent talk. In general, activities that they identified as 'fun' are characterized by some or all of the following: action was involved; it was out of routine; peer interactions took place; cross-sex interactions occurred; adult supervision was minimal; and it gave a sense of accomplishment.

A scene from a non-denominational Campus Life meeting illustrates an occasion most attendees described as 'fun'. Forty to fifty students from Greenfield sat on the carpeted floor of a former restaurant, now converted into a meeting hall. The room was so packed that most participants had little room to stretch their legs. Some of them leaned against walls or their neighbors. The Campus Life director of the Greenfield High School chapter, a Greenfield High graduate, opened the meeting with a game. The students were divided into two groups, and pens were distributed to individuals of one group. Members of the other group were told to take off their socks and go around to get autographs from members of the other group on their bare feet. The rule of the game was that the one who collected most signatures became the winner. Some were at first hesitant to take off their socks but soon drifted into the 'chaotic' mood, running around with bare feet for scribbles.

After the first activity, another game awaited. Three volunteers were called and went into another room. Each was blindfolded separately and asked to identify by touch objects covered with a cloth on two tables. The objects included a tennis racket, a football, clothes, and the head of the fourth volunteer, Jim, squatting between two tables. The first and second volunteers successfully guessed all the objects but the head. When they were touching the head, Jim jumped up to surprise the blindfolded volunteers. For the third volunteer, the director altered the plan; without Jim's knowledge, the director instructed the volunteer to smear a dishful of whipped cream on Jim's face when he popped out. His peers laughed at the double cross. This surprise game was followed by another make-a-fool-of-yourself type of activity, and the telling of a 'horror' story on the theme of Halloween. The two-hour meeting concluded with a group discussion about fear.

This meeting was full of action, surprise, and peer interaction. The double cross broke the routine of the game. The presence of adult staff did not seem to threaten the young people (the staff members regularly visited the school during lunch hour and made close contacts with students). In these casual and relaxed circumstances, the young people said they had fun. Both the adult and the student staff said that many of the attendees probably were not interested in religious messages, but came to the meeting to 'have fun'.

While the Campus Life case represents a light and exciting way of having fun, some teenagers observed that they found enjoyment through more 'heavy-duty' or serious activities. Jill, a sophomore, thought of doing homework as fun, something perceived as a headache and 'no fun at all' to many other adolescents. The pleasure that she found in doing homework derived from a sense of accomplishment as she went through the process of creating ideas, organizing her thoughts, and finally finishing projects.

As discussed above, having fun could motivate adolescents to take action. Since 'fun' was sometimes sought outside daily routines, it could lead young people to pursue pleasure from unusual, present-oriented (temporary) activities. It could be very costly when it was embedded in present-oriented hedonism. Some teenagers said that they drank or experimented with drugs 'just for fun'. Others drove their vehicles fast and made sharp turns at high speed for the same reason. For Prom night, many adolescents were willing to spend several hundred dollars to enjoy the single event. Gwen and her date spent over $200 for their attire ($120 for her dress, matching shoes, and new undergarments; $70 for his tuxedo; and $30 for a corsage), close to $100 for an exquisite meal for two at a first-class restaurant, and about $30 for bowling and snacks after the prom. Probably, the adolescent value of 'fun for now' would explain the willingness to risk lives by speeding, to take illegal substances, and to spend as much as a whole month's pay on one night's fun.

'Getting Popular'

Many adolescents believed that those who were involved in structured activities such as sports or organizations tended to become popular among peers. They often equated 'becoming well known' with 'getting popular', not necessarily synonymous with 'becoming well liked'. Many adolescents believed that popularity played an important role in winning votes in election and awards.

Barbara was convinced that the athletic popularity of her campaign opponent, James, was responsible for his success in winning the election for Student Body President. According to her, people knew John's name because he played sports. Those — especially freshmen

— who did not know about the ability of candidates tended to vote for familiar names. Judith, who transferred to Greenfield at the beginning of her junior year, took advantage (maybe, unconsciously) of this athletic route to gain popularity. In her first term in Greenfield she played volleyball, and in her second term she played basketball. In addition to her attractive appearance, her reputation as a fine athlete and an active student helped her win the crown of Prom princess in the spring. Lisa, voted Girl of the Month for leadership, admitted in an interview with the school newspaper, 'Being vice president for the senior class and being in student government could have had some effect on why I was chosen.' These three adolescents recognized that active involvement rewarded them with considerable popularity.

'Getting Ready for the Future'

Some adolescents got involved in activities in order to build credentials for their future. Students were often told that when they applied for admission to colleges and scholarships, their activity records would play a critical role in their admission. Even when they applied for jobs, their high school activity level would be used as a predictor for their ability and responsibility on the job. Some teenagers believed that their job experiences or volunteer work during high school would prepare them for their future careers. Actually, Cindy, who had volunteered her services in a nursing home, entered a nursing program at a community college after she graduated.

A counselor advised students to gain a wide range of experience in sports, leadership, volunteer work, music, art, newspaper, and yearbook. Her advice basically meant that adolescents should get actively involved in various types of activities and, in turn, prepare to be well-rounded. Her advice was taken more seriously by seniors who had begun to see the potential effect of their activities on their future.

Activity as a Social Virtue

Getting involved in activities was encouraged by the school staff. During a one-day orientation for incoming freshman, an administrator gave a lengthy speech of what they should and should not do in school. His list of *dont's* was much longer than *do's*. Among a few *do's*, he emphasized, '[Do] participate and get involved.' He added, 'Those who get involved have a better life.' The go-and-get-involved rhetoric was well-expressed by a memo sent to parents by the high school administrators who quoted a memo from a US Education Department study, '"The more activities students were involved in, the higher they ranked" in terms of grades and test scores.' Even though the memo carefully warned parents, 'Participation in extracurricular activities does not guarantee improved performance as a student,' the act of sending the memo seemed to represent the school administrator's position on students' active involvement.

Many parents shared a similar attitude toward adolescent involvement. Sue's parents encouraged their daughter to be actively involved in sports, leadership, school clubs, and the church. They also showed their support by attending parent meetings and making commitments to assist with programs beneficial to adolescents. Since they believed that their children should spend more time involved in school and community activities, Sue's parents disapproved of her getting a job during school years. They presumed that employment would cut into Sue's schedule by a substantial amount.

Newspapers often carried articles of adolescent activeness written in tones of approval. A Riverville newspaper featured a glowing article about Kim, a Greenfield High school student, on the basis of her academic and social excellence, despite her unusual living circumstances (she was living independently without an adult guardian). According to this article, 'By rights,' she 'should be cutting classes, haunting the streets and doing drugs.' By contrast, she stayed in school faithfully; moreover, she excelled as an honor student, student body president, and athlete. She also held a part-time job. The article went on:

> She's been captain and most outstanding player of the girls' soccer team. She coaches and referees youth teams. She volunteers for community food drives. She's a regular blood donor. She's won academic awards from the American Chemical Society and from the National Science League.

The article portrayed Kim as a successful teenager. Like the newspaper article about Shirley (see *An Active Adolescent* in this chapter), this journalistic rhetoric suggested that her active involvement be taken as evidence for this recognition. This tacit way of encouraging adolescent involvement by the local newspaper was also used in the high school newspaper whenever any honor recipient was reported. For example, a student newspaper article highlighted Sarah, who was voted Girl of the Month for 'Sense of Humor': 'Sarah is a member of the Honor Society, keeps statistics for the J.V. softball teams and is ending her sixth year in choir.'

Not only school administrators, parents, and media advocated the idea of 'Go and get involved', but also many adolescents themselves believed they should be active. Some of them focused their involvement in the area of organized school and community activities. Others chose to be active with their peers or families. Whatever activities they selected to do, most of them agreed that activeness was better than 'doing nothing'. The role of a performer or an actor was more likely to be respected than that of a listener or being in the audience.

Between Activeness and Stress

The ethos of activity was reinforced by exterior forces and self-consciousness. In school, students hurried from one class to the other, following a tight schedule with four- to five-minute breaks in between classes and a less-than-one-hour lunch time. During this free time many activities took place. After school, sports, rally meetings, dance practices, jobs or informal gatherings with friends demanded students' participation. The school staff and parents also encouraged adolescents to get involved, particularly in organized activities, not only of one kind but several types — the more, the better. Society rewarded those who displayed their activeness. Peers not only acknowledged those, but also often compounded their involvement by voting them for prestigious titles, such as Homecoming and Prom Court members, leaders, and Girl/Boy of the Month. Many Greenfield teenagers felt pressure to get involved and prove their activeness in public. In addition, 'Be Active' and 'Get Involved' messages had been so emphasized since childhood that capability seemed to be assessed on the basis of actions.

The pressure of being both 'actor' (one who actively gets involved in organized functions) and 'performer' (one who displays one's activeness in public) affected adolescent life in two ways. On the one hand, the young people said they learned to manage time efficiently because they had to fit so many tasks into a tight schedule. To accomplish this, they needed to plan time wisely in advance, and not to waste it on secondary interests. On the other hand, many adolescents experienced stress from their overwhelming number of commitments. Even those who managed their time efficiently were not immune to stress. Rather, stress often seemed to affect the time-conscious adolescents who tried to live up to the ethos of activeness.

Managers of Time

It was astounding to see how many activities many students were involved in and how well they seemed to manage them within a limited time. Some seniors questioned my surprise, insisting that they failed to manage time efficiently. However, many others confirmed my observation and shared their strategies with me. I categorized the strategies into four types:

1 'keeping on top of things' (pace keeper);
2 'organizing myself and setting priorities' (list maker);
3 'not getting much sleep' and 'sacrificing weekends' (over-stretcher);
4 'cramming at the last minute' (crammer).

Many young people combined some of these elements in completing their tasks.

Jean, a pace keeper, made conscious efforts not to fall behind her schedule. Her way was to try to finish tasks in advance instead of waiting until the last minute. She resolved to complete each important task — for instance, homework — right away before she became engaged in other activities, such as meetings or watching TV. One afternoon when she accompanied the cross-country team as a statistics keeper for a competition, she spent her spare time between events doing her writing assignments. Even though her peers sometimes called her a 'book worm', she managed to stay on top of her agenda. For this style of time management she was rewarded with excellent grades and activity records.

According to her mother, Lynn was a remarkable organizer: 'She is a list maker. She does organize.' Lynn might not always stay on top of her schedule, and sometimes she put off her tasks as long as she could. She then made a priority list and finished tasks one by one accordingly. Lynn agreed with her mother's observation:

[I make lists] all the time. At the beginning of a year, probably for the first three months of the school, I'd sit every night and make a list out and put it on my desk.

She sometimes 'let everything fly'; however, her inclination toward organization helped her maintain her academic and involvement status.

Marie was an overstretcher type. She was active as a cheerleader, an officer of the French Club and Future Business Leaders of America, a member of the Honor Society, and had a steady boyfriend. She always felt that she did not have enough time for everything. Her strategy was to utilize as many hours as possible from her days and weeks, even by sacrificing night sleep and free time on weekends.

Tom finished tasks by cramming at the last minute. He gave priority to peer interaction over homework and other tasks, but he was concerned about his grades. He often found himself cramming the night before an examination, or finishing homework shortly before a class. He was able to concentrate during those hours. His grades were good, and he was proud of learning as much as he did in that way. He also tended to take care of his club activities at the last minute. He felt that he was rushing all the time to get his immediate needs completed; indeed, he rarely appeared relaxed in school. Tom was so accustomed to this 'last minute' style of finishing projects that he did not seem to be considering alternatives to it.

Victims of Stress

While many adolescents seemed to manage their time efficiently, others were also overwhelmed by the number of activities in which they were involved. The unbalance between the amount of activities and available time and energy frequently created stress or 'burn-out' feeling. Drew, a senior, expressed his frustration as follows:

> My life right now is very confusing. I have to spend time for school, football, family, friends, and my girlfriend. And all of that just doesn't fit in one day's work.

Despite the stress, this boy did not resolve the dilemma by giving up any of his involvement. To him, reduction of commitments was not an option, because they were all necessities in the life of an allegedly successful male adolescent. Therefore, he chose to continue the same life style — trying to be busy with many activities, and to excel in all of them. As he saw it, he did not have the option to give up any of his activities, high grades, or his good relationship with family, peers, and girlfriend.

More seniors than those in other classes articulated their stressful situations. The increasing stress level may symbolize the transition from adolescence into adulthood, because the latter presumably entailed more tasks and stress. In addition to all the *must's* of adolescent life, seniors identified more matters to take care of, as compared to those in other classes. For instance, the seniors contemplated their future. Those who planned to continue their education were concerned about selecting the institutions to apply to and determining how to finance their college education. Ginny and Betty, seniors, explained their stress as follows:

> I have so many things going on in my life right now. I don't even know where to start. First, there's school — high school and the prospect of college. In high school, I am taking Political Process, Accounting II, College English, Chemistry, and I'm also the Senior Class Vice President. I have so many pressures and so much responsibility to deal with. I just want to scream sometimes. Then I have to make decisions about college. I have all these adult decisions to make and then there's my third confusing thing — home!

> I have stayed after school every day for the last two weeks. I finished the newspaper (school). I made a tape for the All-State band two weeks ago. I tried to make my scholarship tape last night and I sounded terrible. That was depressing because I spent so much time and energy on that tape and I *know* I could have done it if I had the *time*. I've been overloaded with homework and I still have to cook dinner when I get home after a long day of school.

Parents' mixed messages sometimes added stress to students. Parents encouraged their children to get involved, only to realize that their teenage offspring then spent less time with their families. Several parents then complained that their children became too involved. The parents noticed that once youngsters started driving, they participated in more off-campus activities and were absent more frequently from family activities.

Some parents expressed concern about their children's increased involvement in informal and unofficial activities with peers. Some of them reprimanded their adolescent children for too frequent peer interactions; others put restrictions on the number of outings. An extreme case was 'grounding' them against going out at all after school. Sue's parents took the first option. According to Sue, 'My parents do not want me to be involved in more things. They said, "Sue, you're gone too much — gone, gone."' Sue expressed her confusion: 'They're contradicting themselves. They told me to go out and become involved. Now they say I'm involved too much.' In addition to stress resulting from all the responsibilities that Sue had, her parents' mixed messages placed extra pressure on her.

The social emphasis on getting involved generated a certain amount of anxiety in many adolescents. Some with sedentary inclinations might feel compelled to keep up an active front. Others might feel obligated to stay for after-school activities against their preference to go home to rest. Both groups of young people knew that the more they were involved, the more recognition they were likely to get. Even those who enjoyed involvement realized that they were limited in time and stamina. In straddling expectations and reality, many young people experienced stress.

Summary

Shirley represented an active adolescent, who was recognized as a successful teenager by both adults and her peers. This involvement was advocated by the school staff and her parents, who believed that activeness would promise 'success' in the school years and in the future. Adults encouraged teenagers to participate in 'structured experiences' such as sports, clubs, and organizations in school and community activities. Teenagers got involved in these structured experiences, and they also became active with jobs or informal activities with their peers.

Adolescents were aware of the social value of involvement, noticing that their active peers were winning awards, honors, and scholarships. When discussing plans for their future lives, they were frequently advised to become engaged in various activities in and outside school. In addition to this future-oriented motivation, adolescents got involved in activities in order to avoid boredom, to make friends and ease into the social network, to have fun, and to gain name-familiarity among peers. At the same time, those adolescents who made multiple commitments often found themselves trapped between the ethos and reality. They realized that they could not accomplish everything within their time and energy constraints. Some said that they had to give up some activities. Others — often 'successful' adolescents — managed to maintain multiple involvements to raise their social credentials. No matter how well adolescents juggled their time and activity schedules, they tended to experience stress because the social expectation of activeness seemed to be imposed overwhelmingly on them.

Notes

1 The activity sheet of an individual student contained information on leadership experiences, honors and awards, and activity participation since the freshman year. All students were encouraged to update this sheet every year and to utilize it in applying for colleges, scholarships, or jobs. While most students could fit the information on the two sides of the printed form, Shirley typed her records on four separate pages, because the form was not long enough for her.
2 The 4-H Club is 'a rural youth organization sponsored by the Department of Agriculture, offering instruction in scientific agriculture and home economics' (Guralnik 1970:551).
3 Holly dropped out of school in her freshman year to take care of her ill mother and returned to school the following year. Then she missed a part of her sophomore year due to her own health problem.

Chapter 10

The Duality of Adolescent Ideals

The dimensions of adolescent ethos identified in the previous chapters — 'getting along with everyone', 'being independent', and 'getting involved' — appear to be rooted in American ideals of egalitarianism, inner-directedness, and competition. Much of the adolescent behavior I have described reflects these ideals. Yet, other behaviors seem to be grounded on contrary ideals such as elitism, other-directedness, and cooperation. In this chapter, I attempt to explain how the youngsters balance the contradictory ideals in everyday operation and how the duality of adolescent ideals guides Greenfield teenage behaviors.

Egalitarianism and Elitism

The adolescent ethos of 'getting along with everyone' reflects the ideal of egalitarianism, in the sense that adolescents believe in equal treatment of their peers, regardless of their socio-economic background, age, and gender. Many of the Greenfield teenagers subscribed to this egalitarian value and tried to live it in their lives. This ideal was advocated not only by adolescents themselves, but also by the school staff and some community members. At the same time, adolescent behavior frequently displayed quite the opposite. For example, these young people were selective in choosing their close friends and sometimes explicitly refused to associate with peers of different circles. The conflicting ideals of egalitarianism and elitism seemed to operate without much conflict in individuals' everyday lives.

Egalitarianism

Many Greenfielders verbalized the importance of showing general friendliness to their peers, without consideration of their status in school. They also tried on some, though not all, occasions to put the ideal into practice. Many adolescents observed that they did not cling to one particular clique or judge their peers on the basis of social labels. The egalitarians often dismissed the social labels — 'popular' and 'unpopular' people, or 'low, middle, and high' class people — which some of their peers used to classify students in Greenfield. The eqalitarians claimed that these labels were 'just concepts'; people could not use them to pigeonhole individuals. They also argued that the labels did not accurately represent the quality of the people in the category. Popularity and unpopularity were seen as relative concepts; popular people might be liked by their own circles of friends but not by other groups. Likewise, those who appeared to be unpopular might be well accepted within their own group of friends. These adolescents, who recognized the relativity of socio-economic status, made a conscious effort to transcend an unequal system by trying to interact with peers from different social classifications.

Marcie, a senior who did not smoke and was academically successful, indicated that she had friends from the Smokers' Shed and special education classes. She discovered that these friends tended to be more honest and more personable than so-called 'popular' people. Jane, who was academically and athletically successful went steady with a boy who 'hung out' with smokers and others who were not interested in school activities. He failed to graduate with his classmates, due to his substandard grades, but their courtship continued after graduation. These girls obviously did not feel restrained by the adolescent social stratification.

Many adolescents reported that age did not pose problems in how they related to their peers. It was not uncommon to see that students from different classes became good friends. Nick, a junior who seemed always to be seen with his sophomore friend, said that they shared many social activities in and outside school. For three years, Julie, a senior, had cherished a best friend, a girl one year her junior, in spite of the difference in age and class schedules. In her senior year, when she had classes only until fifth period, she waited every day for two more periods to give her friend a ride home. Those students who had older or younger siblings at school tended to establish more cross-class friendships. Most extracurricular activities also enhanced chances for teenagers to interact with peers of different ages. I frequently observed that students from different classes intermingled formally and informally. In most cases, adolescents neither discriminated against their peers because of age difference, nor excluded them from friendship.

Many adolescents said that they believed in gender equality. They rejected the idea of treating their peers, or being treated, according to stereotyped sex roles. Both boys and girls participated in activities with close circles of friends that often included both genders. At school dances, they did not seem to mind dancing in a mixed group of males and females or with same-sex friends. Two boys came together to the Prom; girls came with their female friends. In the view of these adolescents, going to a dance with same-sex friends was an acceptable option and just as much fun as cross-sex dates. In dating, adolescents did not necessarily restrict themselves to the traditional social norms, that boys invite girls and pay for all expenses. Several girls who invited their dates to Homecoming or Prom dances told me that either they paid for everything or the couple split the cost.

The young people seemed to take it for granted that boys took home economics classes, traditionally known as 'girls' classes', and that girls participated in a wood workshop that used to be open only to boys. Girls were voted into office as President of the Student Body, of different classes, and of clubs. The principal argued that girls were no longer disadvantaged in elections for Student Body President, which 'might have been the case ten years ago'.

Athletic ability of girls was respected by Greenfielders. All, but a few, sports were available to both genders in single-sex teams, for example, boys' and girls' basketball teams. Many of the female students were involved in sports, and successful ones gained popularity. Athletic girls were often chosen as princesses or queens in Prom and Homecoming Courts.

Some students also argued that female students should be able to participate in the wrestling team as were male students. This egalitarian idea was not supported by the administration. Two junior girls challenged the district policy that prohibited girls from participating in wrestling. They appealed to the school board after their request was denied by school administrators. Even after the final appeal was denied by the school board, several girls expressed unhappiness with the 'discriminatory' decision. A lively discussion between an administrator (A) and a few girls (G) took place in a class:

A: The school district promotes equal opportunities for girls and boys but does not approve co-ed teams for wrestling and football.

G: Why can't girls play with boys?

A: Because of the mixture of body contacts.... It is embarrassing to look at [a girl wrestler pinning a boy down].

G: If there's a team for guys, why not one for girls?
A: There is no place to compete. There are no state wrestling teams for girls in other schools.
G: [repeatedly] Discrimination!

Elitism

While many adolescents advocated the ideal of egalitarianism, some of their verbal and physical behaviors reflected elitism both explicitly and implicitly. Many students were aware of the existence of non-egalitarian social labels: popular/unpopular and high/middle/low class. An individual's social status was often determined on the basis on clique affiliation, types and degrees of involvement in activities, appearance, and academic performance. The students agreed that popular cliques included well-known groups such as athletes, 'brains' (good academic achievers), 'pretty faces' (nice-looking and well-dressed females), and 'good bodies' (muscular males), who tended to be classified as 'high' class. Those classified as 'unpopular' included 'smokers' (cigarette smokers, tobacco chewers, and drug users), 'scums' (untidy people), and special education students, who were regarded as 'low' class people. 'Middle' class referred to non-classifiable ones who were considered neither high nor low class. Adolescents' social classes did not necessarily reflect their families' socio-economic statuses. Thus, those from working class families could achieve higher classification with self-earned money, involvement, appearance, and academic achievement.

Several adolescents acted out their elite attitude in dealing with a certain group of peers, particularly smokers. They looked down upon the smokers and refused to 'go out to the shed even to talk with them'. They thought that association with them would affect their social reputation (see Chapter 7). They strongly argued that smokers ruined the school image and the Smokers' Shed should be eradicated. The smokers were not always passive victims. They formed their own social circle and developed a sense of unity against others. They acknowledged other people's low opinion of them. Some of them expressed their resentment about 'jocks' unfair treatment' of smokers (see Chapter 7). Several smokers criticized the inequality of the social system and the superficiality of so-called popular people. They manifested an elite attitude as well, proudly separating themselves from those who were indifferent about world peace and social justice and concerned only with personal grades and reputation. This elitism on both sides sometimes overshadowed egalitarianism among Green-fielders.

The age-graded class sometime became a criterion for discrimination in the youth society. Although individual freshmen might not be discriminated against, when dealing with freshman as a group, adolescents were not always egalitarian. Upperclass students (sophomore, juniors and seniors) viewed freshmen as immature, unruly, dependent, and imprudent. Some freshmen complained that they were put down with a remark, 'What do you know? You're just a freshman.' The 'freshman hall', where some lockers were located, was stigmatized as a messy and 'lousy' place (full of immature, low-quality people); upperclass people tried to avoid having their locker assignment in that hall.

On a band field trip, a senior girl publicly expressed her elite view against freshmen. Indicating that freshmen in her bus were too loud, she asked passengers on the other bus, 'Would you like to trade some freshmen in our bus for your upperclass people? We have too many freshmen.' Other upperclass students also demonstrated this attitude toward freshmen. Despite the principal's warnings at the beginning of one school year, several junior and senior boys executed an 'initiation' ritual by putting some freshmen boys into garbage cans.

This negative stereotype sometimes prevented freshmen from being taken seriously and participating in activities with upperclass peers. Some teenagers mentioned that the social isolation of freshmen could be a consequence of their having neither a driver's license nor a car. A senior described the freshmen's limited social life: 'Out of school, they (frosh) don't have a car, so that they can't really "go out" or "cruise".' It meant that freshmen either needed to depend on upperclass peers who had cars or could not get involved in these activities.

In respect to gender, many adolescents behaved as if the difference did not matter in peer interaction, but when their interests seemed directly affected, young people switched their position from egalitarian to elite. A few male students complained that some teachers gave favored treatment (grades, in particular) to female students. I also observed adolescent preferences toward same-sex friends as their best friends. Apparently, gender seemed to matter in forming close friendships. Teenagers who called their cross-gender friends 'best friends' often referred to their romantic relationships, differentiating them from same-gender best friends. It was more common for many adolescents to cluster with a group of same-sex peers in the lunchroom, in classrooms, and for assemblies. Grant and Sleeter

Table 3. *Driving and Ownership of Cars among Seniors in the Class of 1987*

	Male	Female	Total
Respondents	37 (51%)	35 (49%)	72 (100%)
Acquisition of Driver's License	32 (56%)	25 (44%)	57 (100%)
Ownership of Car	27 (60%)	18 (40%)	45 (100%)
Regular Driving to School	24 (62%)	15 (38%)	39 (100%)

(1986) suggested that they found the same phenomenon of grouping by sex in a junior high school: 'The students segregated by sex in school whenever given the opportunity to decide where to sit or with whom to work' (p. 48).

Despite their efforts to transcend the traditional sex roles, many adolescents' way of thinking was still influenced by the traditional sex stereotypes: the pretty, slender, blonde, well-dressed 'cheerleader' type for popular girls; the handsome, muscular, athletic, 'real stud' image for popular boys. Many adolescents judged their cross-sex peers on the basis of these criteria. The female sex symbols were exhibited to a certain extent in the Homecoming and Prom Courts, both regarded as 'beauty contests' for females. Girls' League (an organization that included all female students as members and held social functions mainly for them) symbolized patronage for females, whereas no equivalent organization existed for male students.

Both male and female students seemed to take for granted the socially established male 'superiority' in employment and mobility patterns. Males were generally employed for better paying and more physical jobs than females (see Chapter 8). According to the results of the senior survey, 12 per cent more boys had a driver's license than girls; 20 per cent more boys had a car of their own; and 24 per cent more boys drove a car to school. To the extent that the privilege of driving and the amount of spending money symbolized power as in mobility and independence, male adolescents were able to demonstrate more power than their female counterparts. Many male adolescents drove their girlfriends home or to activities and paid expenses for both, which made the girls dependent on their boyfriends. Some girls seemed to favor boyfriends' dominance represented by an automobile and a 'thick' wallet. Parents' double standards also perpetuated male elitism. They often imposed a 'curfew' on their daughters, but rarely on their sons, and they generally regulated girls' social life outside home more than boys. This unequal treatment differentiated between boys and girls in terms of the independence that adolescents coveted.

Inner-Directedness and Other-Directedness

The adolescent ethos of 'being independent' was reflected in the ideal of inner-directedness. The 'inner-directed' character belongs to people 'who listen to their own "inner voice" for guidance' (Riesman, in Bock 1980:122). Those with an inner-directed character resist dependence upon external authority. The concept of adolescents' independence implied that they preferred taking charge of their own lives, becoming independent of adult authority figures, and relying on their own judgments. Adolescents, however, did not always listen to the 'inner voice' of self. They seemed to follow 'others' voices' (conforming to group norms) in certain circumstances. According to Riesman, an other-directed character can be found in people 'whose tastes and decisions are determined by what they think others value' (Bock, p. 122). What others valued was often established by a group consensus or by a limited group of authorities.

Inner-Directedness

Adolescent self-reliance was emphasized by parents and the school staff. Teenagers were advised to stand firmly by their individual consciences instead of being swayed by peer pressure, especially in 'at-risk' areas. A few parents in the Green Lake community had been 'fighting' against teenage 'problems' like drug and alcohol abuse and teen pregnancy. They focused on the issues of self-assurance, independence, and self-esteem. They thought that the act of listening to their 'inner voice' would help teenagers make 'right choices' when they faced challenges.

Greenfield adolescents advocated the ideal of inner-directedness in their own way. Many of them expressed an interest in gaining independence from adult authorities. They believed that individual freedom would come when they could make decisions on their own. When individual freedom seemed to be restricted, they felt resentful and argued with adults. Deanna, a freshman, told me that she became bitter toward her mother and her mother's live-in boyfriend because she was frequently 'grounded'. She said she was constantly told 'what to do and what not to do' around the house. When she violated the rules they imposed, she could not go out after school or use the telephone, and her household chores might be doubled. She acted on what seemed to be her only option — moving out of the house — to regain her individual freedom. When she left, she felt proud because she made decisions on the basis of what she believed to be right for her, not on what others had decided.

Some adolescents expressed inner-directedness by resisting group norms of acceptable dress, hairdos, or mannerisms. Lauri dressed all in black and had dyed her hair black. She said, 'I'm different. I don't want to be a conformist.... I try to change the attitude here, to think it's OK to be different.' To her, being an individual was equivalent to doing things that most of her peers did not typically do. Ginny, a junior who held a student leadership position, pierced her nose and wore a diamond in it, which shocked not only many school staff, but her peers as well. Craig had his long hair dyed black and wore a cowboy scarf on his head; he also dressed in a 'sloppy' baggy shirt, a pair of pants, and a pair of high-topped checked shoes. For Lauri, Ginny, and Craig, their non-conforming appearances and behaviors were a form of self-expression and considered as an indication of listening to 'inner voices'. Some of their peers approved of their individuality, saying that they liked their 'different' and 'unique' appearance and behavior.

At the Junior/Senior Prom, I also observed instances of adolescent inner-directedness. Almost all the boys were dressed in tuxedos; girls wore formal floor-length or knee-length dresses, color-coordinated pumps, and corsages. Within the first hour, several boys took off their jackets, hung loosened bow ties around their necks, and loosened their cummerbunds. Two boys changed from long trousers into shorts worn with the formal jackets. Many girls danced in bare feet and took off corsages. Some adults wondered why the young people paid so much money to rent tuxedos and to color-coordinate their clothing and yet did not take full advantage of it. Adolescents rationalized their acts, saying that the formals were uncomfortable and the hall became too warm. Obviously, they were more interested in comfort and con-venience than in the acceptable norm of why and how to wear the formal attire. This attitude did not raise the eyebrows of their peers. Rather, such behavior was accepted by adolescents as an expression of individuality; a certain degree of inner-directedness was also respected as a sign of self-confidence.

Other-Directedness

In general, adolescents preferred more inner-directedness when they related to adults. Interacting with their peers, however, they followed group norms and sought approval from peers. This other-directedness subjected many adolescents to peer pressure, whether or not they wanted to acknowledge it.

Peer pressure sometimes strengthened a collective sense of unity, as when zealous students and a few student leaders often used pressure to enhance school spirit (pride in the school). They asked their peers to wear school colors on game days. Cheerleaders actively coaxed their peers to cheer for teams during athletic events. Adolescents thought that individuals' degree of school spirit could also be measured by their active participation in school activities. During Homecoming week, referred to as 'Spirit Week', students were encouraged to dress up for each day's theme to 'show their school spirit'. It was not mandatory to wear costumes, but students who did not appear to join the Homecoming mood were subtly pressed with the question, 'Where is your spirit?'

Peer pressure encouraged complaints about institutions, in general, the school lunch program and school dance music, in particular. Bock argued that this sort of complaining is typically American: 'Since respect and awe are highly painful emotions for most Americans, debunking leaders and institutions is a favorite pastime' (1980:120). I suggest that adolescents' frequent criticisms about school lunch and dance music are a reflection of actual dislikes, and, as well, an expression of other-directedness. I observed a few times that they did not really mean to express their dislike; rather, they could not voice their 'real' opinions against 'what they think others value'.

One day, I sat with three freshmen in the lunchroom. Pam selected a taco salad, Angela a hamburger and french fries, and Karen a piece of cake. The following conversation took place at the lunch table:

Angela:	(to Pam) How can you eat the taco salad?
Pam:	No choice. It's yucky.
Karen:	I hate school lunch.
Angela:	What's tomorrow's lunch?
Pam:	Spaghetti.
Angela:	Spaghetti is basically ketchup with water, lots of water.
Pam:	I guess I have to pack a lunch tomorrow.

Pam did not actually mean that her taco salad was 'yucky'; it was a large salad and she ate all. She did not pack her own lunch the next day, but bought spaghetti at the school cafeteria. In the situation in which her friends Angela and Karen put down the food, Pam could not say that she liked it; it was considered 'stupid' to say anything favorable about school lunches.

I heard many teenagers whine about the quality of the food: 'This pizza is like a dirty carpet', and 'This hamburger tastes like plastic'. Ironically, pizza and hamburger were the top selling items, and many adolescents who did not usually eat school lunch bought pizza on days it was served. Finishing food on a tray was not common, hence much food was wasted. They did not *have* to take what they did not want. Yet, many adolescents did not even finish what they chose and threw away what was unfinished. Complaining and throwing away the school lunch seemed to be a pattern created and nurtured by peer pressure.

In similar fashion, I heard many teenagers complain about music at school dances. When I asked students why they were not dancing, they often responded that the music was not good. Some students who were leaving early gave the same answer. As I often observed, however, the real answer had little to do with the quality of music. They did not dance because their friends did not dance. Adolescents who left early did so because their clique of friends left early. In both situations adolescents did not seem to recognize that their behavior was influenced by peer pressure. I suspected that perhaps they did not want to acknowledge their other-directedness because it would hurt their pride in being independent. By criticizing others, they might have felt they were making judgments on their own.

Other-directedness was also manifested in adolescent concerns about appearance. Many Greenfielders conformed to the collective standards of acceptable fashion among adolescents. Greenfielders' fashion styles seemed to depend on regional trends rather than the high fashion of leading magazines. Those who exceeded local norms in favor of high fashion were criticized for being too radical. By contrast, those whose attire was substandard received comments like, 'She looks stupid' or 'He looks like a scum'. Since the young people were aware of the acceptable norms for appearance, they tried to adhere to the norms. As noted in Chapter 2, Marylinn wore make-up because of her peers' views about her 'looks'.

In a choir class, some girls expressed their common opinion about the proper way of dressing. When other high school choir members suggested in a choir competition that Greenfielders would have looked 'tidier' if they had tucked their blouses into their skirts on the stage, they refuted the suggestion by saying, 'It's stupid to tuck in a shirt'. Actually, most girls and boys in Greenfield did not tuck their shirts into skirts or pants. In order to conform to group norms, many adolescents spent a considerable amount of money to buy the 'right' kind of clothes, hairdos, jewelry, car accessories, and music.

Peer pressure also urged adolescents into a certain pattern of social life. When a circle of friends drank alcohol at a party, everyone was expected to drink or at least to pretend to do so. Anyone who spoke out against drinking by minors was likely to be ostracized. Karen was no longer invited to her friends' private parties where drinking alcohol usually took place; her friends knew of her disapproval of drinking.

Competition and Cooperation

The ethos of 'getting involved' often was associated with competition among adolescents. Some activities were, by nature, competitive; limited opportunities to participate also forced adolescents into a competitive mood. In areas such as sports, elections, grades, and contests, competition was encouraged. In friendship and courtship, competition, although discouraged, nonetheless took place. While they were competing as a group, adolescents also cooperated with each other within the group. Adolescents adopted the contrary ideals of competition and cooperation in dealing with their human relationships, depending upon situations.

'A Jungle of Competition'

Many adolescents perceived that competition was far more pervasive in their world than cooperation. A junior girl described her world in this way:

> Our school is a 'jungle of competition'. There are people who compete in sports like football, volleyball, basketball, track, etc. Those people compete for what team they're going to be on, freshman, JV, or Varsity. Those people also compete who's going to be the best on the team. Then there's competing about who gets better grades than so–and–so. There's also competing in who gets the guy or girl to ask them out first and that usually means fighting between friends.

She was describing two types of competition. One type, legitimately accepted and explicitly encouraged by peers and adults, included both individual and group competition, such as interscholastic athletic games, intramural group contests, elections, grades, and award nominations. The other type generally involved competition between friends and was considered undesirable.

In sport events, Greenfielders competed with other schools for better records, with teammates for playing time or more favorable positions, and with themselves for better personal performance. In these cases, it was perfectly acceptable to show explicit concern about scores and records. Coaches, peers, community members, and media paid close attention to the results. A sense of rivalry with other schools was not only accepted but encouraged. The stronger they expressed 'hatred' toward their rivals, the more school spirit they were said to have. In addition to sports, many clubs and organizations participated in off-campus competitions. The rally squad usually entered up to five competitions, and the dance team competed a few times each school year. Members of the Future Business Leaders of America competed in various categories of business skills at a community college annual competition. Vocational classes such as auto-mechanics, metal-working, wood-working, and home economics participated in annual skill competitions in respective areas. Some faculty advisors said that the purpose of these frequent competitions was to motivate adolescents to perform their best in these areas. When students finished the competitions with good records, the participants as well as the student body said they felt proud of their school.

Group competition was incorporated into school activities in both organized and spontaneous formats. For instance, during Homecoming Spirit Week, classes competed with each other to demonstrate their class spirit and, in turn, school spirit. Members of each class encouraged classmates to dress up for each day's theme; competed with other classes in the Spirit Olympics (a tug-of-war, a pie eating contest, an apple passing contest); and designed a class float. The spirit of competition was also stimulated in classrooms. Mr. Lewis divided his class into five groups and gave each group a worksheet every day; students solved the problems on the sheet together. The group that accumulated the most points for a week was treated to pizza by the teacher. This type of group competition for a prize was widely utilized in school to improve performance. When a parent-teacher conference was approaching, the school administrators announced that the homeroom that brought the most parents to the conferences would win pizzas. In another example, the media center staff held a Christmas tree decoration contest among student aides before the Christmas break. The aides from each period (two to three people) decorated a cardboard tree, and the best entry won ice cream sundaes as a prize.

Junior Class Float made and paraded on the day of the Homecoming Game.

Pie-Eating Contest during the class (9th–12th) olympics in the Homecoming Spirit Week.

In addition to group competition, involvement led to competition among individuals as well as among groups. Many students participated in competitions for awards and leadership positions. Since these forms of public recognition were considered as manifestation of their hard work and competitive characters, many students were self-motivated to prove their capabilities and often encouraged to do so by adults. Their successes were often mentioned in the school and local newspapers. While competition worked as an impetus for activeness, some adolescents said that they lost sleep over competitions. Maria fretted in her journal entries about waiting to learn of the recipient of a service/leadership award. Her family asked her every day if the decision had been made, thus reminding her constantly of their high anticipation. She also regarded herself as better qualified for the award than the other nominee, who happened to be her good friend. Her competitive zeal went unrewarded, however, for the decision was made in favor of her 'opponent'. Karrie also seriously hoped to be nominated for a major scholarship for her college education. Her well-to-do parents advised her to try her best to get scholarship money before they would help her financially. The school staff instead nominated Kim, a senior girl who lived alone and needed any kind of financial assistance for her college education. Karrie bitterly remarked that they nominated Kim 'just because she is Student Body President'.

The election of student leaders is another example of organized individual competition. In May, Greenfielders elected student officers of the Associated Student Body and of each class. The election process began with the nomination of students for each position by the student government or by a certain number of signatures from students. The nominees then gathered helpers from among their friends to contact voters and post campaign signs. Most posters presented their candidates straightforwardly; some, however, became overzealous in putting down their competitors. For example, a poster described a high-fashioned opponent belittlingly as a queen bee: 'If you want a worker instead of a queen bee, cast your ballot and vote for Kim, ASB President.'

In addition to the elections, choir audition and tryouts for the rally squad and dance team also posed fierce competition among Greenfielders, because these activities held high status and opportunities were limited. The rally tryout for the coming school year took place on a May day after school. Seven returning cheerleaders and eleven new auditioners tried out together for a new squad of eight members. To prepare for the tryout, the advisor strongly suggested that old members form groups[1] to practice with the newcomers. The old members protested, however, worried that newcomers' unrefined skill levels would hamper their performance in front of outside judges. To protect their positions in the squad, most of them stuck together with their old pals. In the tryout, all seven former members were chosen, along with one new member.

While all the group and individual competitions mentioned above were explicitly encouraged by the staff and adolescents themselves, some forms of competition, although discouraged, were nonetheless subtly manifested in adolescent everyday life. A subtle competition jealously occurred between friends, even good friends. The competition was usually over friendship and courtship. Competing for same-sex or cross-sex friends was common among adolescents. The sense of competition often arose when a new member was introduced into established relationships.

The following cases deal with changing dynamics caused by competition within a group of friends. As described in Chapter 2, Marylinn had a circle of close friends. When she introduced Brandt, her boyfriend, to this group, he fit in comfortably. Soon Linda, her good friend, became interested in Brandt and competed for him. When Marylinn broke up with Brandt within a month, she found herself in the position of competing with him to win her original friends back.

Another case is Peter, who liked Yvonne for a year, although she did not respond to his interest. She began going out with Jim, Peter's best friend, which upset Peter a great deal. Peter sometimes was included in the couple's activities but felt that he was 'tagging along' with them. Whenever problems arose between them, Jim came to Peter for advice. When their courtship broke up, Yvonne and her female friends, who were aware of Peter's feelings, suspected that he 'spoke ill of' her out of jealousy and was partly responsible for the breakup.

A third case is Ruth, who was initially scheduled to sing a solo with the choir in an interscholastic competition, but was replaced by her friend shortly before the competition due to a 'lost' voice. Her substitute performed well and was assigned the role for future occasions. Ruth used to sing with Sarah in a trio; this change, however, turned the cooperative mood between them into a competitive one. She did not overtly express her resentment about being replaced by Sarah, but found herself dissociating from her. All three felt that they had become involved in competition with their friends. Aware also that the overt expression of jealousy toward friends was not condoned, they kept it to themselves.

An 'Ocean of Cooperation'

Even though competition was evident in many aspects of adolescent lives, many young people believed that cooperation should be more strongly emphasized. The following journal entry shows yearning for cooperation, but pessimism as to its attainment:

> A jungle of competition seems to fit our world the best.... I think that the world should be an 'ocean of cooperation' but it's not. I don't think that it ever will be, either.

Despite many teenagers' complaints of extreme competitiveness, cooperation also took place in their everyday lives. Ironically, cooperation often resulted from competition, particularly between groups. In the case of competition between groups, cooperation refers to unifying efforts within a group. Most competition between the groups mentioned above prompted cooperation among group members. When adolescents competed against other schools, groups, or classes, they worked together with their teammates and built camaraderie.

The cheerleaders agreed that competition often nourished congenial relationships among themselves. They, as well as their advisor, admitted that the members usually argued a lot over cheer routines when they choreographed by themselves. At every practice someone disagreed with another's suggestions because, as some said, 'Everyone thinks she is the best and knows the most.' However, when I visited them at a summer camp where fifty or more high school cheerleading teams were attending, they reported that they were having the 'best-ever' relationship with each other. They had to make up routines and perform them every day and were evaluated on that basis. They therefore became cooperative in creating, implementing, and analyzing new ideas. The conduct as well as performance of each team was constantly watched and scored. This competition appeared to put pressure on them but also forced them to cooperate.

Some adolescents cooperated with peers when they shared responsibility for a common project, such as the school newspaper or a yearbook. Members of journalism and yearbook classes often needed a division of labor to cover multiple tasks efficiently. Sometimes these tasks could be done concurrently. For instance, Greenfield photographers developed pictures in the school darkroom. When they worked together, coordinating efficiently among themselves was extremely important, because one's developing paper could be easily damaged by even dim light from another's enlargers. When they moved to chemical trays, they often had to wait patiently until the person ahead of them had finished. At other times, one task could not be undertaken properly until others were completed. If a photographer did not cover an athletic event, a reporter's effort to write an article on the game was most likely to be in vain. Or, until pages were properly laid out in the journalism class, they could not be sent to a printer. In these situations, students became aware of the importance of cooperation in completing their individual tasks and in meeting deadlines for the group's sake.

Peer cooperation was also observed when seat work or homework was assigned. Some seat work required collaborative efforts, a group presentation of the daily news in Political Process class, writing a paper as a group in an English class, and a 'trivial pursuit' contest between groups in Resource Room classes. Adolescents also helped each other with individual projects. When given problems to solve in a math class, students immediately formed groups and worked together. This natural grouping for seat work was common during classes. Sometimes it created not only a working-together mood but bordered on what might have been termed 'cheating'; since some students used it to copy the entire project from their teammates with minimal input of their own. In other cases, adolescents volunteered to help with friends' projects, although the final results would be compared with their own. For example, Brian and Rick were eager to help classmates with a biology project. The project was to find a dead animal, remove its tissue by natural decomposition or boiling, retrieve the bones, and reassemble them. Brian and Rick picked up a few dead animals along highways for their classmates and helped them with the most 'yucky' process of removing tissue.

Pragmatic Negotiators within the Duality of Ideals

The Greenfield adolescent ethos of 'getting along with everyone', 'being independent', and 'getting involved' reflects in microcosm the American ideals of egalitarianism, inner-directedness, and competition. Yet, the young people's daily behaviors manifested not only these ideals, but also seemingly contradictory ones, such as elitism, other-directedness, and cooperation. The six ideals can be paired up into three sets in terms of their conceptual contradiction, yet practical coexistence: egalitarianism/elitism, inner-directedness/other-directedness, and competition/cooperation. Conceptual properties of two elements in each set were mutually exclusive. However, each set of contradictory ideals functions as a continuum as the ideals interplayed in individuals' daily behaviors. Instead of being consistently guided by either ideal, adolescents positioned themselves somewhere in the middle of this conceptual continuum.

One reason for the intertwined ideals in the adolescent life is that a consistent adherence to one pole of each continuum was not easy, and was probably impossible. More importantly, however, over-conformity to either pole was not favored in their daily interactions with other peers. Social sanctions — criticism, rumors, peer pressure, negative labels, and social exclusions — functioned as counter-forces that discouraged adolescents from conforming 'too much' to either side of dual ideals. This is where discrepancy between ideal and reality comes into play. Most adolescents neither observed these ideals in the extreme nor advocated their practice in every situation.

Adolescents who behaved like 'pure' egalitarians were criticized for being idealists. This label could cost them privileges in their social lives. The adolescents who transcended the age barrier for friendship ran the risk of being severed from interactions with their own classmates. Elitist interactions restricted to one's own classmates could become critically important at various times, in particular during class functions. Those who acted out their ideal of gender egalitarianism also experienced their share of frustration. In a teenage society where courtship was glorified, the image of being 'liberated' deprived some teenagers of the pleasure of being treated like males or females. They complained that their peers were not interested in them as potential boy/girlfriends.

In addition, when teenagers tried to be equally friendly to people of different socio-economic backgrounds, their friendliness was suspected of being 'fake'. Also, people who denounced discrimination against the 'low' class people and criticized elitists were accused of acting self-righteous. Extreme elitism was also criticized. When upper-class people mistreated underclass students, the older ones were accused of being unfair and arrogant. People who adopted traditional sex roles were called sexists. Boys and girls, alike, who discriminated against peers on the basis of their social status were criticized for being 'stuck-up'.

Criticism was also leveled for being too inner-directed or too other-directed. Those who dressed or acted too differently from others were regarded as strange and weird. They were likely to be avoided by peers. Lauri, who dressed like a 'punk' complained, 'Teachers ignore me because I'm different.' A sophomore boy also experienced subtle rejection from his peers due to his expression of individuality:

> [People think] because my hair is long, I am into drugs. I am strongly against drugs. I am still a great basketball player. A lot of people also think I gave that [basketball] up just because I have long hair.

In both cases, too much inner-directedness invited unwelcome treatment from peers and the staff. This social and emotional alienation often functioned as powerful sanction against the extreme individualistic behaviors. As much as the noticeable deviation from the group norm was discouraged, extreme other-directedness — blind obedience to group norms — was also disapproved. For instance, people who seemed to follow group norms all the time were criticized for being too conforming or were called 'air-heads' (referring to those who lack intelligence and individual opinions).

Regarding competition and cooperation, adolescents responded negatively to those who showed too much of either. On the one hand, teenagers who became very competitive toward their peers were criticized for being self-centered and hard-headed. Those who were too self-conscious about their performances in school activities also gave an impression of being tense, not-fun-to-be-around, or selfish. They tended to have poor reputations and were most likely to be shunned by their peers. On the other hand, adolescents who seemed too cooperative were discouraged by negative labels such as 'brown-noser', 'goody-goody', or 'wishy-washy'. In this case, co-operative behaviors referred to subservient as well as compromising behaviors. Teenagers who appeared to agree with adults readily or be open to various opinions could be subject to these unfavorable reputations.

Young people realized that an unswerving and exaggerated adherence to these ideals would hurt their social life. In adolescent society in which individuals' social acceptance among their peers was crucial to leading an enjoyable life, most would not risk jeopardizing their social lives by violating social rules. Consequently, most Greenfielders consistently tried to avoid observing one ideal over the other.

How do the young people resolve the internal paradox between the ideals when they follow them? Instead of adhering to either pole, they seemed to shift their positions between them. In the continua of contradictory ideals, many Greenfielders steered a moderate course, leaning toward one pole in some situations and toward the opposite in other situations. Those who were able to pick appropriate ideals for situations and to behave accordingly were considered successful. In any situation, however, they avoided going too far to one end and tried to stay in the mid-range as much as possible. I would call the surviving 'actors' in the adolescent society successful negotiators among contrasting and contradictory ideals. Those who followed a middle route with flexibility were more likely to evade criticism from peers and to be regarded as potentially 'successful'. This pragmatic ability to compromise was viewed as an indicator of their social adequacy. Most 'average' adolescents preferred an opportunistic adjustment to individual situations, rather than a more consistent commitment to certain ideals. These adolescent social dynamics seemed to produce a 'middle-of-the-road' mentality and to discourage young people from consistently adhering to particular ideals. Only a few of them appeared to commit themselves to being 'idealists', a role which was not favored among adolescents.

Note

1 Contestants tried out in groups of two to four people, which enabled them to build a pyramid. Points were given on the basis of individual performance rather than group performance.

Part 4

Reflections on Ethnographic Experiences

Chapter 11

Reflections on Ethnographic Experiences

The process of doing ethnography does not limit ethnographers to the scholarly tasks of describing and interpreting cultural data. Until recently, ethnographers' field experiences tended to be reserved for dinner table conversation. Since Malinowski's field diary was published in 1967, more anthropologists have been liberated to discuss publicly their actual field experiences, both pleasant and abhorrent, in writing. In most cases, though, their 'confessions' have been kept separate from ethnographic texts that have been devoted chiefly to cultural descriptions. Under the umbrella of interpretive anthropology, some anthropologists have bravely experimented with incorporating the personal dimension of field experiences into ethnography (see Crapanzano, 1980). This confessional mode of ethnography swings ethnographers from a positivistic, 'objective' orientation to the humanistic, subjective one.

Taking a moderate stand between these two orientations, George Spindler, editor of *Being an Anthropologist* (1986), collected essays of field experiences from eleven authors who had already published case studies in the series, Case Studies in Cultural Anthropology. He carefully warned readers that 'fieldwork is not all feeling, self-criticism, and identity search' (p. v). Fieldwork needs a balance between the 'significant aspects of field research methods' and the 'personal dimension' of fieldwork. The former, referred to as the 'procedural' aspect, pertains to 'what one did to obtain what kinds of data'. The latter, the personal aspect, is concerned with 'the struggle to survive as a person with a personal identity forged in another culture, one's own, while trying to grasp the outlines and meanings of someone else's' (p. v). Spindler criticizes contemporary humanistic anthropologists for overemphasizing the personal dimension of fieldwork in 'violent swings of mood and mentality' (p. iv).

By its nature, anthropological fieldwork does not allow ethnographers to remain as objective observers and mechanical researchers. Fieldwork is a 'lived' experience in which ethnographers subjectively encounter other human beings — often unfamiliar ones — who put forth their own subjectivity. Intersubjectivity between self (researcher) and others (natives) in the field provokes an inquiry of self as well as others; the dynamics between self and others are also subject to examination. The period of writing an ethnography forces ethnographers to relive their field experiences as they review recorded data and unrecorded memory. During the process of doing ethnography, ethnographers reflect on, examine, and critique their own field experiences in both personal and methodological aspects. This 'experiential, reflective, and critical activity' is considered as 'the very strength of anthropology' (Rabinow, 1977:5) that separates this discipline from 'objective' and positivistic social science orientations.

This chapter is devoted to a discussion of personal experiences in a confessional mode. Vignettes illustrate my reflection on field experiences in terms of examination of self, dynamics between myself and natives, 'the inequality of languages',[1] and after-effects of the fieldwork.

Examination of Self

Identity Search

I began my fieldwork as a loner in the midst of an unfamiliar crowd. I often had to make very specific decisions about associating with certain adolescents. My ambiguous identity was both a blessing and a curse. Accepting this ambiguity as a blessing, I tried to build friendships with different groups of students. One of the first students who approached me attempted to strike up a friendship. She initiated various activities by inviting me to her house, suggesting we go out for lunch or go shopping in town, asking for rides, and showing off her horse, which was kept in her aunt's barn. After we had taken part in several activities together, she told me I was her 'best friend'. Initially I appreciated her acceptance, but I soon began feeling burdened. I did not want to commit myself to such an intense friendship with one student for two reasons: I planned to get to know a wide range of students, and I was afraid that she would become too dependent on our friendship and be deprived of contacts with her peers.

While making contact with a variety of students, I was conscious of my public image, because this image would influence my further association with certain students. After learning about the stigma about smokers, for example, I tried to avoid identification with them as a group, although I did get to know them as individuals. I stayed away from the smokers' shed for the first term.

My effort to associate with a wide range of students was partially rewarded with a reputation as a friendly person. However, I sometimes found myself in awkward situations, where some of my friends saw me interacting with others with whom they did not socialize. Some students ignored me in that situation, and others tried to take me away. Such complications cost me the friendship of several students.

My ambiguous identity was also a curse, for it was difficult for me to penetrate already established circles of friends and develop close relationships. The following incident illustrates my emotional limbo. One day when school was 'blacked out' due to a temporary power failure, students came out from classes and congregated in their own groups in the hall waiting for the administrators' decision on the possibility of early dismissal. I tried to join these groups for conversation but felt like an intruder. My journal of that day recorded my feelings as follows: 'For the first time, I felt lonely. I felt I needed my group. Everyone belonged somewhere, but not me.' Recognition of my concern about a sense of security and belongingness partially answered the question — 'Who am I?' — that had persistently followed me during the two years of doing ethnography. For me, this was not so much an existential question as a relational question; I was seeking my social identity in relation to others.

I also search for an identity by transposing myself as an imaginary Greenfielder. Had I been a high school student in Greenfield in 1987, whom would I be like? With whom would I hang out the most? Would I be perceived as a nerd, a socialite, an active future citizen, or a jock? To my surprise, these questions elicited multiple similarities between myself in high school days and the Greenfielders. Crapanzano suggested that this similar-seeking endeavor is a part of fieldwork:

> The ethnographer's entry into the field is always a separation from his world of primary reference — the world through which he obtains, and maintains, his sense of self and his sense of reality. He is suddenly confronted with the possibility of Otherness, and his immediate response to this Otherness is to seek both the security of the similar and the distance and objectivity of the dissimilar. [1980:137]

My longing for security was reconciled by finding key informants. Among a few key informants, I found Marylinn extremely helpful and personable. Fortunately, she was also well-informed, articulate, part of the 'in-crowd', and considerate. Above all, we felt comfortable with each other; we shared similar values, personality, and concerns. This mutual comfortableness facilitated our working relationship and strengthened our personal friendship. I am still amazed at the fact that I could see myself in my informant. I learned about myself through her: for example, how other-directed I was, and how much my mental well-being relied on social acceptance. This process clearly illustrates the hermeneutic wisdom of 'the comprehension of self by the detour of the comprehension of the other' (P. Ricoeur quoted in Rabinow, 1977:5).

'Spoiler Role'

During the ethnographic process, I noticed myself playing a 'spoiler' role (Beals, Spindler, and Spindler, 1973:359). Wolcott elaborated the role as that of 'contradicting broad generalizations by providing exceptions from the ethnographic record, of the sort: "It's not so in my village"' (1981:4). Anthropological 'spoilers' challenge authority established on the basis of limited facts or persistent myths. I realized my ethnographic data presented many examples counter to stereotypic images of adolescents and to my preconceived notions of ethnographic research methods. My spoiler role was activated when the discrepancy appeared obvious between what I was led to believe by other sources and what I learned firsthand.

My previous understanding of American adolescents has been amended. The stereotypic image of American youngsters has often been reinforced by mass media, focusing on 'at-risk' areas such as drug and alcohol abuse, teen pregnancy, and adverse effects of peer pressure. Greenfielders were not immune to these problems. But I have found that many young people were *not* involved in these 'pathologies' in Bennett's term (1988:10). Even among the 'at-risk' teenagers, I found young people open-minded and personable. In addition, cliques were neither a reproduction of students' socioeconomic classes nor were they fractional. For example, cheerleaders in Greenfield High School were not all from well-to-do families or 'air-heads'. As a matter of fact, most of them were serious students with a 3.5 GPA or higher (above 'B+' average) and they did not usually 'flirt' with football players. Not all Greenfield football players were so masculine and boastful as to intimidate non-jocks. Academically and socially 'in-crowd' students were not always from middle- or high-class families; in fact, many students from working-class families were high achievers at Greenfield.

The field experiences challenged my preconceived notions of doing ethnography. I began fieldwork with an ideal type of ethnographer in mind. Successful ethnographers appeared to

1 stay in a field for a long period of time — often more than one year;
2 chase after numerous activities frantically in the field;
3 keep notes ceaselessly;
4 sustain their excitement about acquiring new knowledge and meeting new people throughout the whole period;
5 be so involved as to dream about the fieldwork.

This image of ethnographer was often invoked in books of anthropological fieldwork. I assumed that this type of super ethnographer had written valuable ethnographies.

My reality, however, did not seem to match these characterizations of the super ethnographer. I did not live in the fieldwork community. Doing participant observation and interviews, I spent an average of eight to ten hours a day in the field for the first few months; as time increased for data organization and writing, my involvement in the field decreased. I sometimes could not keep notes on site because of inappropriateness of note-taking and difficulties of simultaneously participating and recording in some situations. In addition, fatigue often consumed me by the end of the day after several hours of intensely listening, observing, and trying to maintain rapport. I was able to sustain excitement about getting to know new people and learning different aspects of their lives to a certain degree, but sometimes a sporadic emotional withdrawal overshadowed the excitement. Finally, although I did think about my fieldwork while traveling, eating, and even sleeping[2] at times, I also had to accept that fact that I had another life as a non-ethnographer.

Another example of my preconceptions pertained to the image of teenagers as 'welcoming natives'. The endorsement of American scholars, friends, and school administrators for my research idea led me to believe that the teenagers would receive me with open arms because I was new to their culture, from another continent, and interested in learning about them. At the beginning of my fieldwork, some students approached me to inquire into my identity and nationality.

Their initial responsiveness to my presence seemed to prove my expectation to be correct. As my novelty wore off, most Greenfield students became rather indifferent to my presence. I also had an expectation at the beginning that these young people would be eager to talk about themselves and be thrilled to have someone listen to them for many hours with patience. My expectation turned into disappointment; they seemed too busy with their own lives to spare time for me. And even when they did so, visiting with me was not a top priority; it was, rather, doing me a favor.

Through ethnographic fieldwork, I certainly encountered a different reality from what I expected from my readings. Doing ethnography also provided opportunities to enact the anthropological spoiler role and search for self-identity in the unfamiliar crowd. I discovered myself as a human being, as well as a researcher, and I came to intellectualize my personal experiences throughout the process.

Dynamics Between Self and Others

Impression Management

'Impression management' (Berreman, 1962; Goffman, 1959) appeared to be a survival strategy employed by both adolescents and me in the process of building up a relationship. Techniques of impression management included the 'discourse of politeness' (Campbell, 1987:246–248), minimization of dire consequences, and preclusion or withdrawal from possible embarrassment. These attempts are attributed to human inclinations to protect one's self-image and to test the limits of possible relationships with strangers.

First, students constantly demonstrated the discourse of politeness. During the first two months, many students asked questions about me and my country. I assumed that their curiosity grew out of genuine interest and took it as a personal welcome. I had continued exchanging greetings with most of them after our first encounters. After having spent several months in the field, and been introduced as a researcher in the school newspaper, I was amazed at the students' ignorance of who I was. I was also puzzled by the fact that the same adolescents who had greeted me earlier subsequently ignored me at school or in the community. I took it as a personal rejection at first, but later understood when I realized that the initial friendliness of some teenagers was not necessarily an invitation for friendship but was an exercise in the discourse of politeness, and sometimes mere curiosity. Their effort at politeness was also demonstrated when young people changed their 'earthy' language into more formal English in front of me. This switch of language was more noticeable when they were engaged in conversation with me than when I was just a bystander to their conversations with peers.

The second technique of impression management, minimization of dire consequences, is illustrated in the following cases. After the first few weeks at the school, I had a chance to sit with a group of students for lunch in the cafeteria. A freshman girl stated, 'I'll be a cheerleader', actually meaning that she was planning to try out for the following year rally squad. Other girls, juniors, dropped the corners of their lips to show their disapproval of her idea and tried to dissuade her. A boy sitting with them soon started to joke about the appearance of some cheerleaders, 'Bonnie has legs as big as this' (indicating their size with his open hands) and 'Liz has thick lips. She puts on a lot of lipstick.' The junior girls soon looked uncomfortable about my presence, while he continued to ridicule the cheerleaders. They turned to me and asked, 'Do you talk about others in your country, too? We don't gossip all the time.' On another occasion, I asked a boy if there were many categories of students. He identified groups such as smokers, jocks, and nerds and then added, 'I don't belong to any clique. I basically get along with everyone.'

Both examples illustrate the minimization of effect; the former case deals with a group impression and the latter concerns an individual impression. With remarks such as, 'We do not gossip all the time' and 'I basically get along with everyone', the teenagers acknowledged their gossiping and categorizing, but attempted to assure me that the problems were neither serious nor common. These impression-managing remarks purported to minimize the negative effect of some phenomena by presenting counter examples. In this way, teenagers kept the outsider from making a negative generalization about US teenagers and themselves.

A third type of impression management is to avoid possible embarrassment by precluding others from activities or withdrawing oneself. The two following stories show precluding and withdrawing, respectively. In an overnight field trip of ten students (four girls and six boys), a few boys engaged in shenanigans against the girls. While the girls (including me) left their tent unattended one evening, the boys 'raided' it, 'stole' the girls' underwear from individual bags, and hung them up on a camping kitchen stand set in the middle of our camp site. All of our party saw them; needless to say, the 'victims' of the prank were embarrassed, but laughed about it. Fortunately my own belongings were exempted from the raid; later, I learned that the 'gentlemen' had searched my bag but decided to exclude me from the embarrassment.

On some other occasions, I voluntarily withdrew from certain activities in order to maintain my image. One example took place at an all-night party after the graduation ceremony held in a student's house. I attended the party to get a glimpse of an informal adolescent party, but I did not want to get involved fully in their private activities. As time went by, more teenagers got drunk and some of them began 'throwing up'. I had also become conscious of my non-conforming dress (I was still dressed for the graduation ceremony, while students had changed into casual clothes) and behavior (I drank only a few sips of beer). When I finally left the party, I felt relieved, because I did not have to give the impression that I was 'policing' them or, alternatively, that I was approving of their behavior.

Through these three techniques, I found myself testing limits to how close I, as a professional stranger, could enter teenagers' lives and how much of their inside stories the adolescents were willing to reveal to a stranger. Impression management also helped both parties sustain a sense of trust toward each other by establishing guidelines for interaction.

Reciprocity

I returned favors to my informants in various ways: verbal gratitude, material items, monetary rewards, food, rides, and speeches about Korea. Since the students were the major helpers in my study, I tried to reciprocate with them more than with adults. I verbally expressed my thanks to all informants, whether their assistance was intended or not. I also gave some teenagers rides home or to go shopping, treated them to sodas or snacks, bought small gifts for birthdays, and paid a small amount of money to my key informant for regular interviews conducted during the summer. In addition to my intended reciprocity, the teenagers might have felt that they received social and/or intellectual rewards from my attention to them. They asked, 'Why did you choose us living in a small town?', showing their surprise at my interest in them despite their 'remoteness'. They were also given opportunities to observe me, an Asian ethnographer, while being observed, and to satisfy some curiosity about a foreign land while being asked about themselves. When I visited students' families, I sometimes brought baked goods or fixed Korean meals for the families.

For the school staff, I expressed my appreciation by bringing baked items to the faculty lounge. Such a gesture seemed to communicate my appreciation, and evoked increased interest in my research from certain staff who had earlier appeared indifferent to my presence. Another form of reciprocity was in providing information about Korea: I gave presentations about Korean communication styles in classes. I also offered some administrative assistance to counselors, but unfortunately the assistance was not as often as I wished, due to my time constraints.

Returning favors was often spontaneous and sporadic. I could not respond properly to all the favors I received, because it would have been endless. I constantly asked myself if I was unconsciously exploiting the students. My ethic of reciprocity kept me mindful of returning favors directly and in a more recognizable way to my informants, either as material or verbal rewards. My limited resources — time, money, and energy — prevented me from expressing my thanks in more tangible ways. Verbally expressed gratitude, albeit intangible, was more affordable to me. In response to my concern with conscious reciprocity, my colleagues stated, 'Teenagers will be happy to find someone who is willing to listen to them for hours with patience' and 'The adolescents will benefit from this kind of study.' Despite some truth in these statements, I could not stop seeing a potential danger that ethnographers could abuse this to rationalize their exploitative behaviors.

My next question was 'Do I try to reciprocate with adults more than adolescents, because the former hold more powerful positions as gatekeepers?' In the hierarchy of an educational institution, administrators had higher positions than teachers and teachers than students. In home settings, parents tended to have 'final say' over their children. Consequently, if the higher authorities had refused to approve my study, I was aware that the study would not have taken place. Thus, the assistance of adults could not be underemphasized. At the same time, I wondered if it was appropriate to be more concerned about reciprocity with adults than with teenagers because of the power structure. Since my study focused on youth culture, and the young people were my immediate informants, I often felt that they deserved more of my appreciation and reciprocity.

Marginality: Blessing or Barrier?

Although I was generally well received by the young people and gradually slipped into the natural scenes of the youth culture, I was only partially accepted as being their 'kind'. My spotty attendance in their classes affirmed that I was not exactly like them. No teachers asked me to show a hall pass when I was seen out of class during periods. No detention was given to me for absence from classes. They observed that I turned in no homework, took no exams, and received no grades. They found my name under one of faculty mail slots. They also saw me writing notes all the time, even during the Veteran's Day Memorial ceremony. I might have exhibited too many 'deviant' behaviors from those of 'typical' teenagers.

I was, however, differentiated from school staff and other adults. The adolescents sometimes accepted me as a semi-student and semi-adult. On a field trip, teenagers considered me not as a chaperon but as a 'kind of counselor'. My presence did not seem to threaten the adolescents in various settings where adults were not normally present. A senior boy later talked about me in a meeting, 'She was not like an adult who told us what to do. She blended with us. It was nice.' Other times the teenagers did not seem to know how to deal with me in 'liminality' or 'the period of margin' (Turner, 1967:93). Then I was pushed into an in-between status, marginal to both teenagers and adults. For example, on a field trip bus, students left a seat for me between theirs in the back and chaperons' in the front. This example symbolizes boundaries drawn for me in between these groups. On another occasion, my informant, who became a good friend, told me a lot about her birthday but invited only her teenage friends for the party. During the fieldwork, my status often drifted from the semi-student/semi-adult to neither one, depending on situations. I was at the adolescents' mercy.

I played more of an adult role in the community, while I concentrated on associations with adolescents in school. Parents of students, school district staff, and community members expected this of me. The adult role legitimated my attendance at school board meetings and parent meetings. My presumed identity as a 'responsible' adult gave me access to information unavailable to adolescents. The adult image also earned me parental trust: parents who would not allow their daughter to drive with 'irresponsible' peers did not mind her riding with me. Since giving a ride to teenagers gave me time to talk, this trust often was to my advantage.

Adults' acceptance of me sometimes created a role conflict. Especially when I was with both parents and teenagers, my dual roles clashed with each other. Despite my effort to keep my priority on friendship with the teenagers, I was often treated as a friend of their parents. If we rode together in a car, I was given a seat next to the parents or was addressed more frequently by the parents than by the adolescents. Both parties seemed to take my role as an adult for granted. For example, after the graduation ceremony, I was standing with a number of students, listening to them plan what to do next. They decided to go to a boy's house, and I was invited to come along with them. The male student added, 'Oh, Mom is at home. You can talk with her', affirming my role as a partner to adults. I followed his car with my own. As soon as we arrived at his house, he and his mother seemed to expect that I would visit with her in the family room while the others made other plans for the evening in the kitchen. I wished to be with these young people; I felt 'trapped' with an adult. While I was conversing with the boy's mother and his older brother who attended a college, the teenagers left without informing me of their plan. They might have thought that I was in the appropriate place with my kind of people — adults. I was assumed to be a 'responsible' adult who could take care of herself in that unfamiliar household.

'The Inequality of Languages'

Asad proposed that the activity of doing fieldwork in other cultures resembles that of translating a text in a foreign language:

> In the field...the process of translation takes place at the very moment the ethnographer engages with a specific mode of life.... He learns to find his way in a new environment, and a new language. (1986:159)

In the process of cultural translation, inequality between the languages of the ethnographer and the natives interferes with a fair representation of a native culture. In this section, I discuss the inequality of languages in three dimensions as I have experienced it: 1) between myself and natives in the field, 2) between the teenage culture and its textualization in an adult academic perspective, and 3) between my text and American readers.

First, I experienced inequality between my English and American teenage English. When I began my fieldwork, I had acquired competency in the language with over ten years of school learning in Korea and four-and-a-half years of living in the United States. My English vocabulary, however, included mainly standard expressions and academic jargon. I first found myself incompetent in the high school language to the degree that I was sometimes unable to respond properly to teenagers and to copy their remarks verbatim. The following incident in a class illustrates my initial incompetence with teenage slang. In a class of juniors, I was sitting behind a girl whom I had not met before. She sent me a note reading as follows:

Are you stoned?   yes__ no__
Do you get stoned?   yes__ no__
Why?
Because I _____ like it.

I understood neither the meaning of 'stoned' nor the intent of her inquiry. Upon my request, she reworded the term as 'smoking dope', which still did not come across to me. I finally guessed that it probably meant taking illegal drugs. Even though its meaning was cleared to a degree, I continued to wonder about her actual intention behind asking the questions. When I finally asked about it, she responded that the question, 'Are you stoned?,' could be addressed to someone who was being too quiet. Her response satisfied my initial curiosity at the time. Yet, I still wonder if her question was supposed to mean an invitation to a certain clique, knowing her associates in school. In addition to slang that teenagers used, I realized that young people used many colloquial expressions that my knowledge of proper written English did not cover.

The second type of inequality of languages was recognized in the process of translating the culture of adolescents into a text: namely, writing. As Asad correctly suggested, language inequality became obvious at this step even though it had not been recognized before. My textualization underwent the following stages: 1) I recorded what I observed through my eyes, the eyes of a foreign adult; 2) I interpreted the lively experiences from a scholar's framework; and 3) I textualized the materials to make the cultural data palatable to academics. In addition, having Korean as my first language put limits on my cognitive frame. My advisor, Harry Wolcott, noted that in fieldnotes my American teenagers 'all seemed to be speaking Korean English'. His remark reminds us of the constructiveness of ethnography. All ethnographers develop fieldnotes on the basis of what they hear and what they see. This constructive process inevitably includes ethnographers' language and world view in a controlled academic manner. The disparity between my text and the American language may appear more apparent to native readers, because this ethnography was written by a non-native author. The same problem would be less recognizeable when American readers come in contact with ethnographies of other cultures written by American anthropologists, because the texts are presented in their native tongue. During their fieldwork, however, the English-speaking ethnographers might have experienced a similar degree of language inequality, when they studied foreign cultures with minimal competency in their informants' languages or worked through translators.

My third type of language inequality concerns 'distance' between my text and my readers. Many ethnographies present cultures unfamiliar to US readers. Cognitive distance between the foreign cultures and readers is distinctly noticeable. Consequently, readers take the distance for granted. This ethnography of American adolescents may not pose the same kind of distance between the text and readers because the text is too familiar to readers. Rather, the inequality of languages expresses itself delicately when the ethnographer's version is compared with the natives' version of their own culture. Varenne, a Frenchman who studied a mid-western town in the United States and wrote an ethnography in English, pointed out the tactful task as follows:

> The task is more delicate when the observer addresses himself to the very people whose culture he is reporting on, for how useful the type of knowledge an outsider has to offer is not obvious. [1977:xi]

It is not an easy task to present an ethnography to natives because these two parties — ethnographer and natives — may represent different constructed reality. The notion of 'propriospect' (Goodenough, 1981) also indicates that people construct individual versions of their own world. Thus, no one's cultural version stands as *the* authority. The variant versions among natives and between natives and ethnographers can create controversy over whose version or interpretation is most fair to the real world. It may be almost impossible for ethnographers to receive favorable responses from all natives to their ethnographic texts. The difficulty of presenting a text to natives may come from the 'we-know-it-all-and-so-what' attitude. While I am convinced that there are many interpretations of a culture, it is a challenge to assure my American readers that one more interpretation — even that of an outsider — can contribute to the understanding of themselves.

After the Fieldwork

The completion of my fieldwork marked the beginning of a new chapter in my professional and personal life. Professionally, I devoted the following year to writing this ethnography. In the course of writing, I continued to search for the cultural meanings of adolescent life by reviewing notes and collected documents and by relistening to taped interviews. I also tried to maintain 'faithful' contacts with some adolescents and their families through telephone conversations or visits.

Personally, I have clung to the unanswered questions regarding my acceptance among adolescents, the effect of my presence on their life, and of my experiences with them on my life. After the fieldwork was over, I discovered that the two realms of my life as a professional researcher and a human being still interplayed just as they did during the fieldwork. In a sense, post-fieldwork contacts with the informants have turned out to be a continuation of the ethnographic research to a certain degree. Differing from the period of the fieldwork, however, I have been able to play more of the role of friend than of researcher and I continue to cherish personal friendships with them without professional guilt.

Continued Friendship

I officially completed the fieldwork at the end of December 1987, as I originally proposed to the school district. Since then, particularly during writing this ethnography, I have maintained contacts with teachers, students, and their families, and attended some school functions. I especially enjoyed my friendship with Marylinn and her family. Her family and mine visited each other's home for dinner. Marylinn invited me to a few school functions and telephoned to inform me of happenings in school: a new principal, a strengthened tardy policy and a students' protest against it, and unexpected breakups and romantic match-ups among her peers. During several telephone conversations with her mother, I learned about changes in her family: her husband's new job, her new affiliation with a community women's choir, and her daughter's new boyfriend. Since my physical departure from the field, our friendship has grown out of the original working relationship as a researcher and an informant. My inner conflict about my dual roles has been eased because I neither have to deal with it on an everyday basis, nor am I compelled to behave like a strict researcher. I have felt more relaxed about telephoning, visiting, and corresponding after my move to the East Coast; I no longer feel like an investigator.

However, from time to time, the pattern of the relationship that we set at the beginning has influenced our friendship. I have sometimes restricted myself from expressing opinions or encouragement, fearing that they might unduly influence Marylinn and her family's natural course of life. For instance, at the end of her junior year, Marylinn was planning to run for a major student leadership position. I personally felt that she was well qualified for the position. I offered my unofficial endorsement for her decision, but I soon regretted it, because the ethnographer in me warned, 'Don't try to influence your informant.'

I sometimes wished that I could become more of a true friend who gives advice. The educator in me said that Marylinn had a potential to pursue a professional career successfully if she wished, and she needed some positive input: she had intelligence, leadership, public skills, and sensitivity to others' feelings. Even at the beginning of her senior year, Marylinn knew only that she would go to a community college; she did not know what to do with her life. Her parents agreed that she should go to a community college and possibly to a university, but they did not seem to envision concretely that her life could outgrow their socioeconomic status. Looking at Marylinn's potential, I was tempted to advise her to apply for scholarships for colleges, to show her options for future careers, and generally to encourage her to look for the best opportunities for herself. However, the researcher in me seemed to win the battle, detaching myself from these commitments. Despite my struggle between detachment and humanism, I am convinced that a friendship which began with scientific incentive can continue to exist with more of an humanistic interest. This is a beauty of ethnographic research — a scientist is allowed to remain a human being while committed to his/her profession.

Continued Puzzles

While I kept in touch with Greenfielders after the completion of the fieldwork, unresolved puzzles lingered in my mind. The puzzles revolved around the questions: 'Was I accepted by the adolescents?' and 'What impression have I left with them?' Even after a year of fieldwork, I did not fully understand how to interpret responses from the adolescents regarding my presence among them. As I have noted, on some days in the field they recognized my presence and warmly received me at their school and in the community. They initiated brief greetings or struck up long conversations. On other days, the same people totally ignored me. I had often been confused about my status among the adolescents.

This confusing phenomenon was repeatedly observed during my post-fieldwork contacts with the Greenfielders. Three occasions within a month — a prom, a National Honor Society banquet, and graduation — raised my bewilderment to a peak. One afternoon in March after the fieldwork was completed, I received a telephone call from a girl who informed me that members of the National Honor Society had selected me as a guest speaker at that year's annual banquet. She added that I should not feel pressured to accept their invitation, but that my acceptance would please everyone in the group. She was calling on behalf of the organization, because she knew me better than the others. She also indicated that it was originally her idea to nominate me. Even though I took with a grain of salt her statement that 'everyone' wanted to have me as a speaker, I felt honored and welcomed by the adolescents. I gladly accepted the invitation and confirmed my decision with the faculty advisor in late April.

Then, at the beginning of May, I accompanied a junior girl from the student leadership class to help decorate a prom hall. Since I had met most of the student leaders before and many of them were in the National Honor Society, I expected they would recognize my presence after a long absence. Surprisingly, none of them paid attention to me, and some acted as if they did not hear me when I greeted them. My confusion did not cease there. In a week, the banquet took place and those who ignored me on Prom night attended the meeting. After I delivered a seemingly 'well-received'[3] speech, several students, including the 'unfriendly' ones at the Prom, came to greet me and have pictures taken with me. One boy, known as being 'stuck-up', and who had never greeted me at school and had refused my request for cooperation during the fieldwork, even struck up a conversation with me. What a change!

In early June, I attended the graduation ceremony to express my good wishes to graduating seniors. At graduation, I again coped with the 'cold shoulder' from those who had treated me in a friendly manner at the banquet; at the same time, I was surprised at the unexpectedly friendly greetings and hugs from boys and girls who had not shown an interest in me during my fieldwork. I have not been able to understand the reason for the students' seemingly inconsistent behavior.

Regarding the incidents of alleged inconsistency, several questions were raised: Was the feeling of acceptance or unacceptance subjective? Did my status change from nobody (a quiet student of a new culture) to somebody of importance (a guest speaker and active performer) after the 'successful' speech? If so, did the change affect adolescent impressions of me? Did I happen to catch them in different moods; or were the varying responses to me mere coincidences? I do not have an answer for this puzzle yet. However, I continuously remind myself of the ethnographer's mission to distinguish cultural phenomena from mere coincidence (consider the difference between a wink with an intent and a twitch in the eye, as discussed by Geertz, 1973:7) and to search for the cultural meanings of social phenomena.

Influencing and Influenced

Another unanswered question is 'How has my presence affected the world view of adolescents, and, conversely, would my experiences with them influence my perspective on young people?' An inquiry into this question poses a difficulty because effects may not be revealed quickly nor explicitly.

Joy's mother telephoned one day to tell me about her daughter's new friendship with a Chinese-Hawaiian boy. Joy met him in a leadership camp during the summer after my fieldwork was finished. Since the boy lived over a hundred miles away, they did not meet often, but they did correspond and telephone each other. They invited each other to their respective Homecoming dances. Although her mother suspected that the long-distance relationship might grow into a serious one in the future, she accepted the fact that at the present time her daughter regarded him as a special person in her life. In this overwhelmingly white community and school, intercultural dating was rare and unusual.[4] I recalled an earlier conversation with Joy about intercultural dating. The talk was spontaneous and concerned a hypothetical situation. She neither had any intercultural friendships before nor was seeking one at that time. I sensed from our talk that both she and her mother were neutral about the subject. When this girl actually chose a boyfriend from a different ethnic group, I began to wonder how much the family's good friendship with my German-born husband and me had affected their view of intercultural courtship.

Another concern about influencing informants is based on sharing the ethnography with them. I showed Marylinn and her mother a draft of Chapter 2 in order to check on the accuracy of my description, as well as to abide by my professional ethics. I was conscious of my analysis of Marylinn's friendship with Linda because it might sound somewhat negative. Both Marylinn and her mother 'approved' of the chapter. In addition, I shared the descriptive chapters of the high school and the community with Mr. Smith, the now-retired principal. His response to the chapters was also positive. I was pleased with their responses; however, I wondered if their looking at their own lives through my lens of reality influenced their perception of themselves. I was reminded of an anecdote that an anthropologist discovered, with terrible disappointment, that his informants provided him with information on their kinship system on the basis of an ethnography done by his predecessor in the same community.

Not only might I have unintentionally influenced the world view of adolescents, but I also sense that my experience with them has affected my view of young people. My personal encounters with different categories of adolescents, ranging from so-called 'good' to 'at-risk' students, have taught me to regard them as human beings first, before considering any social and academic labels given by the system or others. It is clear to me now that those who 'hung out' in the smokers' shed are 'John' or 'Nancy' first, before being 'smokers', and those who cheer for sports teams are 'Mary' or 'Joan' before being 'cheerleaders'. I do not know how these invaluable experiences with the young people will shape my 'propriospect' (Goodenough, 1981:98), but they will undoubtedly affect it.

My Goal of Understanding Adolescents

Have I accomplished my original goal of understanding US adolescents by the end of the study? My answer is both 'yes' and 'no'. My positive answer is based on my concept of understanding that was summarized in my speech addressed to the National Honor Society banquet. An excerpt follows:

> What is understanding? When I began my research, I was determined to learn about adolescent culture and to understand these young people. In order to understand them, I felt it was necessary to make myself closer to them. In order to bridge the gap between myself and the teenagers, I wore more of

their clothes — jeans, tee-shirts, and sport shoes — and did what students usually did in school. You might have seen me going to classes, having lunch in school, and going to school dances. I believe that my effort helped me come closer to many young people and become friends with them. However, looking like them and acting like them did not guarantee my understanding of them.

I needed more than that. I realized that the more important thing was to make the psychological gap between them and myself smaller. What does it mean to close a psychological gap? I could see the answer from the word 'under-stand'. A real 'under-standing' of others could not come until I was able to stand under others. 'Standing-under' others required four stances: 1) coming out one's own shell of values and judgments, 2) lowering oneself and elevating others, 3) opening one's mind and tuning into others' voices, and 4) trying to look for what others have, not what others lack.

Based upon this concept of understanding, I believe that I have made considerable headway toward my goal of understanding the adolescents. I have learned something about the culture of US youth within my intellectual and cultural limitations.

However, I do not claim that I have fully accomplished the goal; this is not a complete portrait of US adolescents. What I have obtained is perhaps a silhouette of the whole, or a close-up picture of a few parts. I doubt that any study, even an extremely extensive one, would succeed in the task of drawing a complete, perfect portrait of US adolescents. What each ethnographer of adolescents tries to achieve is to make a fractional contribution to the whole understanding of young people. I would be content if my bit of understanding made a contribution to the on-going task of understanding adolescents. I also gladly admit that this study has set a stepping stone for my further commitment to expeditions into the adolescent world.

Notes

1 I adopted the concept of 'inequality of languages', introduced by Asad, in order to include various translating acts from one language to the other, observation to recording, and adult view to adolescent view and vice versa.

2 At the beginning of my research, I occasionally dreamt of my fieldwork.

My dreams often reflected anxiety. For instance, some of the students who became friends turned into monsters who gave me troubles in my dream.

3 After the banquet, many parents and students approached to give compliments on my speech: for instance, 'We enjoyed your speech', 'It was the best speech that I have ever heard in the Honor Society banquet', and 'We could relate to your speech well.'

4 I only noticed one case of intercultural dating in school. My intercultural marriage seemed to confuse, maybe surprise, some community members. A few days after I visited a student's house and met her grandparents, (her guardians), whom she told about my intercultural marriage, she told me, 'My grandparents have a prejudice against a mixed marriage, but I don't.' But I did not encounter any direct prejudicial treatment due to my intercultural marital status during fieldwork.

Appendix

Senior Survey Questionnaire

This survey is to learn more about the life of seniors in your high school. The information you provide in the survey will be used for a paper on American high school youth culture. **Please answer following questions seriously and honestly.**

I appreciate your cooperation very much.

Heewon Chang

Please Write Your Answers

1 What **words** come to your mind to describe your senior year?
2 **If** you had your senior year to do over **again**, what would you change?
3 What are the **differences** between freshman social life and senior social life? (not only in school but also out of school)
4 **If** you were a **parent** of a high school student, what would you do to help your son or daughter and why?
5 **How** did you manage to get things done during your years of high school?
6 Describe the kinds of things you have been **involved** with and **enjoyed** most this past years. (formal and informal, in school and out)
7 a. **Who** do you usually pal around with at school?
   b. **Who** do you usually pal around with out of school?
8 What are some informal or formal **groups**?
   a. **At school**
   b. **Out of school**

9 a. How do you spend your morning **before** school begins?

  b. How do you spend your **lunch time** during school days? If you **go somewhere** for lunch, where?

  c. How do you spend your time **after school** during school days?

10 a. What did you do **last weekend** (Memorial Day holiday)?

  b. Was that weekend typical? If not, what do you **usually** do on weekends?

11 What did you do **last summer** vacation? (Please be specific)

12 a. What are the characteristics that you think make a person **'popular'** in school? (please be specific)

  b. What are the characteristics that you think make a person **'unpopular'** in school? (please be specific)

13 Please list your **sources of income** for meeting personal, social, and school expenses during school year? (e.g., allowance, cash gift, babysitting, part-time job, full-time job, etc.)

14 **If you work** for money during school year,

  a. **What** do you do?

  b. **How** did you find the job?

15 **If you don't work** for money during school year, please explain why not.

16 a. What is your opinion about **working** during the **school year**?

  b. What is your opinion about **working** during the **summer**?

17 **How much** do you spend on the average in a month?

18 Please list **5 of your expenses**, starting with what costs you the most.

  1

  2

  3

  4

  5

19 With whom do you **stay** when you are attending school? (Please list **everyone** specifically, children as well as adults.)

20 How do you **get along** with the adults (parents or guardians) that you stay with?

21 What are some **personal and private matters** that you feel high school students do not want to discuss in public?

22 When you have **personal problems**, who do you like to **talk to** about them? (Please link the type of problem with the personals you might talk to)

Please Check or Write Down Your Answer.

1   Sex: Male __ Female __
2   Your birthday? (ex. Aug. 1, 1959) _____
3   Where do you live?
Greenfield __   Peaceland __   Newland __   Woodland __
Other _____ (please indicate)
4   Which year have you attended Greenfield High School?
Freshman __ Sophomore __ Junior __ Senior __
5   Have you attended other high school(s)? yes __ no __
If yes, which high school(s) (name and location).
6   Do you have a driver's license? yes __ no __
7   Do you have a car of your own? yes __ no __
8   Do you regularly drive a car to school? yes __ no __
9   Your name? (optional) _____ (please print)

Thank you for your help.

Bibliography

AGAR, M. (1980) *The Professional Stranger: An Informal Introduction to Ethnography*, New York, NY: Academic Press.

ALLEN, B. (1987) 'Youth Suicide', *Adolescence*, **22**, 86, pp. 271–90.

ASAD, T. (1986) 'The Concept of Cultural Translation in British Social Anthropology', in CLIFFORD, J. and MARCUS, G. (Eds) *Writing Culture: The Poetics and Politics of Ethnography*, Berkeley, CA: University of California Press, pp. 141–164.

BEALS, A., SPINDLER, G. and SPINDLER, L. (1973) *Culture in Process*, New York, NY: Holt, Rinehart and Winston.

BENNETT, W. (1988) *Our Children and Our Country*, New York, NY: Simon and Schuster.

BERREMAN, G. (1962) *Behind Many Masks*, Lexington, KY: Society for Applied Anthropology.

BOCK, P. (1980) *Continuities in Psychological Anthropology: A Historical Introduction*. San Francisco, CA: W.H. Freeman and Company.

BOCK, P. (1979) *Modern Cultural Anthropology: An Introduction*, 3rd ed., New York, NY: Alfred A. Knopf.

CAMPBELL, J. (1987) 'Cultural Contact as University International Students Provide Service in American Schools and Communities', Unpublished Ph.D. dissertation, Eugene, OR: University of Oregon.

CHANG, H. (1987) 'American High School Students' View of Peers: Ideal Versus Reality', Paper presented at the 86th Annual Meeting of the American Anthropological Association, November 18–22, Chicago, IL.

CHANG, H. (1988) 'Adolescent fund raising as a reflection of American ideals', Paper presented at the 87th Annual Meeting of the American Anthropological Association, November 16–20, Phoenix, AZ.

CHANG, H. (1989) 'Schooling for Upward Mobility or Social Tracking?: A Study of Korean Adolescents', Paper presented at the 88th Annual Meeting of the American Anthropological Association, November 15–19, Washington, DC.

CLIFFORD, J. and MARCUS, G. (1986) *Writing Culture: The Poetics and Politics of Ethnography*, Berkeley, CA: University of California Press.

COLEMAN, J. (1961) *The Adolescent Society*, New York, NY: The Free Press.

CRAPANZANO, V. (1980) *Tuhami: Portrait of a Moroccan*, Chicago, IL: University of Chicago Press.

CRAPANZANO, V. (1986) 'Hermes' Dilemma: The Masking of Subversion in Ethnographic Description', in CLIFFORD, J. and MARCUS, G. (Eds) *Writing Culture*, Berkeley, CA: University of California Press, pp. 51–76.

CSIKSZENTMIHALYI, M. and LARSON, R. (1984) *Being Adolescent: Conflict and Growth in the Teenage Years*, New York, NY: Basic Books.

CUSICK, P. (1973) *Inside High School*, New York, NY: Holt, Rinehart and Winston.

ECKERT, P. (1989) *Jocks and Burnouts*, New York, NY: Holt, Rinehart and Winston.

GEERTZ, C. (1973) *The Interpretation of Cultures*, New York, NY: Basic Books.

GEERTZ, C. (1983) *Local Knowledge: Further Essays in Interpretive Anthropology*, New York, NY: Basic Books.

GERTH, H. and MILLS, C. (1958) *From Max Weber: Essays in Sociology*, New York, NY: Galaxy Books.

GOFFMAN, E. (1959) *The Presentation of Self in Daily Life*, New York NY: Doubleday.

GOLDMAN, S. and McDERMOTT, R. (1987) 'The Culture of Competition in American Schools', in SPINDLER, G. (Ed.) *Education and Cultural Process*, 2nd ed., Prospect Heights, IL: Waveland Press, pp. 282–299.

GOODENOUGH, W. (1980) *Culture, Language, and Society*, Menlo Park, CA: The Benjamin/Cummings Publishing Company.

GRANT, C. and SLEETER, C. (1986) *After the School Bell Rings*, London, UK: The Falmer Press.

GURALNIK, D. (Ed.) (1970) *Webster's New World Dictionary*, New York, NY: The World Publishing Company.

HOLLINGSHEAD, A. (1975) *Elmtown's Youth and Elmtown Revisited*, New York, NY: J. Wiley.

KEESING, R. (1976) *Cultural Anthropology: A Contemporary Perspective*, New York, NY: Holt, Rinehart and Winston.

LITTLE, K. (1970) 'The Social Circle and Initiation Among the Mende', in MIDDLETON, J. (Ed.) *From Child to Adult*, Austin, TX: University of Texas Press, pp. 207–225.

MALINOWSKI, B. (1967) *A Diary in the Strict Sense of the Term*, New York, NY: Harcourt, Brace, and World.

THE NATIONAL COMMISSION ON EXCELLENCE IN EDUCATION (1983) *A Nation at Risk*, Washington, DC: United States Department of Education.

NORBECK, E. (1986) 'Changing Japan: Field Research', in SPINDLER, G. (Ed.) *Being an Anthropologist*, Prospect Heights, IL: Waveland Press, pp. 238–66.

OFFER, D., OSTROV, E. and HOWARD, K. (1981) *The Adolescent: A Psychological Self-Portrait*, New York, NY: Basic Books.

PESHKIN, A. (1978) *Growing Up American*, Chicago, IL: The University of Chicago Press.

PESHKIN, A. (1988) *God's Choice: The Total World of a Fundamental Christian School*, Chicago, IL: The University of Chicago Press.

RABINOW, P. (1977) *Reflections on Fieldwork in Morocco*, Berkeley, CA: University of California Press.

SPINDLER, G. (1986) *Being an Anthropologist: Fieldwork in Eleven Cultures*, Prospect Heights, IL: Waveland Press.

SPINDLER, G. and SPINDLER, L. (1986) 'Fieldwork Among the Menomini', in SPINDLER, G. (Ed.) *Being an Anthropologist: Fieldwork in Eleven Cultures*, Prospect Heights, IL: Waveland Press, pp. 267–301.

SPRADLEY, J. (1979) *The Ethnographic Interview*, New York, NY: Holt, Rinehart and Winston.

SPRADLEY, J. (1980) *Participant Observation*, New York, NY: Holt, Rinehart and Winston.

SULLIVAN, M. (1989) *Getting Paid*, Ithaca. NY: Cornell University Press.

TURNER, V. (1967) *The Forest of Symbols*, New York, NY: Cornell University Press.

US BUREAU OF THE CENSUS (1989) *Statistical Abstract of the United States*, 109th ed., Washington, DC: United States Department of Commerce.

VAN MAANEN, J. (1988) *Tales of the Field: On Writing Ethnography*, Chicago, IL: University of Chicago Press.

VARENNE, H. (1977) *Americans Together: Structured Diversity in a Midwestern Town*, New York, NY: Teachers College Press.

VARENNE, H. (1983) *American School Language*, New York, NY: Irvington Publishers.

VIGIL, J. (1988) *Barrio Gangs*, Austin, TX: University of Texas Press.

WOLCOTT, H. (1981) 'Anthropology's "Spoiler Role" and "New" Multi-Cultural Textbooks', *The Generator*, **12**, 2, pp. 1–12.

WOLCOTT, H. (1982) 'Differing Styles of On-Site Research, or "If it isn't ethnography, what is it?"', *Review Journal of Philosophy and Social Science*, **7**, pp. 154–169.

WOLCOTT, H. (1990) Writing up Qualitative *Research*, Newbury, CA: Sage Publications.

Index

academic areas, 63, 65, 70, 146, 169
achievement, 1, 65, 124, 125
  and independence, 124, 125
active involvement
  see involvement
activities, adolescent, 49–51, **93–107**,
  119, 140
  see also extracurricular; family;
  involvement; voluntary
  activities
activity records, 158, 161, 165n1
adolescent ethos, 5–6, **109–85**
  see also activities; ethnographer;
  ideals; student(s)
adult(s), 126–8, 129, 138, 142, 156–7
  relationships/attitudes, 124, 125,
  173, 179, 184, 198–9
adulthood, 125, 140–2, 163
  social privileges of, 124
Agar, M. (1980), 14, 23
age, social aspects of, 170, 183
alcohol, 2, 95, 176
  abuse, 53, 157, 172, 192
alienation/isolation, 122, 184
  see also rejection
Allen, B. (1987), 2
ambition, student, 61–2
American ideals: adolescent ethos,
  126, 166, 182–5
  ethnography, 11
anti-social behavior, 114
appearance, 78, 82, 85, 169, 175–6

Asad, T., 200
  (1986), 199
ASB
  see Associated Student Body
Asia and US: culture/education, 4–5
Associated Student Body (ASB), 70,
  71, 73–4
athletic matters, 69, 147, 168
  see also sport(s)
'at-risk' adolescents, 2, 3, 4, 52, 192,
  206
attendence, school, 67–8, 77
authority, 124, 128, 129, 130, 142
automobile driving
  see car
autonomy/self-government, 70, 74,
  124, 128–30, 134, 140
awards, 32–3, 52, 61, 65–7, 71, 177,
  179
  and active involvement, 146, 151,
  159–60, 164

Beals, A., Spindler, G., and
  Spindler, L. (1973), 192
behavior, 65–6, 77n6, 114, 118, 173
Bennett, W. (1988), 1, 2, 192
Berreman, G. (1962), 122, 194
biology, 63, 80, 82
Bock, P. (1979), 111
  (1980), 174
boredom, 153–4, 164

For Product Safety Concerns and Information please contact our EU
representative GPSR@taylorandfrancis.com
Taylor & Francis Verlag GmbH, Kaufingerstraße 24, 80331 München, Germany